ART

OF

THE

BOOK

GINGKO PRESS

Art of the Book

GINGKO PRESS

First Published in the United States of America, March 2015
In cooperation with SendPoints Publishing
© SendPoints Publishing Co., Ltd.

Gingko Press, Inc.
1321 Fifth Street
Berkeley, CA 94710, USA
www.gingkopress.com

ISBN: 978-1-58423-589-7

EDITED & PUBLISHED BY SendPoints Publishing Co., Ltd.
PUBLISHER: Lin Gengli
PUBLISHING DIRECTOR: Lin Shijian
EDITORIAL DIRECTOR: Sundae Li
EXECUTIVE EDITOR: Christina Hwang, Kate Yu, Ye Guangqian, Yuanwen Zhong
ART DIRECTOR: He Wanling
EXECUTIVE ART EDITOR: Peng Lingbo
PROOFREADING: Sundae Li, Heart Fensch

ADDRESS: Room 15A Block 9 Tsui Chuk Garden, Wong Tai Sin, Kowloon, Hong Kong
TEL: +852-35832323 / **FAX:** +852-35832448
EMAIL: info@sendpoints.cn

DISTRIBUTED BY Guangzhou SendPoints Book Co., Ltd.
SALES MANAGER: Zhang Juan (China), Sissi (International)
GUANGZHOU: +86-20-89095121
BEIJING: +86-10-84139071
SHANGHAI: +86-21-63523469
EMAIL: overseas01@sendpoints.cn
WEBSITE: www.sendpoints.cn

All rights reserved. No part of this publication may be reproduced, stored in a retrieval system or transmitted in any form or by any means, electronic, mechanical, photocopying, recording or otherwise, without prior permission in writing from the publisher. For more information, please contact SendPoints Publishing Co., Ltd.
Printed and bound in China

Foreword

The book, for most, is an absolute given. It is a constant in the reshuffle of our things. We have observed and continue to participate in the ongoing discussion about the role of the printed book against the backdrop of its impressive history and against new advances in information distribution and consumption. With many discussions on the subject behind us and many more to come, it's important to remind ourselves that our familiarity with our surrounding objects tends to diminish our perception of their potential. It is often when we disturb an object from its established system or traditional environments that it motivates a response that sparks new ideas and possibilities. The various projects featured in *Art of the Book* acknowledge this. They readdress and test convention. They remind us that we need not remain fixed in our cultural perceptions of the book's ability to aid, excite or inform its user, reader or viewer. This publication invites you to appreciate the structures, materials and techniques that form and create the printed book.

Art of the Book offers commentary from the makers about their motivation and intent, alongside technical illustrations of each publication's construction. It details precise terms for many facets of the book's form and includes actual paper swatches. Typical print production processes are also explained, which helps in building an appreciation for the artistry in making publications of this nature.

At a juncture when the acts of reading and watching are in a state of unrest, we are operating in an extremely exciting period for the printed book. The designers, authors and publishers of the material presented within these pages have woven physical and conceptual threads together to bind varied and disconnected elements. Formulated into complete physical artifacts, these books exist as active agents amongst a broader, networked "content economy"[1] made up of blog posts, social media feeds, conversations, events and more. They operate as anchors, prompts, and as points of entry and departure for future readings. They maintain an invaluable and lasting presence. This movement through media, material, structures and forms distinctly mirrors our habitual ways of reading the world we encounter every day and resonates with our nature as multi-modal and multi-sensory creatures. This collection of publications, in their innovative use of materials, narrative structures and variant forms acknowledges this and celebrates the aptitude of its users. More often than not, the featured projects strive to redirect the users' typical engagement with content. They interrupt, confuse and destabilize experiences, with a view to inspire new engagement with the material. They invite the users to form independent interpretations and to arrive at their own conclusions. This exchange is binding, as much as any thread holding the pages together.

Maria Fusco proposes that a book not only provides structure for content, but also builds relevant social ties with its maker, as well as with its reader. Whilst you hold this book and delve further into the pages that follow, take a moment to contemplate the correspondence you are establishing between the fore-edge of one publication and the paper stock of another, but also look past the frame of the page and outward into the spatial, political and cultural context you are reading/viewing within. This is where you will recognize the value of the printed book—in its connection to that which surrounds us.

Paul Bailey

Graphic Designer, Researcher, Educator
www.misterpaulbailey.com

1 Daniel van der Felden, "Content Economies," I Read Where I Am, www.ireadwhereiam.com

Chapter One
6~99 ·········· **Structure**

Chapter Two
100~133 ·········· **Materials**

Chapter Three
134~253 ·········· **Technique**

● Introduction

⋯ Details

Chapter One
Structure

The publishing industry assigns every detail of a book terminology to facilitate description and understanding. In general, the structure of a book can be roughly divided into 19 parts, which are illustrated as follows: spine, head band, hinge, head square, front pastedown, cover, foredge square, front board, tail square, endpaper, head, leaves, back pastedown, back board, fore-edge, turn-in, tail, fly leaf, and foot.

◼ Structure

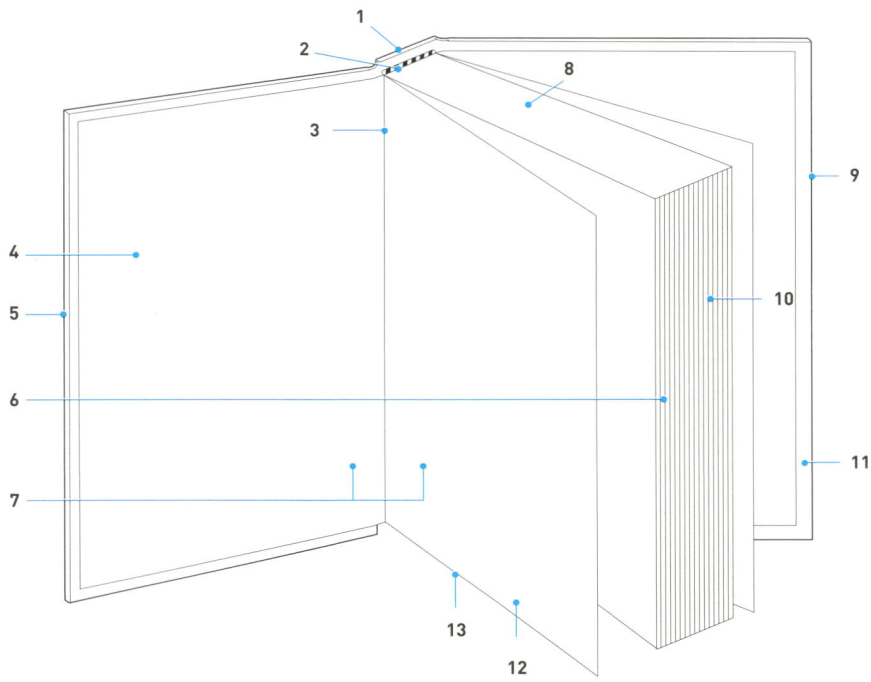

1. spine - Binding edges of a book or publication.

2. head/tail band - A functional or ornamental cloth band at the head and tail of a book attached before the covers are applied, usually complementary to the cover decoration.

3. hinge - A folded gap in the endpapers designed to prevent tearing.

4. front/back pastedown - Individual parts of the endpaper, attached to the front or back covers. There are two for every endpaper.

5. cover - Also referred to as the case. Part of a book which covers the content paper on the front, ridge, and back.

6. book block - The body of the book. The book block is composed of the leaves bound into signatures, which are individually bound sections of 8, 12, or 16 sheets.

7. endpaper - Thick paper attached to the inside of the cover to protect it and the interior pages. Every book has four endpapers, comprised of the pastedown attached to the cover and the pastedown that serves as fly leaf in both the front and back of the book. For production purposes, the endpaper is regarded as separate from the book block.

8. leaves - All of the sheets a book contains, divided into odd or even pages. There are twice as many pages as leaves in a book.

9. front/back board - Hardboard used for front or back cover, respectively.

10. fore-edge - Front part of a book block where the book is opened.

11. turn-in - Location where end of cover material is folded over the edge onto the inside of the board and covered by the pastedown.

12. fly leaf - Flexible part of endpaper, glued to bookblock.

13. foot - Flexible page of endpaper, glued to the book block.

Some readers may find it helpful to reference the terminology on page 136 for definitions of binding and printing techniques.

FEDRIGONI ISPIRA VISUAL BOOK

Spot color
Foiling
Silk screening
UV varnish
Embossing
Die cutting
Hand bound

Paper Material: Fedrigoni Ispira
Size: 200mm x 260mm

Happycentro [Italy]

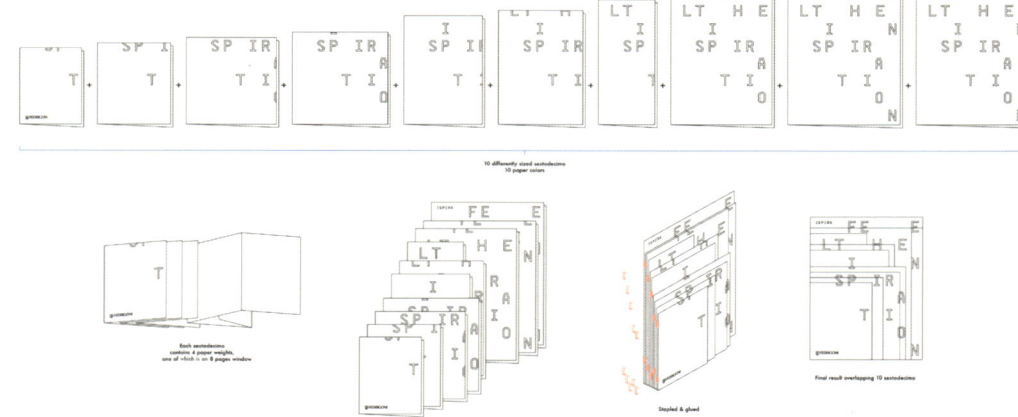

Structure

The new "Ispira Visual Book" for Fedrigoni is no common catalog. The smooth texture of the paper is enhanced with a special paper treatment. Each paper presents a different visual experience in which everything changes, including the color of the paper, the weight, the size, the inks used, and the printing techniques.

The design team's initial idea was to create a book that was designed to be touched rather than looked at. Then a color system was developed directly from the Ispira collection's 10 colors, which was then applied to the spreads after two offset white layers. The purpose was to show the new Ispira paper range at a glance with the support of a consistent layout system. When the book (which looks like a stack of folders) is opened, the reader can find a visual game going on. Each page is treated with embossing and transparent varnishes on one side and is printed on the other. The book uses 10 differently-sized sextodecimos, 10 paper colors, 10 Pantone inks and 100 patterns. Each sextodecimo contains paper in 4 different weights.

HYBRID NOVELS

Slip-open jacket

Pamphlet stack

Paper Material: Context paper, tracing paper
Size: 148mm x 210mm

Alberto Hernández [UK]

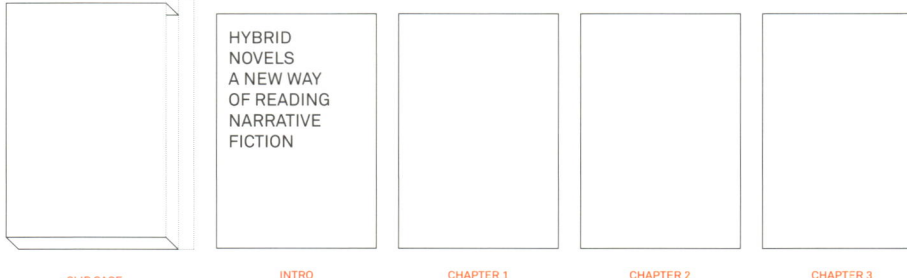

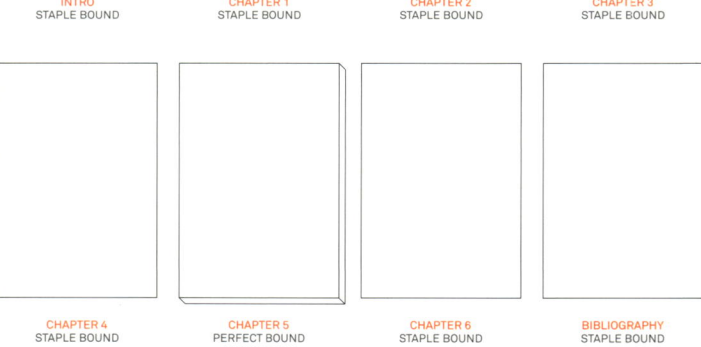

● The main idea of hybrid novels is to enhance the experience of reading, engaging readers in a more dynamic narrative experience, and at the same time helping them to understand the story more easily by adding engaging graphic devices to the original novel. As such, a hybrid novel is a book that needs to be handled and experienced and also requires the readers' actions to be fully understood.

◉ Structure

This publication, printed mainly using duotone and set in Univers typeface, is divided into different booklets which are perfect bound with white staples. These booklets are kept together in a semi-transparent slipcase that features a perforated spine that has to be torn off by the reader in order to open it and access the booklets.

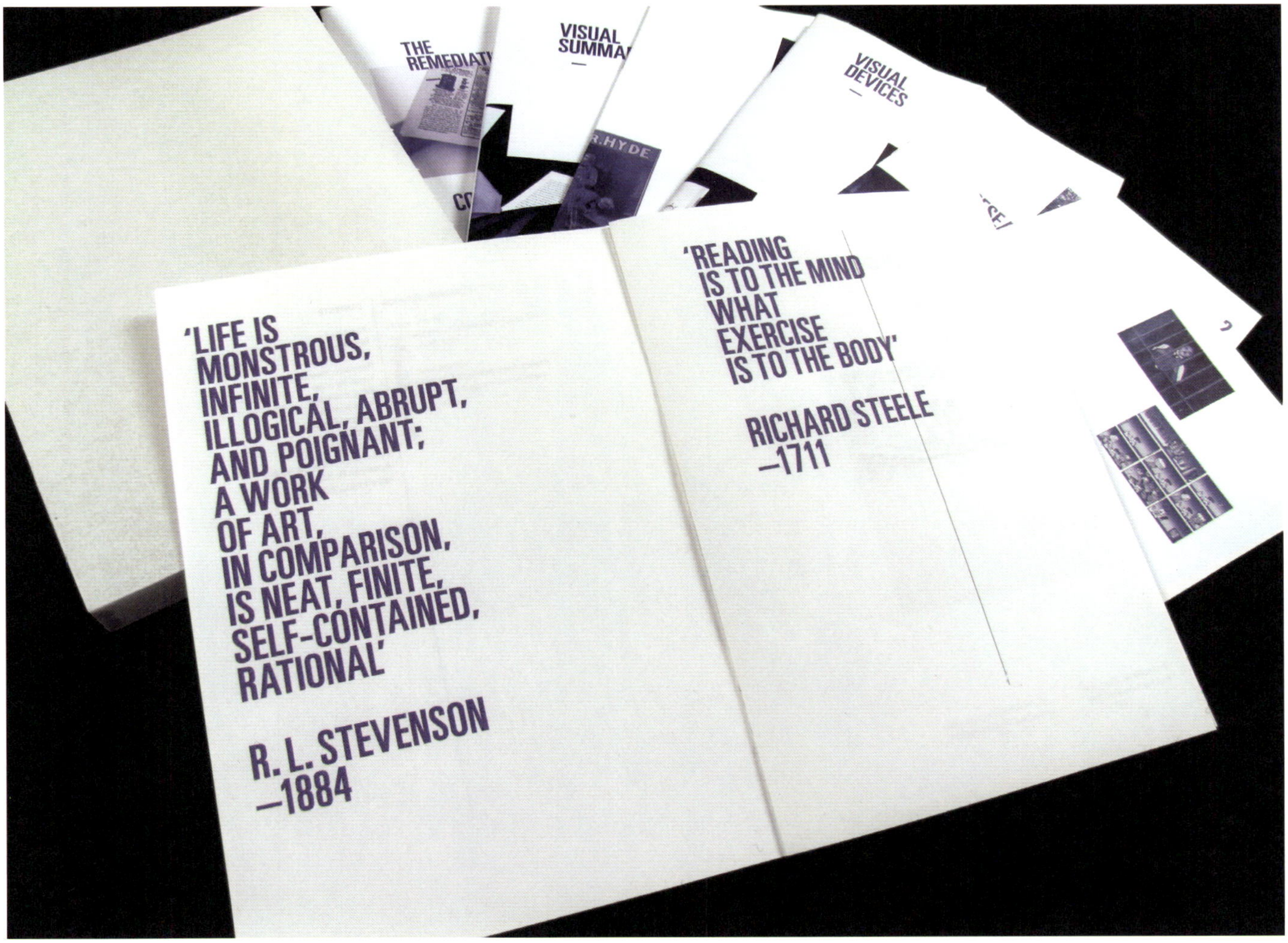

NINETTE Y UN SEÑOR DE MURCIA

Screen printing
Tear-open slipcover
Folded inner page
Special binding

Paper Material: Japanese paper
Size: 185mm x125mm

Jorge Fernández Puebla [Spain]

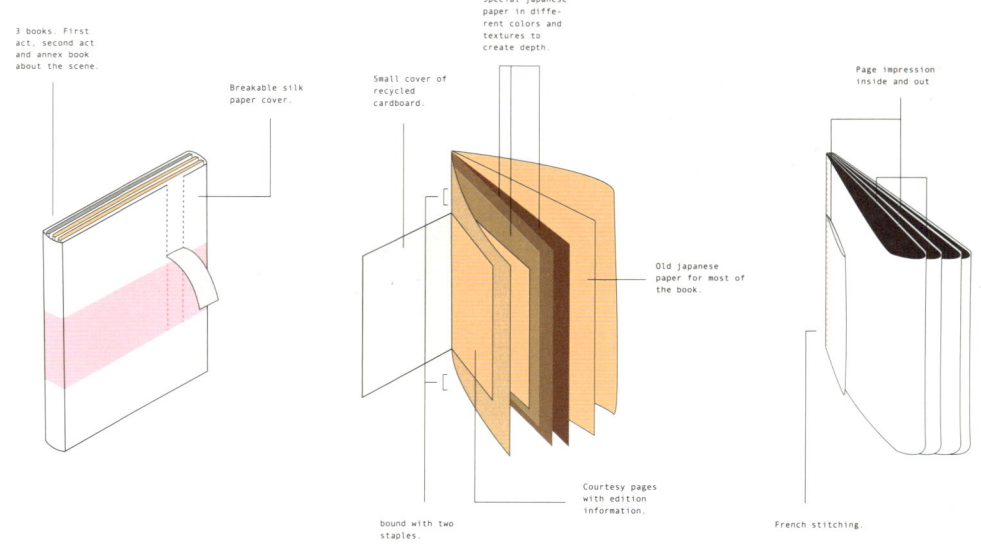

Structure

●

Ninette y un señor de Murcia encloses a reflection on the essence of the play and establishes a dialogue with it. The designer sought to create a visual translation of mise-en-scene, using basic theatre elements such as the ticket, curtain, the play's acts, and the reflection taking place in the spectator's mind as metaphors. In using all of these devices, the author has created a unique hybrid book.

⁂

In order to emulate the low-cost Spanish novels of the '60s, this book is stapled by hand using Japanese paper that matures with time. One page, however, has been sewn to create a gap within the pages to represent the reader. All of the pages are printed using laser technology.

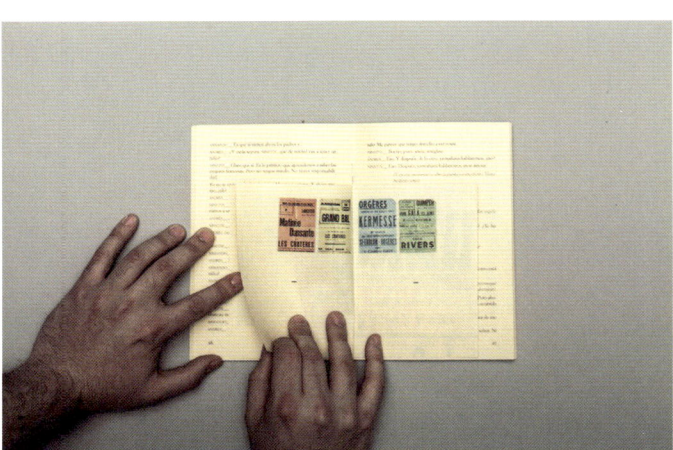

PIXO

Screen printing
Hand-lettering
Cutting

Paper Material: Cyclus offset
Size: 210 mm x 290 mm

Say What Studio [France]

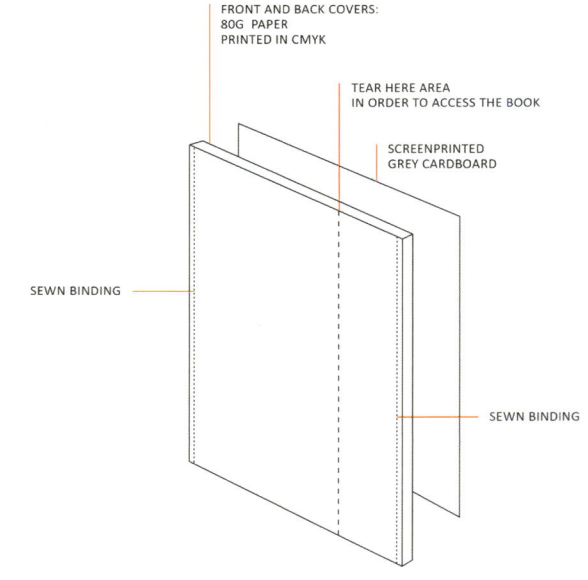

photo© François Chastanet

Structure

● This is a fanzine, printed in both English and Portuguese, revolving around pixaçao and cholo writing—two movements that treat cultural issues through typographic expression.

⋮ *Pixo* was conceived to match the book's content. As the fanzine is about an artistic and cultural underground, the access to the book had to be challenging. The designers decided to sew the book both on the spine and on the opposite side so that one would have to cut through the pages in order to read the contents. What readers get first is the regular fanzine, while the left part is a collection of cholo writing.

FMP - ILLEGALITY

Special book case
Accordion binding
Book set
Laser cutting

Paper Material: Recycled paper, plastic paper
Size: 300mm x 240mm

Stefen Clark [UK]

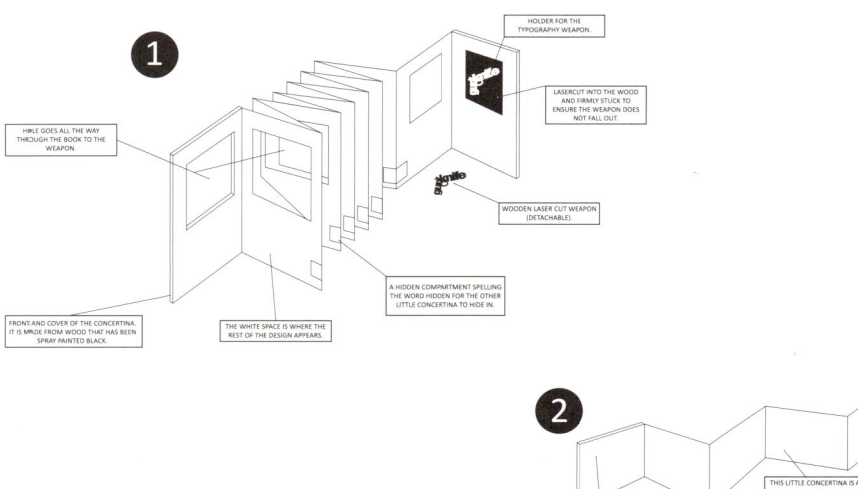

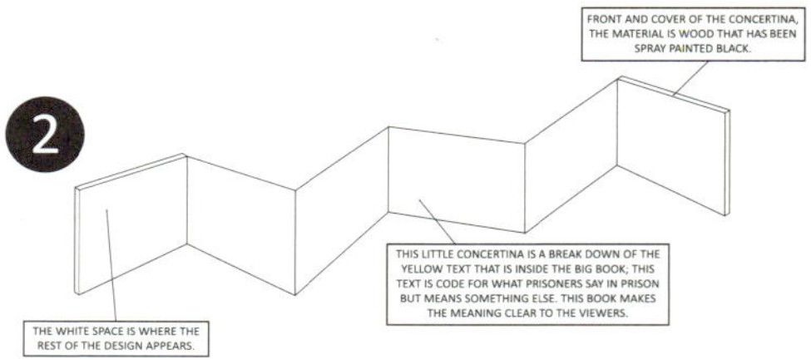

Structure

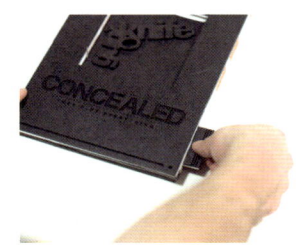

Structure

● This impressive project tackles the subject of prison and the prison system. Inspired by real prison visits as part of his research, the author managed to see contraband weapons firsthand, as well as discovering the techniques used by inmates to smuggle them around the prison. This research is evident in the project, which features many hiding places and hidden messages. It even includes a book that is smuggled inside a book that is smuggled inside another book that is inside a safe!

⁝ This book is metal bound with a matte suede finish for the front and back covers. The techniques used are laser jet printing and laser cutters. Lovely, rough feeling recycled paper from Paperco is the primary material. For the padding at the back and the bars, the designer used thick card stock.

THE SHIT BOOK

Half case

Headband

Hand-glued tag

Paper Material: Curious Touch Soft, Cardboard, Munken Polar Rough, Caribic Black, Colorplan Harvest

Size: 290mm × 335mm

Halbye Kaag JWT [Denmark]

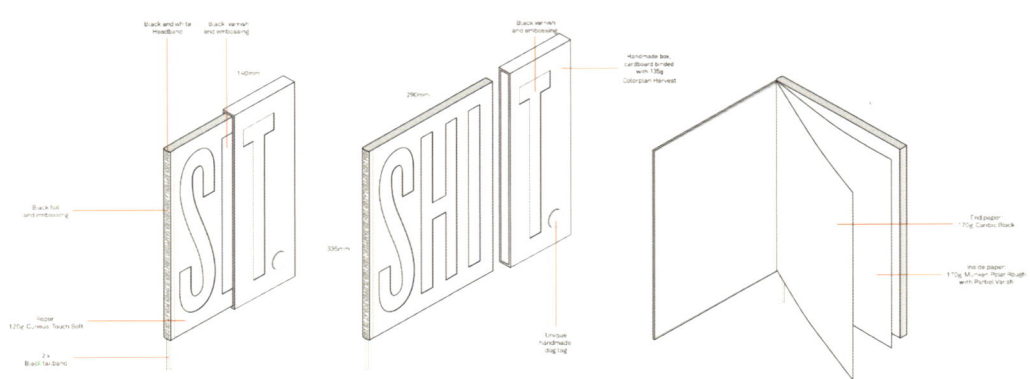

Structure

A record 73,000 tons of dog poop was removed from city streets last year, impacting businesses, the tourist industry and the city's reputation. Traditional paid media anti-poop campaigns had failed. A new strategy and campaign was developed and it required an extensive use of earned editorial media. The creative challenge became finding a way to excite and engage a very select group of decision makers in the media. *The SHIT Book* was a press pack designed as an exclusive coffee table book. The graphic photographs and data provided all the necessary campaign information and the book itself became the catalyst for the campaign's success in editorial media.

This book was printed using offset printing and bound by hand. Each book has a custom-built box sleeve that gave the cover a surprising twist: when closed the book says "SIT," but when opened the "SIT" becomes "SHIT" insert em dash a clear reference to the theme of the book. Each book is also personalized with a unique dog tag.

8 SOLES DE VIAJE/ EL INVENTARIO DE PALABRAS

Special accordion fold

French binding

Fluorescent color

Paper Material: Beige bond, vellum paper, postcard cardboard
Size: 150mm x 150mm

Festina Lente Libros   [Colombia]

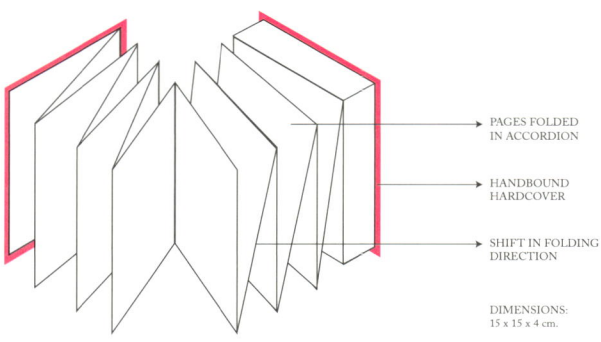

- PAGES FOLDED IN ACCORDION
- HANDBOUND HARDCOVER
- SHIFT IN FOLDING DIRECTION

DIMENSIONS: 15 x 15 x 4 cm.

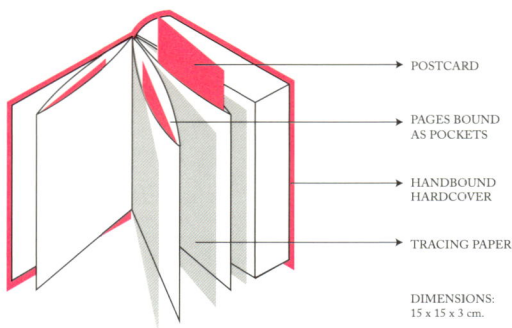

- POSTCARD
- PAGES BOUND AS POCKETS
- HANDBOUND HARDCOVER
- TRACING PAPER

DIMENSIONS: 15 x 15 x 3 cm.

Structure

● These two books are meant to carry the reader through an imaginary journey. The first book, *8 soles de viaje* (8 travelling suns), is an anonymous travel diary left behind by an explorer who travels to imagined places. The book itself is a metaphor for the journey as it unfolds indefinitely. The second book, titled *El inventario de palabras* (A word inventory), is an A through Z bestiary of the discoveries the explorer has made throughout his adventures.

 8 soles de viaje is hand-bound in an accordion-like structure. The trick to this book is in its twists, for as the story changes direction, so does the book, flipping at a 90º angle. Each turn corresponds metaphorically with a plot twist in the story. The binding of *El inventario de palabras* allows each page to become a sort of pocket that holds a secret message. The distance that the 26 postcards can travel is a metaphor for a journey that continues outside the fiction with the reader. Both books have hand-drawn calligraphy and pointillist illustrations. 300 copies of each of these hand-bound books were printed in Colombia, using only black and phosphorescent pink ink.

ASYMETRIC TYPOGRAPHY
– ANDERS KRISÁR

Plexiglas case
Foldable cover
Trompe-l'oeil effect
Elastic band
Embossing

Paper Material: Scandia 2000 white uncoated
Size: 255mm x 290mm

Caroline Andersson [Sweden]

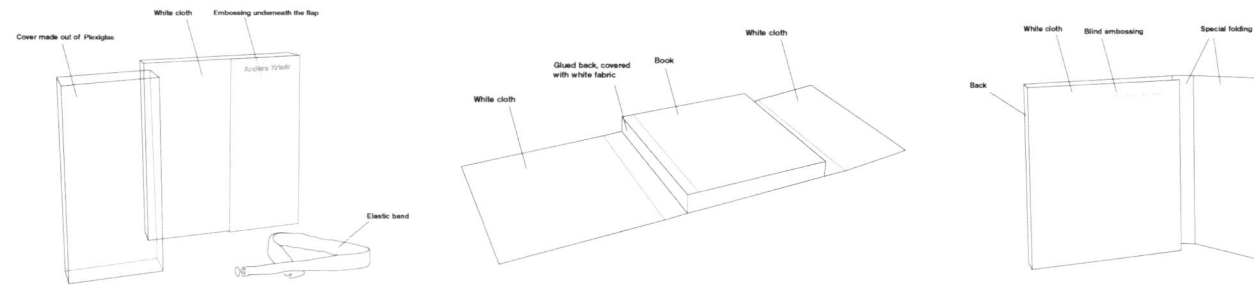

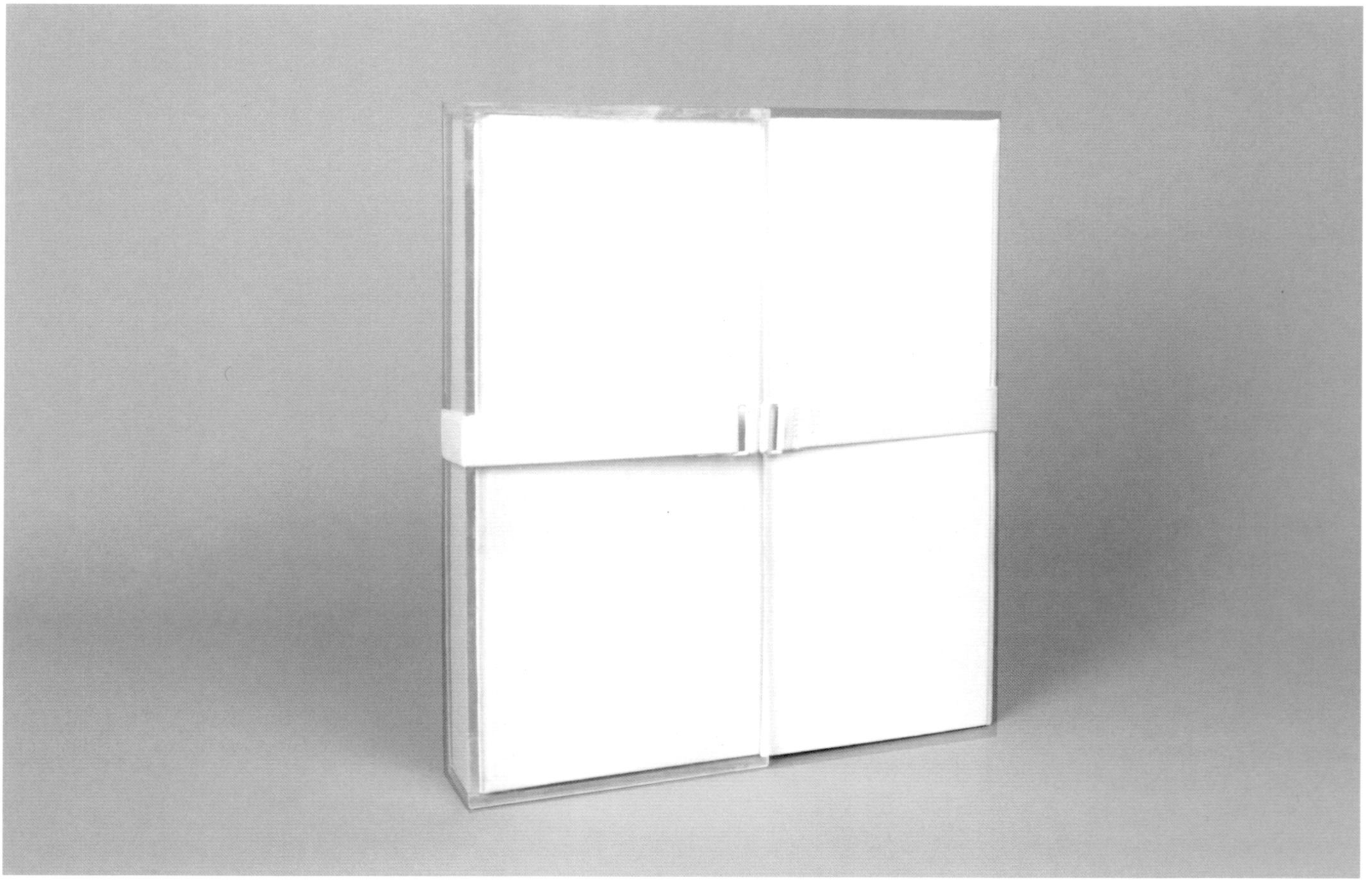

Structure

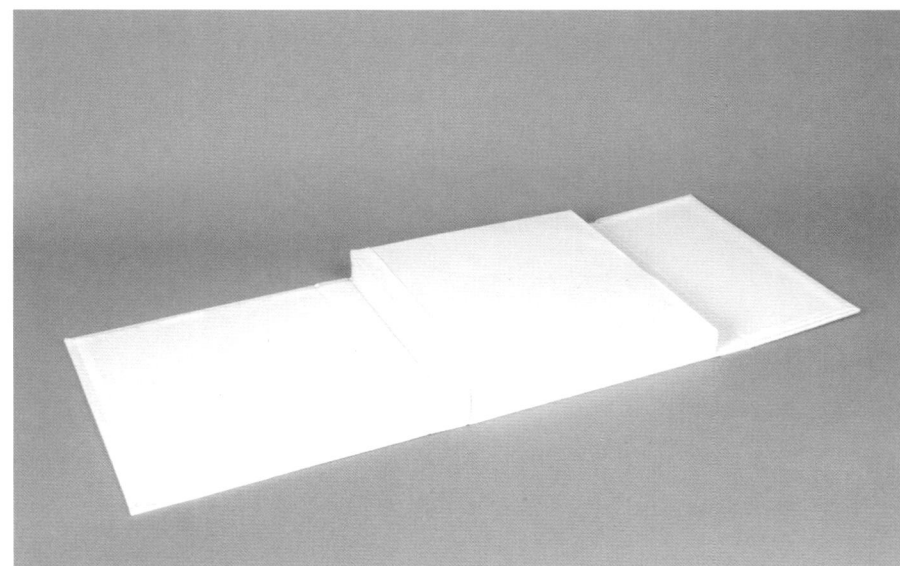

● This book design builds on the contrast that Anders Krisár presents in his works, that is, the contrast between the works (omit comma), and their meanings. The designer created as clean a design as possible so the focus could remain on the artist's work.

∴ This book is encased in Plexiglas to symbolize the psychological aspect of the artist's work while the white fabric symbolizes the physical aspect of his works. Still, it is hard to distinguish where the book ends and the case begins. The result is a sense that there is no clear border between the physical and psychological. The elastic band that holds the case parts together is another ambiguous symbol that represents the observer's hesitancy to decide the book's meaning.

ENLIGHTENED

```
Watercolors
Special binding
Screen Printing
Foiling
Solid color
```

Paper Material: Kraft paper
Size: 192mm x 220mm

KAN & LAU DESIGN [China]

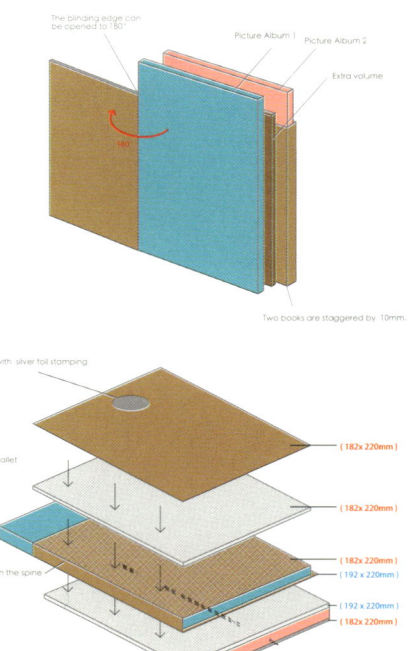

● *Enlightened* is an archive of Shenzhen-Hong Kong Design Exhibition (2009 & 2011), a biennale exchange platform for designers in the two cities. The book is a design history document of both cities. The design concept was inspired by the set design of the events.

26

Structure

 The designers tried to imitate the gradation and texture of the plywood that was used for the exhibition's display platforms by using thick cardboard and kraft paper. The entire book is comprised of two separate booklets that share the same back cover. This special book binding is the best way to describe the relationship between Shenzhen and Hong Kong—connected but independent.

SUNSET PARK

Rubber band

Folded calcic paper

Special binding

Paper Material: Calcic paper
Size: 148mm x 105mm

*JvV by Joost van Vredendaal
[The Netherlands]*

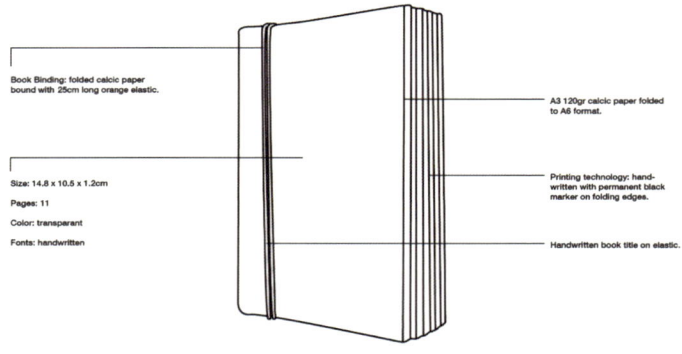

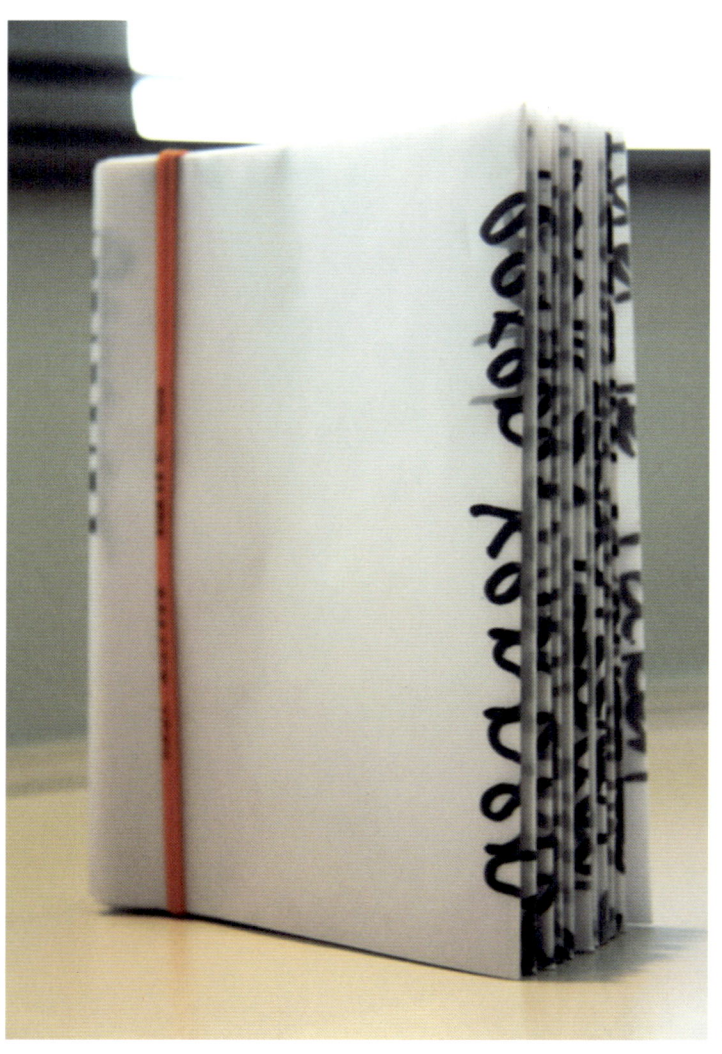

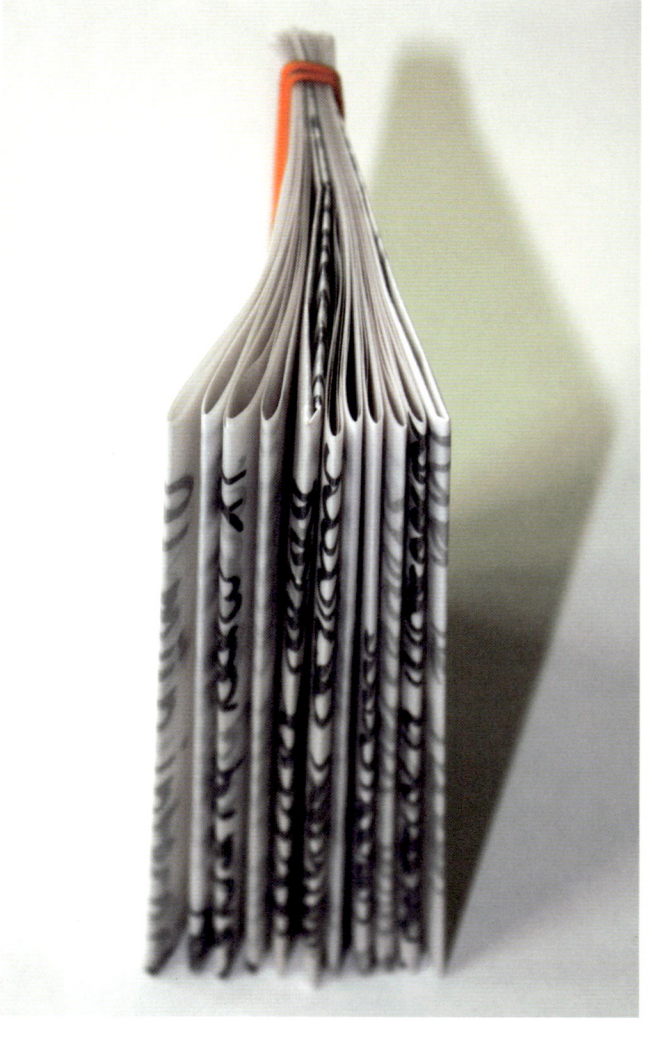

● Structure

- This is a redesign of the novel *Sunset Park*. The collection contrasts the main character with the book itself. It looks at his way of thinking, which is characterized by developing tactics to hide himself and his secrets from the outside world, and places that in juxtaposition with the book itself, which is transparent, open and light.

⁘ The subject of this novel is one that can really touch readers emotionally. In order to keep the author out of the spotlight, the designer reserved his name for a spot on the rubber band that holds the book together.

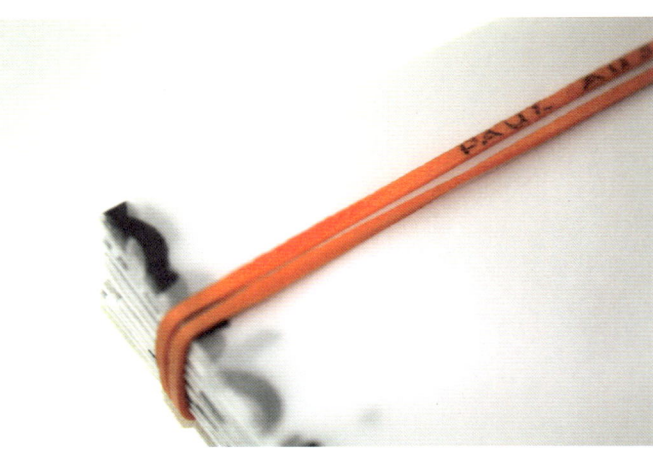

29

ÉÉN

Spot varnish
Duotone
Singer stitching
Double printing

Paper Material: Pastel green paper, pastel pink paper
Size: 160mm x 130mm

Luc van Kan   [The Netherlands]

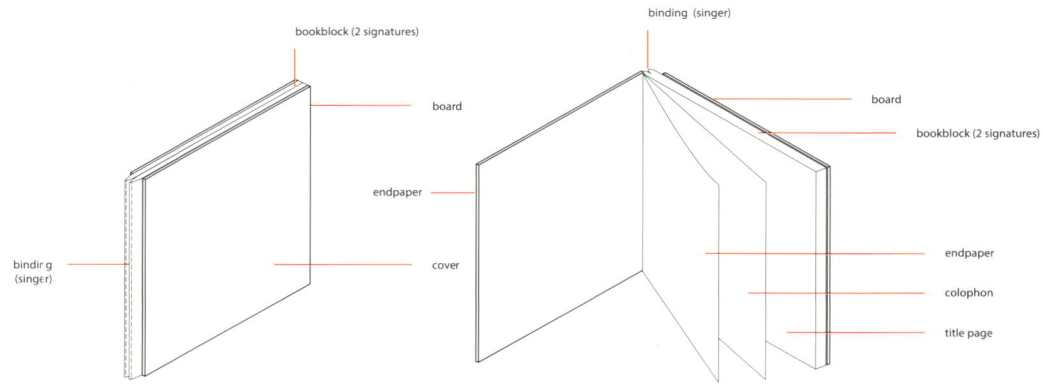

Structure

 ÉÉN (which means "one") is a set of two books made for the Dutch fashion designers Viktor&Rolf. Viktor and Rolf are virtually inseparable partners who work together to infuse the fashion brand with vitality. That is why this project consists of two books. The two different paper colors underline the fact that they are different. At each spread, the reader has to find out how the books differ and complement each other. At the end, the reader discovers the real layers in Viktor&Rolf's working relationship.

The books were stitch-bound with a Singer sewing machine as a link to fashion design. Pastel green and pink paper was used for the contents of the respective books, but the covers of the books are similar and feature the same color. The covers were printed with spot varnish consistent with the mysterious characters of the fashion designers.

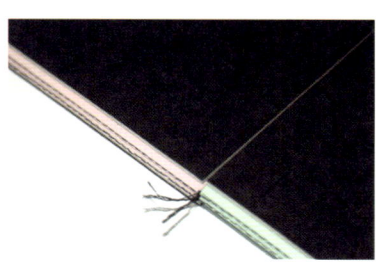
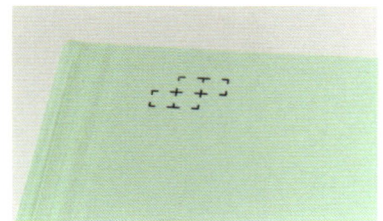
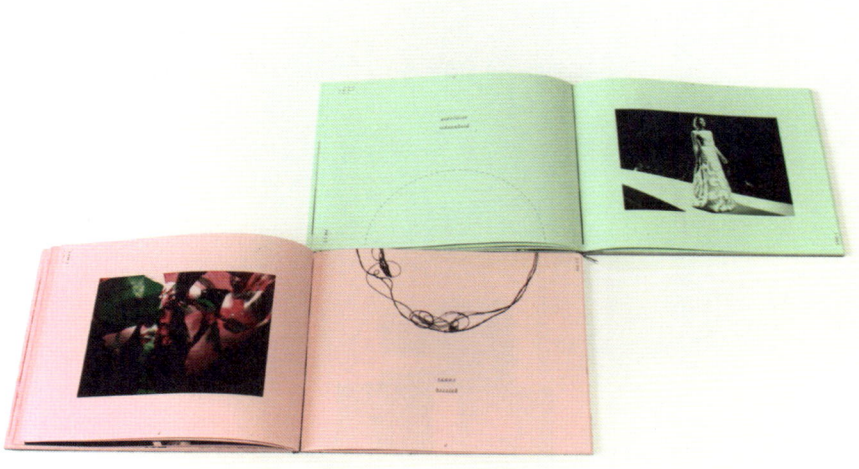

31

WINDOW FARMS

Accordion fold
Insert
Saddle stitch

Paper Material: Off-white paper stock, recycled craft stock
Size: 145mm x 220mm

Jiani Lu [Canada]

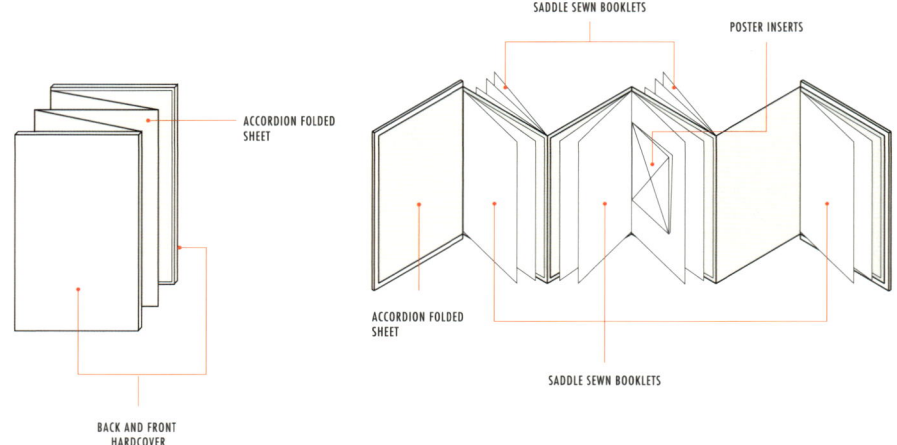

●

This personal project draws inspiration from the urban farming movement. The hand-bound book acts as a reference guide on the indoor, year-round, urban farming method Window Farming. The book illustrates various types of data and instructions covering everything from assembly and mounting to coming up with a "growing plan."

This book features fold-out posters, illustrations, information graphics and an interactive gardening journal. Each of the 5 chapters is saddle-sewn between the folds on both sides of a long, accordion-folded sheet. The format allows for different approaches to reading it. When collapsed together, it reads front-to-back like a regular book. When expanded, it reveals the entire length of the book and a panoramic view of the book's contents. The foldout posters, illustrations, information graphics and interactive gardening journal create a reading experience that is interactive, playful and experimental.

Structure

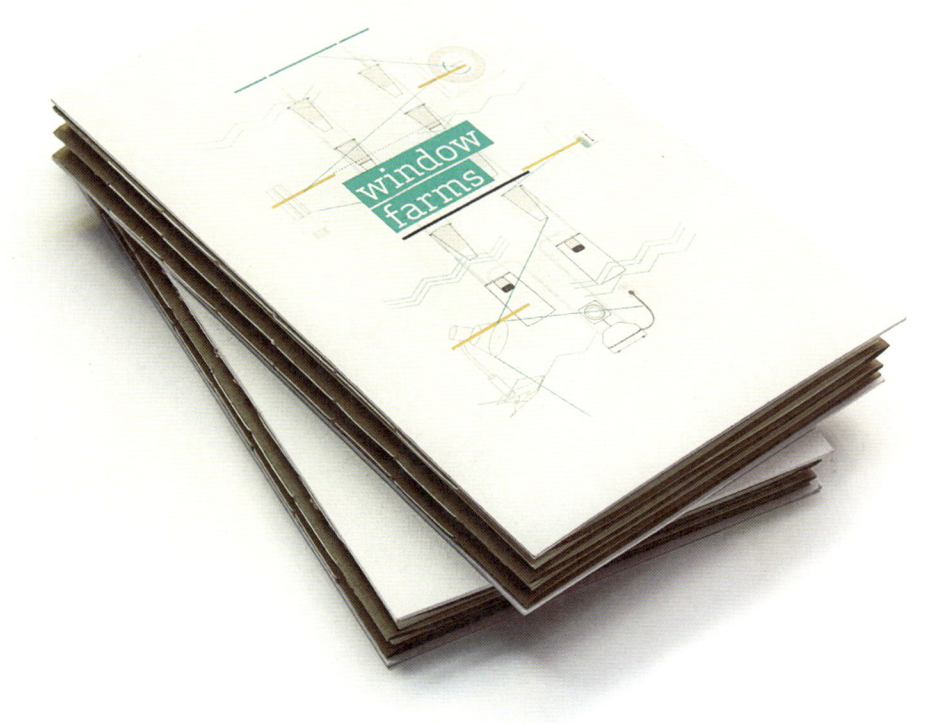

3 STORIES BOOK

Inserted vertical book
Special binding
High-gloss lamination
Unique layout

Paper Material: Matte black paper, high-gloss lamination
Size: 175mm x 160mm

JvV by Joost van Vredendaal
[The Netherlands]

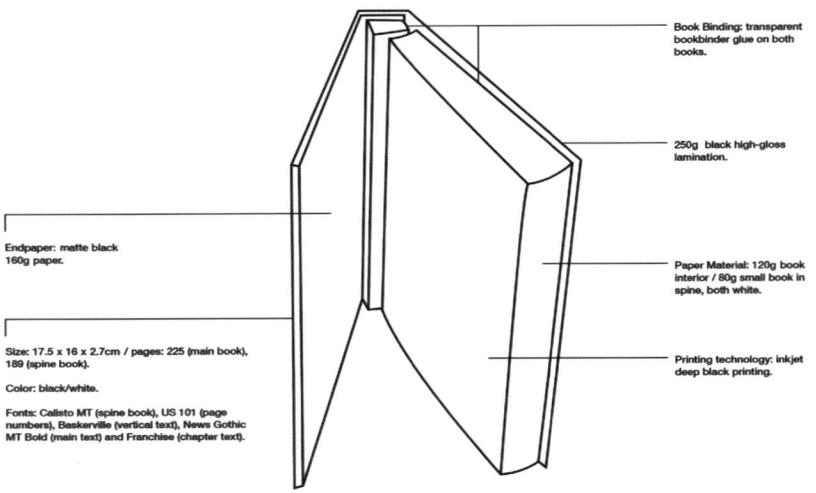

◨ Structure

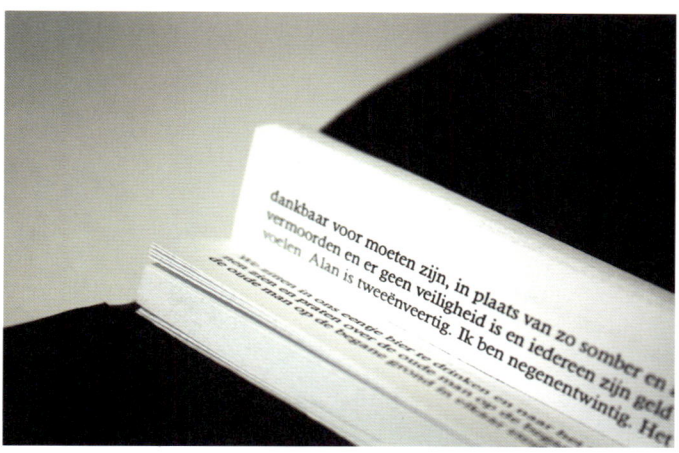
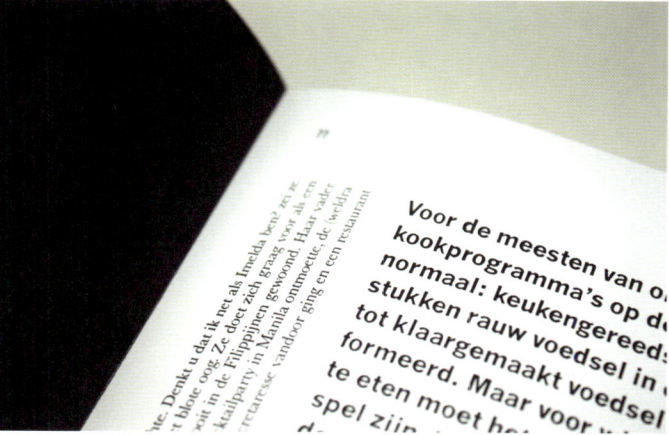

● This book contains three different story lines that all have their own unique place within the design. The small vertical book on the side is especially designed for one of the main characters. Inside the book are the vertical and horizontal texts for the other characters. Once the book is closed, the external book in the spine is not visible anymore. This way the three characters are united.

 The entire book is printed in black and white. For the binding, transparent bookbinder glue was used on both books. The printing technology is inkjet deep black printing. Calisto MT was used for the spine while US 101 40 was used for the page numbers and Baskerville was used for the vertical text. News Gothic MT Bold was used for the main text and Franchise was used for the chapter text.

PHANTASMAGORIA

Vacuum packaging

Debossing

Manuscript

Size: 210mm x 297mm

Wang Zhi-hong [China]

• Phantasmagoria is a Chinese translation of *The Little Prince*, a fictional memoir that touches on topics such as life, culture, art, politics, and love.

Structure

LI DE

Stamping

Special spine design

Size: 210mm x 280mm

Wang Zhi-hong [China]

● This three-volume set chronicles the life of Taiwanese artist Li De. It includes faithful documentation and an in-depth discussion of his more than 200 works of art that include sketches, oil paintings, watercolors and literary creations.

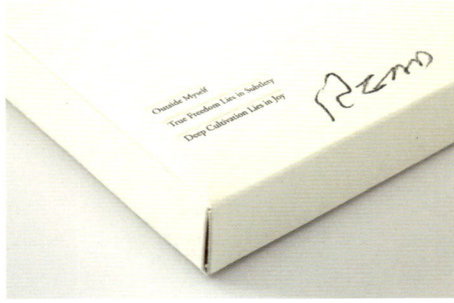

Structure

EYE OF THE TIMES

Unique jacket design
Open spine

Size: 210mm x 280mm

Wang Zhi-hong [China]

- This was designed for "An Age Through Lenses" photography exhibition in Taiwan.

Structure

TEAM CAMELOT ON THE RALLYE ALLGÄU-ORIENT

Accordion binding

Book case design

Paper Material: Flora by Igepa
Size: 260mm x 330mm

Mircea W. Gutu   [Germany]

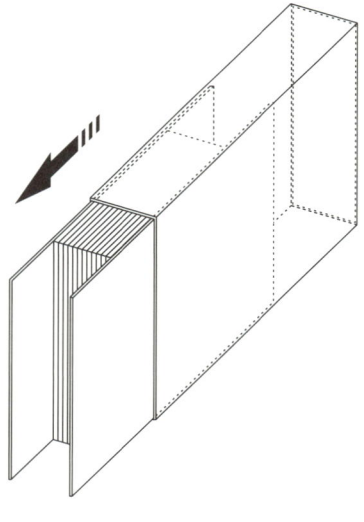
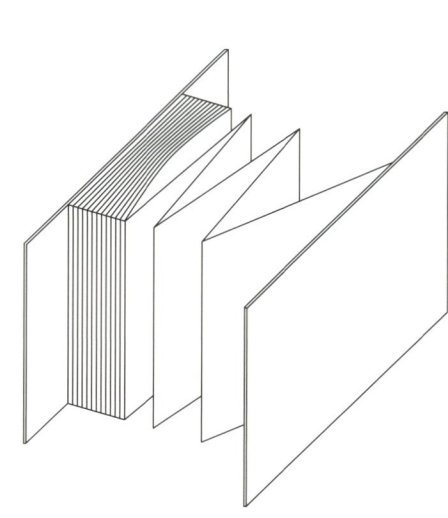

In 2010 the designer participated in the Rallye Allgäu-Orient, a car rally that starts in Southern Germany, goes through countries like Slovenia, Bulgaria and Turkey, and finishes in the Wadi Rum desert of Jordan. On the way every team has to follow strict rules while completing some amusing quests. In exchange they get the chance to win a real camel! This book covers this special event.

The book has a total of 340 pages, each glued together by hand to form a very large leporello-folding, with a total of almost 100 meters of paper, which might make it the longest book in the world. The book was printed manually on a DIN-A3 ink printer. In addition each page was cut manually because the format is quadratic. The paper is 10% cotton, which gives it a natural and dirty look that fits the theme of the book. The photographs in the book are also not glossy but rough and sometimes shaky. While most photographers pay a lot of attention to the correct representation of colors, in this book the opposite happens: the dirty paper adds a special character to the images.

Structure

DEPARTMENT OF GRAPHICS VAA

Coptic stitching

Special case

Paper Material: Cardboard, black paper, tracing paper
Size: 180mm x 240mm (book), 205mm x 255mm (case)

Viktorija Leleive   [Lithuania]

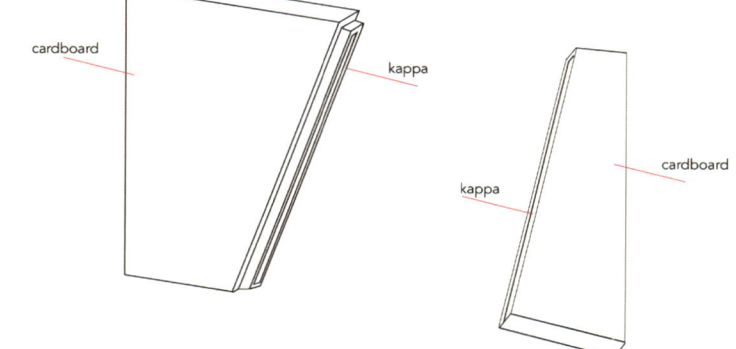

• This is a historical book about Vilnius Academy of Arts' graphics department. The book covers its development, professors, directors, classes, students etc.

Structure

The chapters in this book are organized chronologically, from the school's foundation, up to the present. In order to emphasize the content, the layout and book packaging were given a diagonal design to symbolize movement and change. The book case is made up of two parts, and the cover of the book features tracing paper.

APOPTOSIS

Triptych editorial structure

Perforation

Paper Material: grey recycled paper, matte finished machine coated paper
Size: 105mm x 148mm

Jasper Jongeling   [The Netherlands]

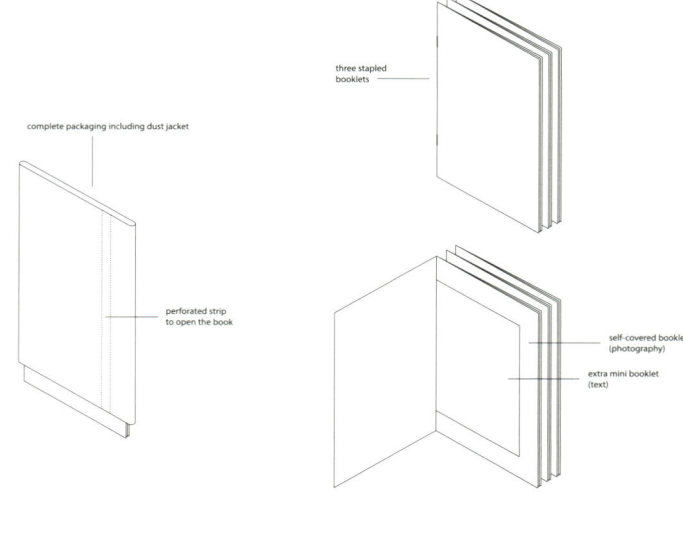

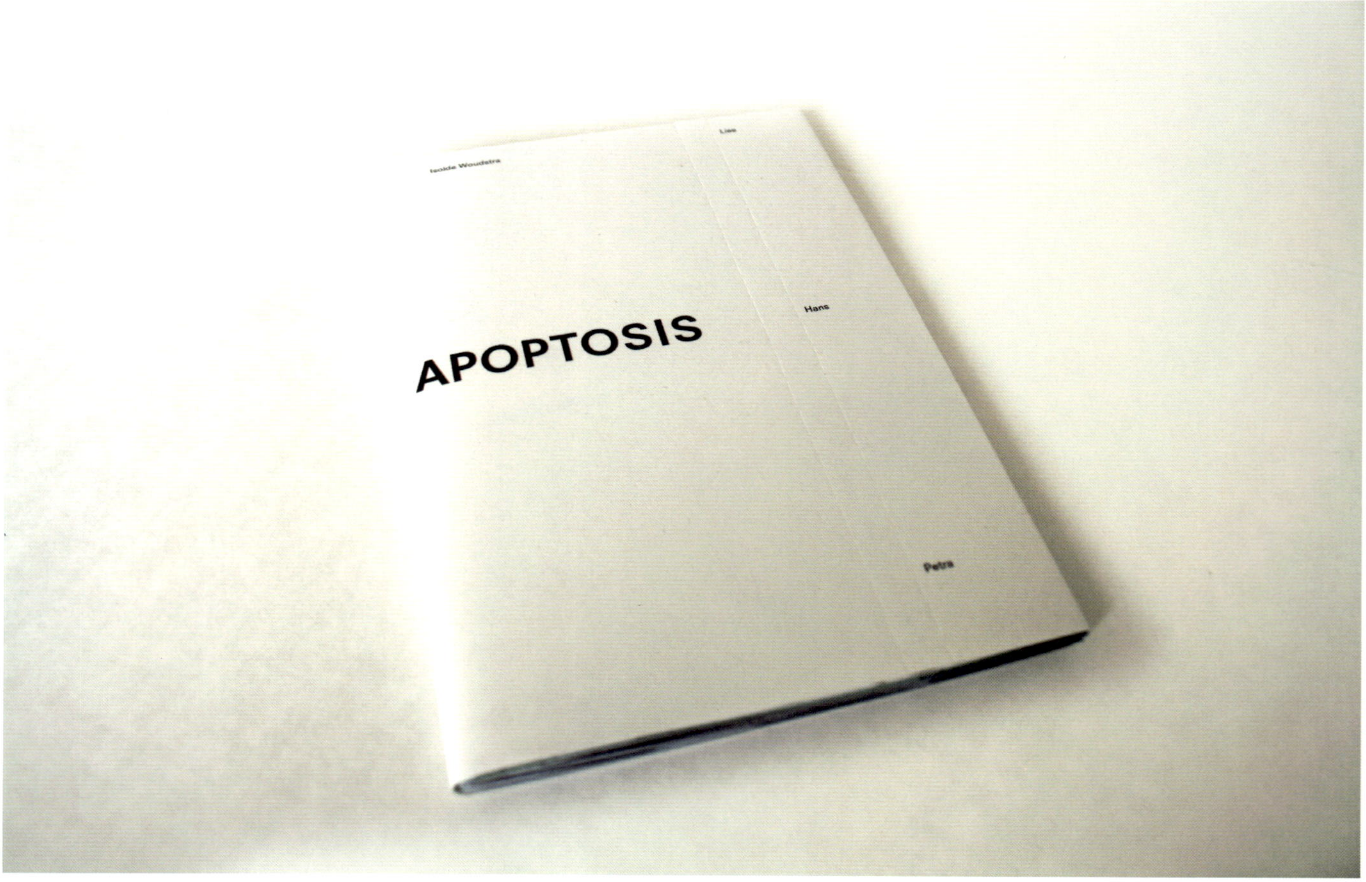

Structure

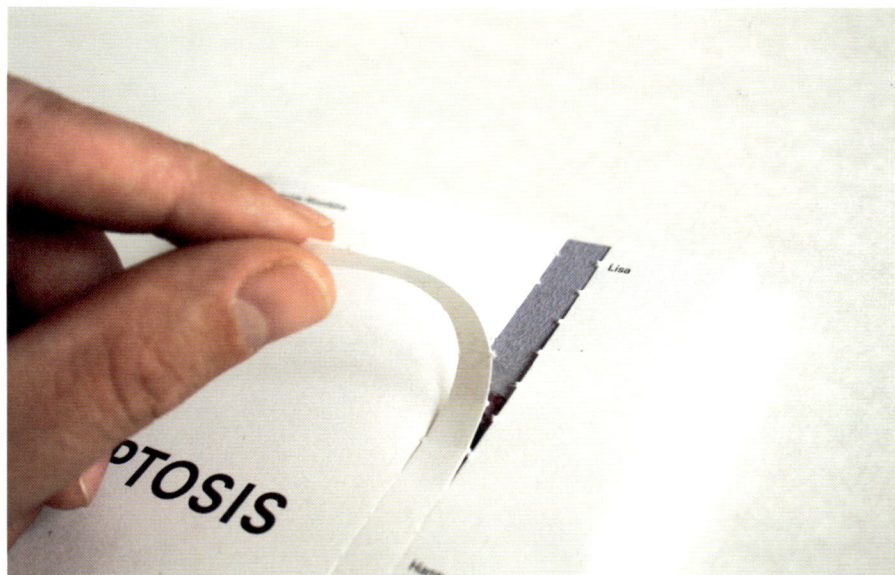

• This triptych contains a series of portraits about people who have a desire to end their lives. The design and structure of the book was inspired by the process of apoptosis (the process of how cells die). It aims to be respectful and in a simple way, to create awareness and understanding of this sensitive and emotional subject.

⋮ The structure, design and dust jacket packaging are all based on the phenomenon of apoptosis. A clear description of this phenomenon can be found in the book *De milde dood* by Maurits Verzele. In the book, Verzele defines apoptosis as "A type of cell death or cell suicide mechanism in which the cell uses specialized cellular machinery to kill itself." He goes on to state that "As a group, cells are able to resist this urge, but once isolated, they all die."

LONGMARK

Stamping
Foiling
Spot color
Accordion binding

Paper Material: Cardstock, offset paper
Size: 175mm x 255mm

Shenzhen Huathink Design Company
[China]

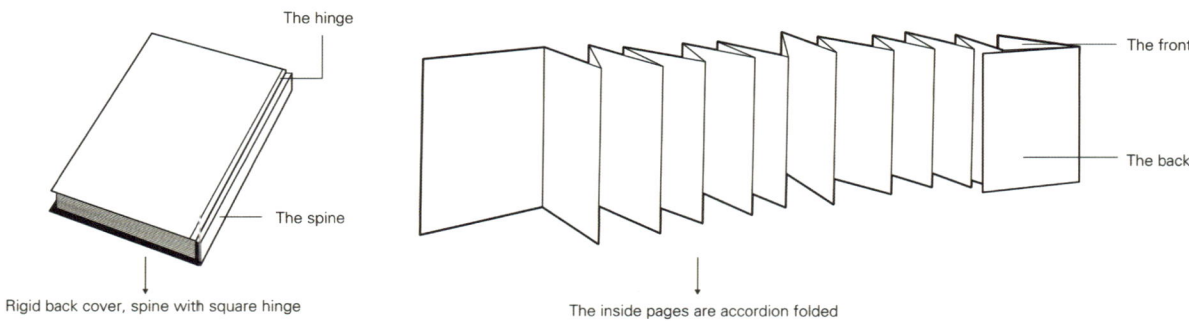

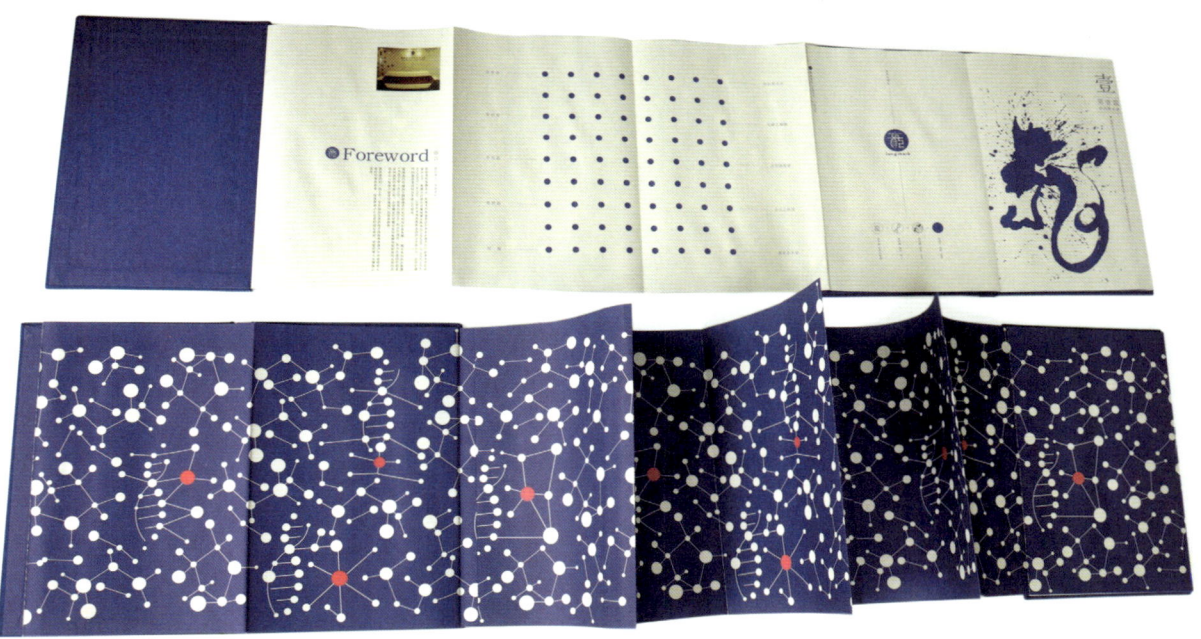

●
Longmark is a group founded by a batch of outstanding Chinese scientists and marketing specialists. Working with United Gene, it is dedicated to the promotion of gene technology, products and services.

The texture of the blue linen cloth on the cover represents genetic combinations. This is mirrored by the translucent full-page Longmark genetic patterns on the inside. The content is presented on paper that has been folded using a Japanese technique.

ALU COMPANY BOOK

Special band
Embossing
Cutting

Paper Material: Black cardboard, Arcoprint White
Size: 200mm x 200mm

Happycentro [Italy]

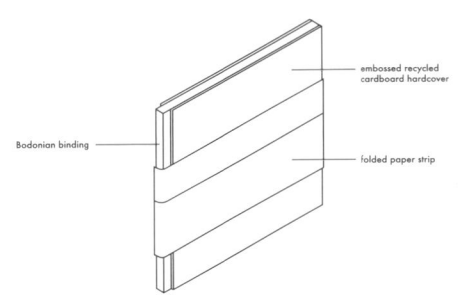
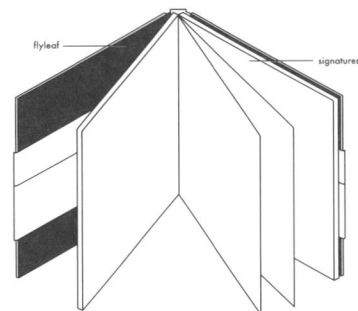
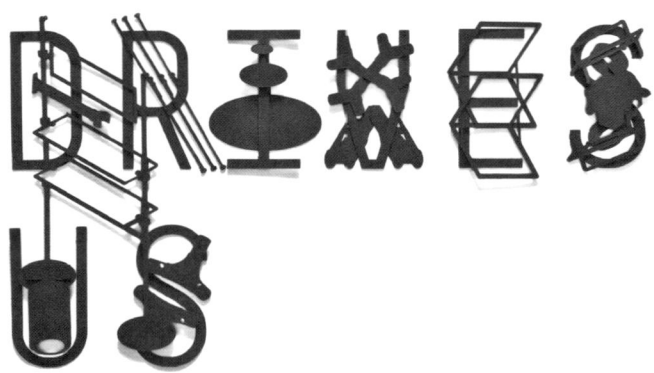

Structure

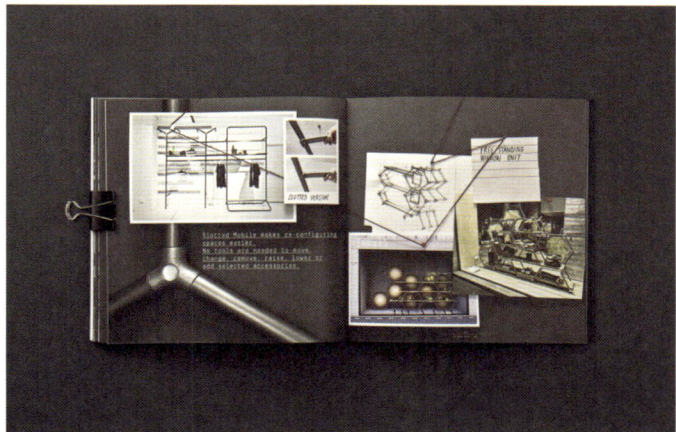

This book was designed for ALU, an international retail company. The task was to redesign the company profile for EuroShop 2011, where the brand's new products were going to be presented. As ALU's products are primarily made of basic materials like aluminum, the designers took inspiration from the soul of these elements to develop ALU's ID. They used pieces of art to present the brand's identity and its products through a series of keywords and by working with materials with a strong tactile element and neutral hues.

All illustrations and typography elements were made by cutting paper and assembling all those tiny pieces into several pieces of art. Product pages, on the other hand, are spreads containing photos, original sketches and real products arranged as big mood boards. A red thread connects the identity and products through the entire project. For the binding, the designers chose Bodonian. The combination of these elements gives the book a refined elegance, as if it were a monograph.

SAMUEL URIA EM DESCANTE

Inserted accordion

Hand sewing

Paper Material: Matte paper, cardboard
Size: 210mm x 148mm

Ivo Ferreira, Bruno Viegas   [Portugal]

●
Intended for a new album by Samuel Uria, this design tries something different from the beginning to the very end, adopting a grid system to explore a different approach to layout.

Cardboard was used for the cover, while in the core of the book, the viewer can find two foldable accordions with lyrics and some of the artist's reflections on his songs. At the end, an index of the album and the CD can be found. The booklet was made using 135g matte paper and digital offset printing.

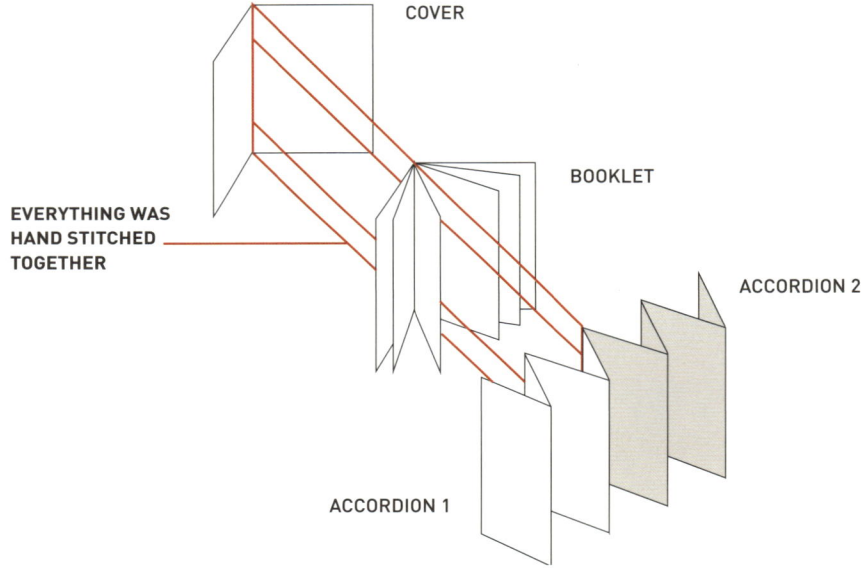

NEEDLEWORK NO MORE

Special jacket

Open spine

Inside cover pocket

Paper Material: Recycled paper, unbleached paper
Size: 210mm x 270mm

Urban Tribe [China]

• Urban Tribe is a fashion brand that strives to create natural and original designs. This book was inspired by the Miao people of Guizhou Province, China. The Miao are known for their traditions and elaborately embroidered costumes, which are handed down from mothers to their daughters generation after generation. This publication explores the exquisite embroidery work of these artisans, particularly that of 34 pairs of daughters and mothers. The work is accompanied by interviews and discussions with local villagers about their life in Guizhou.

Needlework No More contains 177 pictures and a CD of folk songs. Printed in CMYK, the design supports the book's topic with an open spine and the use of gauze and rustic materials throughout. The jacket is the hallmark, made of dyed fabric made by the Miao people as an essential representation of their wisdom and culture.

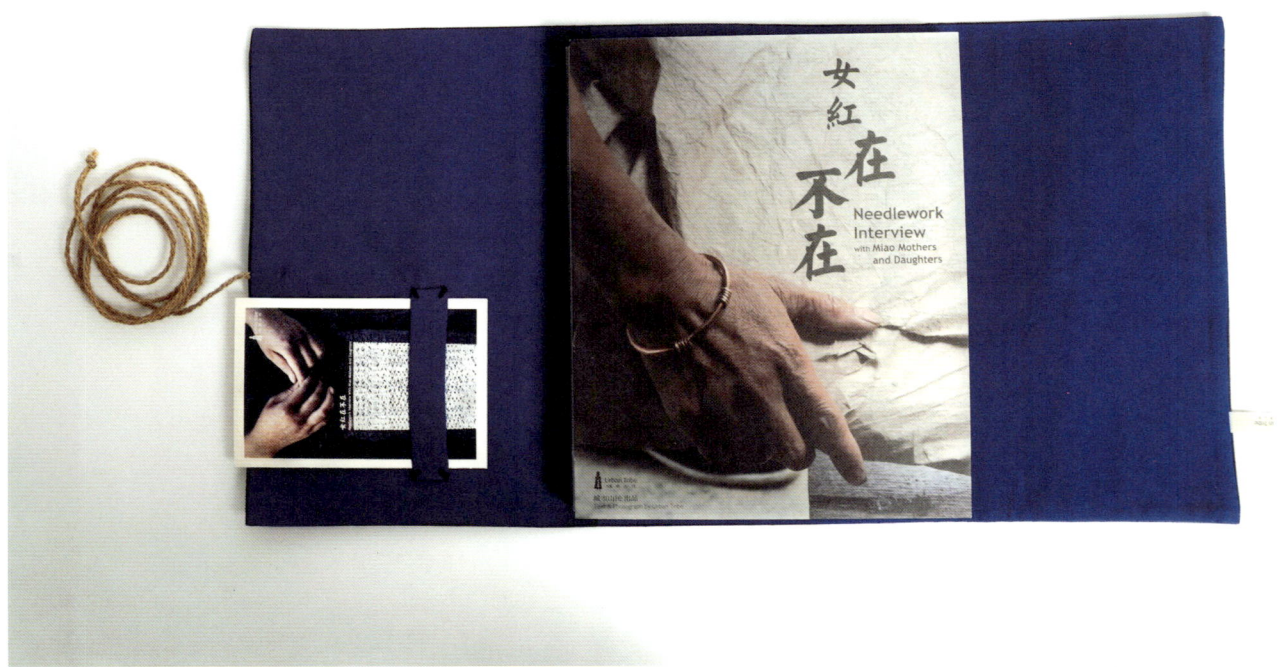

Structure

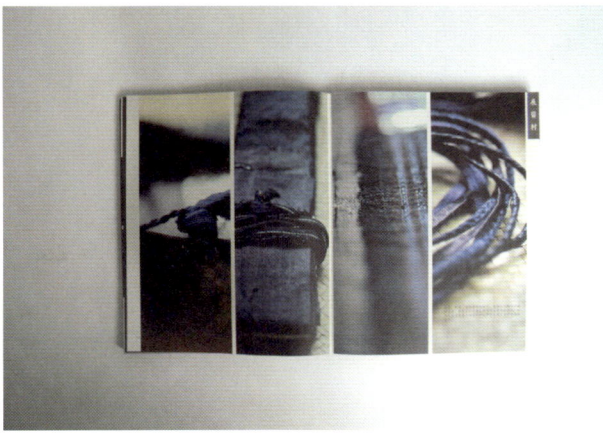

TEA-HEE

Coptic Binding

Fluorescent color

Hand sewing

Paper Material: Canvas fabric, paperboards, matte off-white stock
Size: 160mm x 200mm

Jiani Lu [Canada]

Tea-Hee is a playful and lighthearted hand-bound reference guide for tea lovers and enthusiasts. It introduces readers to a world of tea and tea craft through three chapters. It sets a friendly and accessible tone through inviting colors and organic lines, but the technical and instructional side of tea-making is not compromised. The book uses a systematic visual approach with hard-edged illustrations, and vector-based infographic visuals to make things clear for the reader.

The craftsmanship involved in producing the book was inspired by the art of tea making, which is a slow process that calls for patience as well as hands-on technique and creation. It features an illustrated, handmade, canvas hardcover. The book is Coptic bound and features four signatures.

Structure

TERSAS: ONTVOUWD

Triangular flap
Special binding

Paper Material: Coated paper
Size: 200mm x 200mm

Karolien Pauly [Belgium]

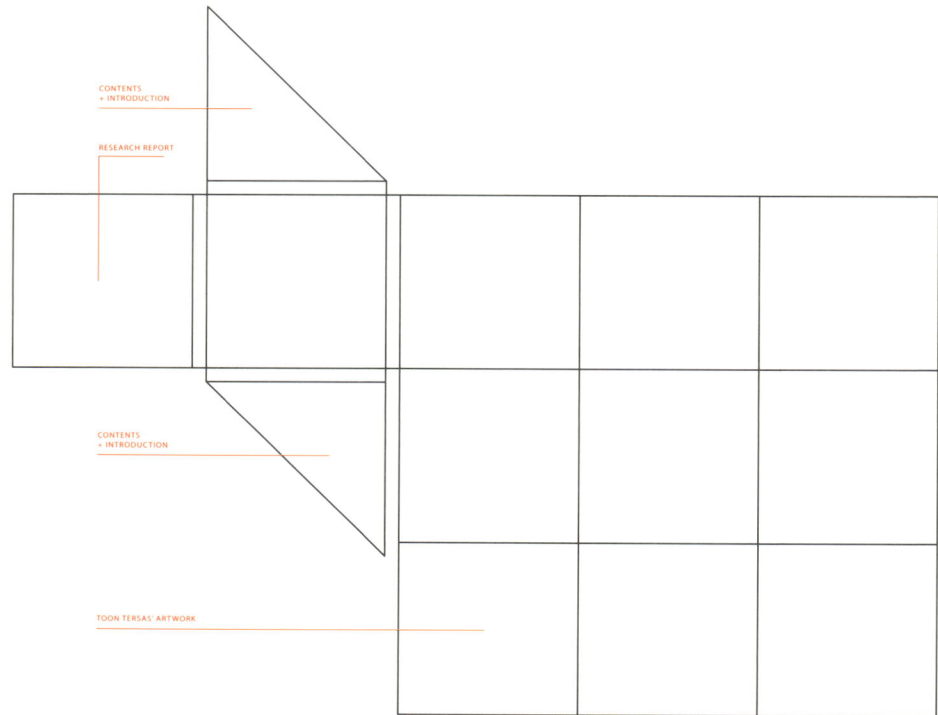

●

The title of the book is *Tersas: Ontvouwd* (*Tersas: Unfolded*), which reflects the complex form of the book. The designer wanted to create a book that readers have to fold themselves in order to read it. This is an experimental book on the works of the Dutch-Belgian artist Toon Tersas.

The book *Tersas: Ontvouwd* consists of three parts. The first component is the two triangular flaps, which are also the cover of the book. They contain the index and the introduction. When these two flaps are spread out, the second part of the book becomes visible. This part contains information about the research for the concepts of an exhibition on Toon Tersas. Those concepts were created by the students of the graphic design department of the MAD-Faculty in Genk, Belgium. The third part is a presentation of a selection of Tersas's work. When completely unfolded, this component resembles a labyrinth.

58

Structure

DIE GROSSE KUNSTAUSSTELLUNG NRW DÜSSELDORF 2013

Fluorescent color
Special binding
Shortened title page

Paper Material: Pure white natural paper
Size: 210mm x 170mm

Morphoria design collective [Germany]

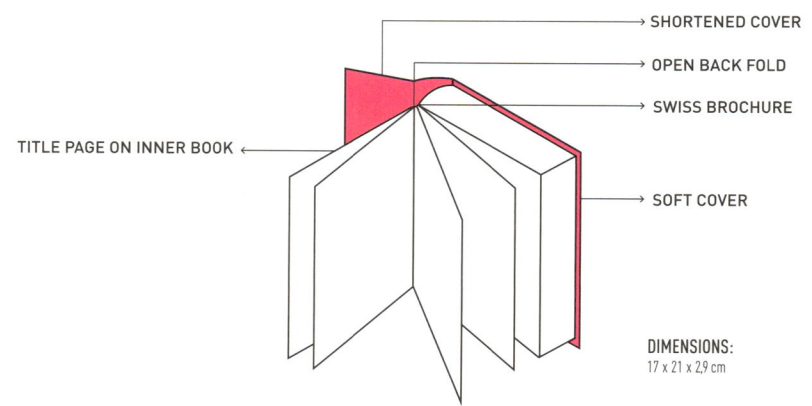

SHORTENED COVER
OPEN BACK FOLD
SWISS BROCHURE
TITLE PAGE ON INNER BOOK
SOFT COVER

DIMENSIONS: 17 x 21 x 2,9 cm

 Structure

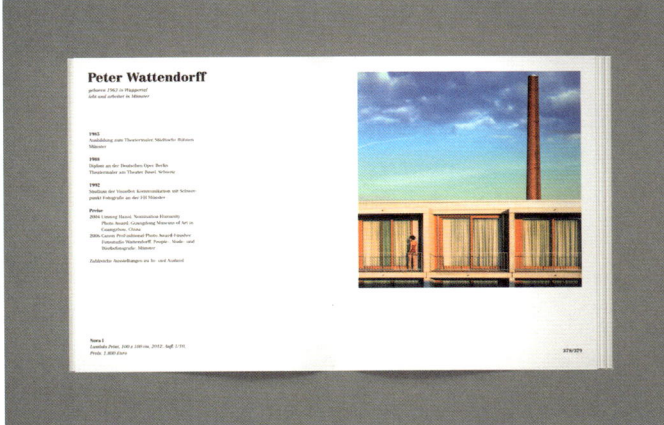

This catalog was created for an annual exhibition of local artists in Düsseldorf, Germany, called DIE GROSSE Kunstausstellung NRW Düsseldorf 2013. It includes the history and stories not only of the sponsoring foundation and the exhibition, but also a portrait of and some stories about the winning artist. Furthermore, it is a collection of all the exhibited work from the 175 participating artists.

It was produced using offset printing technology in a run of 1,300 copies. For the binding of the inner book, the designers used a technique called Swiss brochure. The soft cover is fixed only to the back side of the book, creating a loose spine and shortened cover. The award winner of 2013 is featured on the first page of the inner book. These techniques allowed the creators to draw a distinction between the two layers of visual identity.

CSAC 1971–1980
MOSTRE FOTOGRAFICHE

Special binding

Double covers with a shared back

Paper Material: Uncoated Fabriano paper, colored Fabriano paper
Size: 140mm x 187mm

Riccardo Zecchini & Giorgio Fanecco   [Italy]

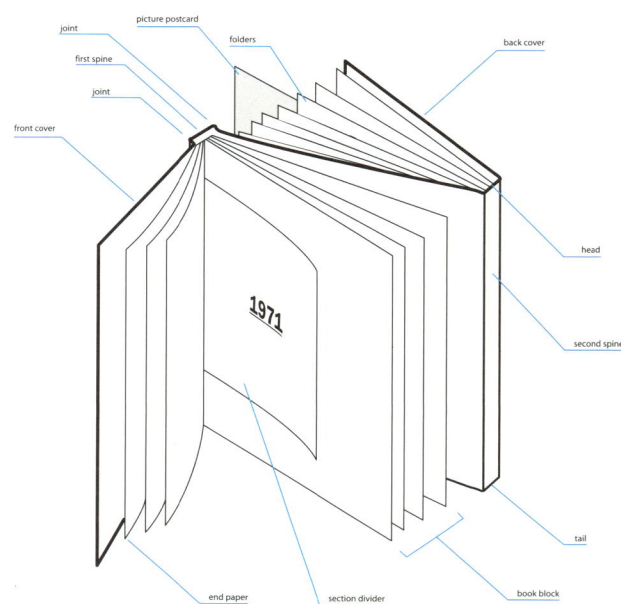

Structure

This book tells the story of CSAC, an Italian archive. CSAC collects, preserves and presents a wide range of different materials from different types of visual communication. The book focuses on photographic exhibitions between 1971 and 1980 and underlines an important aspect of the exposed works: its dimension. All these exhibitions have in fact allowed the visitors, who were used to dealing only with photo reproductions inside magazines, to analyze the original prints, including aspects like their size and material.

For this story, the designers decided to emphasize social aspects in two ways. First they highlighted the size of the original photographs, then they highlighted the function of gathering and cataloging the archives. These special points lead the designers to create a book that is split into two parts. The first part shows the photos of the exhibitions in their original size. The second part presents the same photos as shown in the archive folders, including all their classification data.

MYTHOLOGY OF VIOLENCE

Folded pages
Tritone printing

Paper Material: Munken Print Cream
Size: 130mm x 170mm

Beste Bibi   [Turkey]

● *Mythology of Violence* is a book that covers the concept of violence in cinema by analyzing six film directors and their films. The designers used this book as a source and redesigned it as a set containing six books.

⁞ All the books juxtapose the characteristic features of the directors. Different folding and cutting techniques are used for separators and design elements. The main logo contains elements from each of the six books, giving the set continuity.

Structure

65

APTE

Special jacket design
Book set
Foiling

Paper Material: Alto paper, GC1 carton, offset paper
Size: 160mm x 200mm

Marcin Hernas/tessera – graphic design
[Poland]

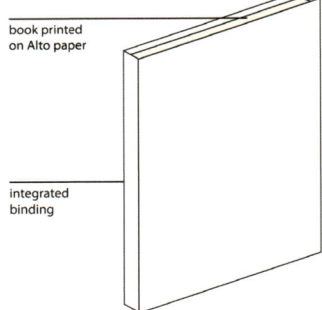
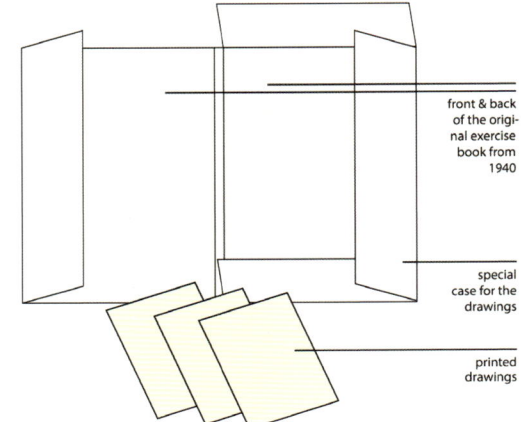

 This publication consists of two parts. The first is a non-fiction work about the writer, poet and painter Ryszard Apte. Apte was a Polish Jew who was killed during World War II in the labor camp in Stalowa Wola. The second part consists of a reproduction of Apte's school exercise book, which lay hidden in an attic for 50 years. This exercise book is filled with previously unpublished drawings.

The two volumes are bound together with a strap of paper and foil for protection. The second volume containing the set of drawings is a very special and unusual type of publication. The drawings are preserved the way they were found—on loose and separate pages. Fifteen drawings appear on separate sheets and are enclosed in a case that was designed to look like the cover of Apte's exercise book. It is a unique style of publication in that readers are granted access to the series in the most unaltered way possible.

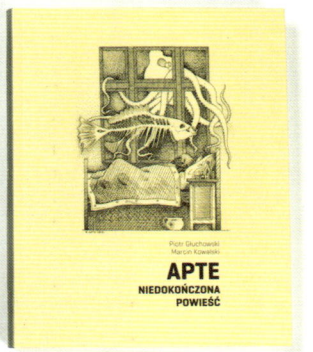

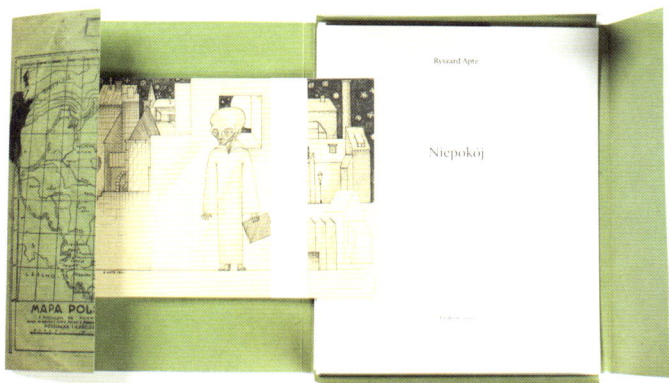

FREEDOM

French binding

Laser cutting

Printed flap

Paper Material: Antalis Arktika, Antalis Ecco Book Cream
Size: 135mm x 195mm

Marcin Hernas/tessera – graphic design
[Poland]

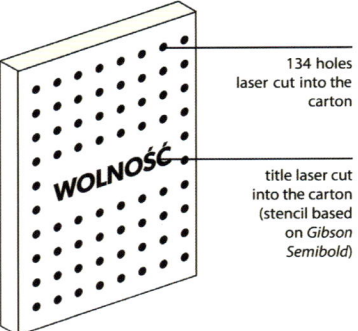
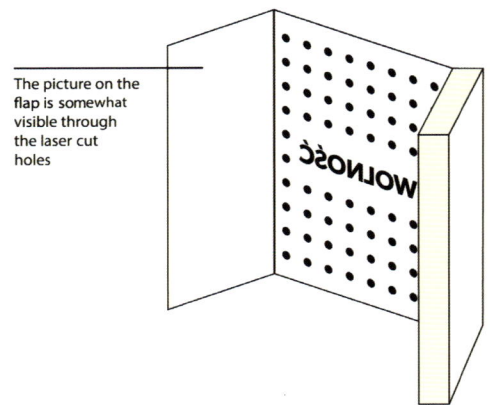

• This anthology entitled *Wolnosc* (freedom) consists of various texts on modern sociopolitical and cultural life. The designer transposed Giorgio Agamben's take on the concept of homo sacer into a graphic concept. To illustrate the Italian philosopher's elusive concept of freedom, the designer used an ambiguous image of a wolf intertwined with that of a Guántanamo prisoner deprived of all human and civil rights. The wolf is printed on the front cover, while the image of the prisoner can be found on the cover's interior side, on the flap.

The cover is based on two colors: black and Pantone orange (orange represents the publisher's logo and the color worn by Guántanamo prisoners). The book's title is laser cut into the carton of the front cover, as are 134 circular holes. These empty spaces suggest that something disturbing always lurks below the surface. A Guántanamo prisoner is barely discernible through the holes, which can be interpreted as the irreducible connection between freedom and lack of freedom, between free people and prisoners, between masters and servants, and between the socially priviledged and the socially disadvantaged.

DOES TURKEY NEED DESIGNERS?

Shortened cover with lamination
French binding
Printed fore-edge
Special ink

Paper Material: Soft cardboard, photocopy paper
Size: 148mm x 210mm

Umut Altıntaş [Turkey]

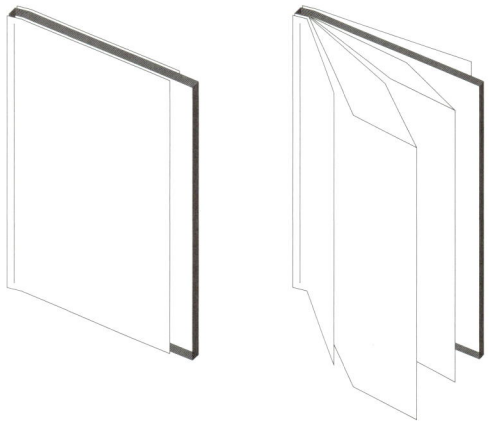

- *Does Turkey Need Designers?* was written by Esen Karol. The text was translated into Turkish from the original English text and both languages are represented in the layout. The goal was to create a text that would allow the book to be as expressive as possible.

- A piece of cardboard with a bright red outside and dull grey inside was used for the book cover. It was inspired by the sentence "We are more concerned about how the package looks from the outside but don't much care about the inside." The title of the book appears both on the edge of the book and inside along the pages, so as to constantly remind the reader of the question the title poses. This limited edition A5-sized book was printed in a photocopy machine on fax paper and features a hand-sewn binding.

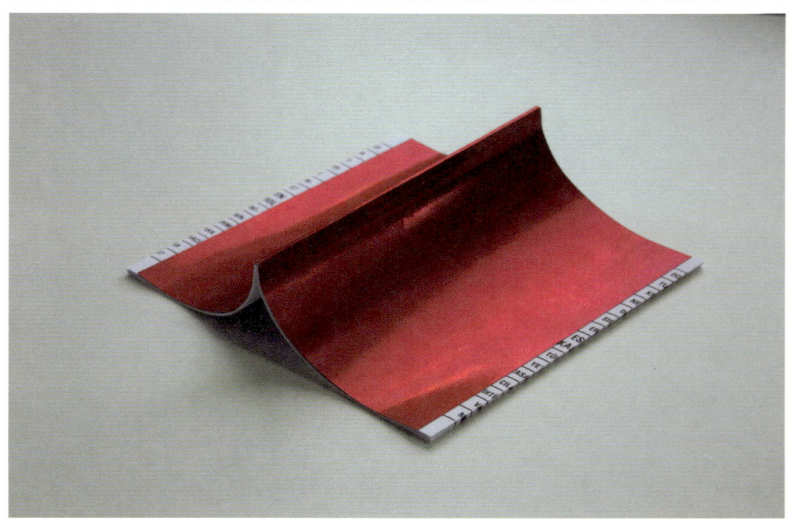

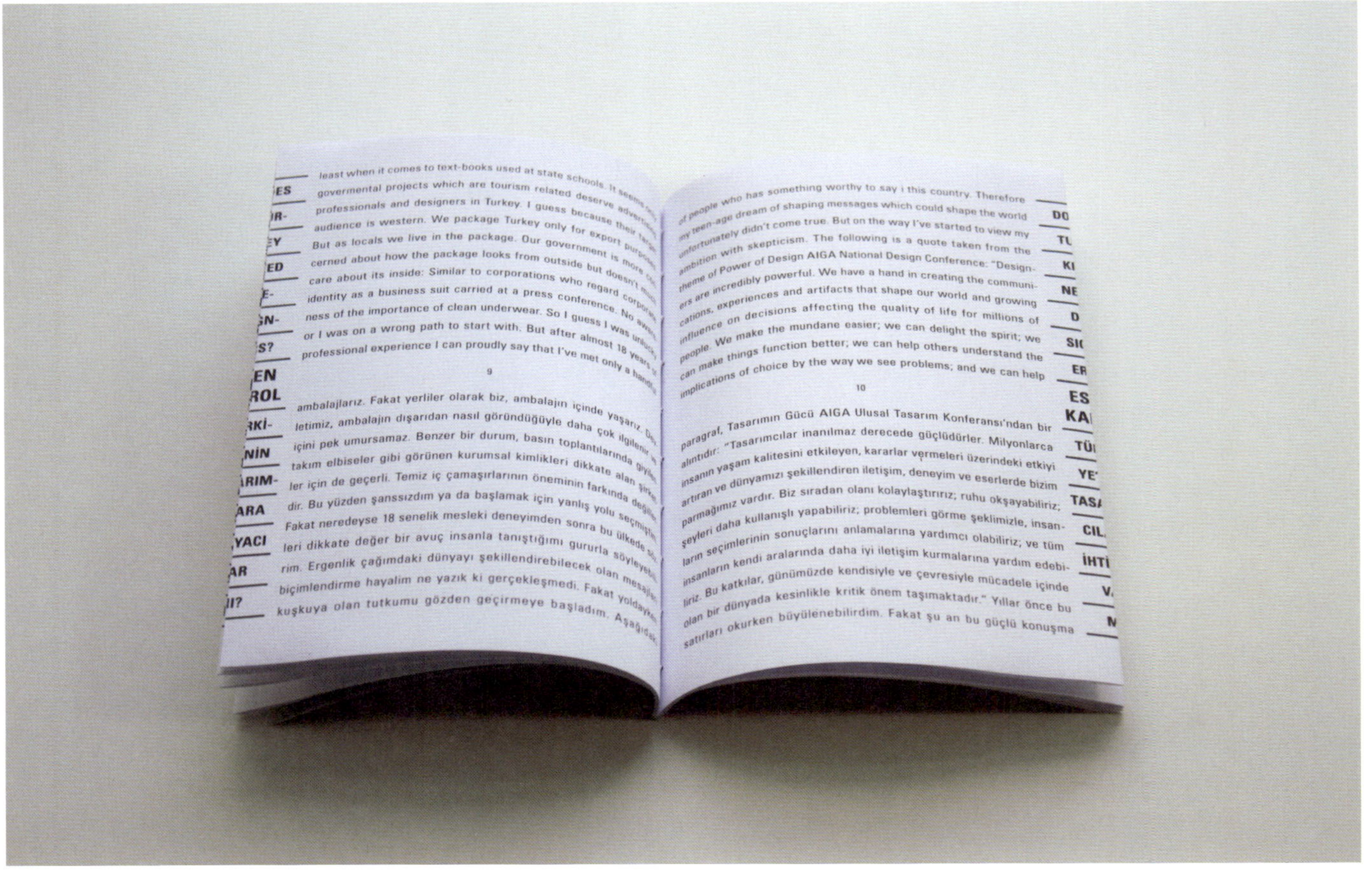

Structure

71

THE COLLOCALIA CITY

Jacket with band
Die cutting
Special book case

Paper Material: Coated paper, matte coated paper
Size: 140mm x 210mm

Ye Sheng-hao [China]

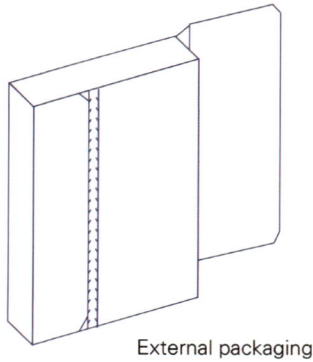
External packaging

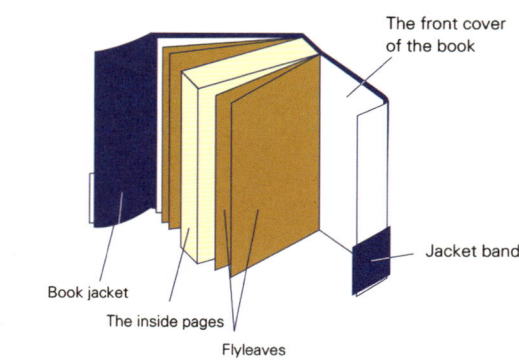
The front cover of the book · Jacket band · Flyleaves · The inside pages · Book jacket

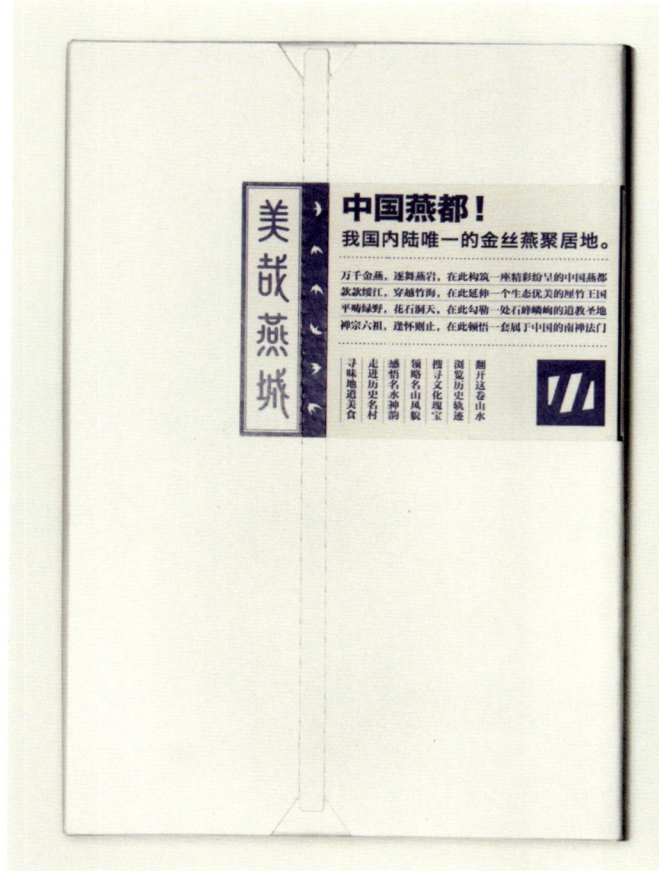

Structure

Huaiji, China is known as the "swift city" due to the great number of birds that can be found there. One of its towns, Qiaotou, attracts flocks of swiftlets that have come all the way from Hainan. The name of this publication is derived from this phenomenon. The book covers the history, culture, and tourist attractions of the city, and includes descriptions of local ancient villages.

The Collocalia City is divided into six chapters, each of which centers around swiftlets. The limited number of chapters lends simplicity and creativity to the book. The book reads from right to left and consists of the case, jacket, cover, an additional dust jacket band, content pages and an inserted feedback card. The contents of the book is displayed on a printed sticker on the jacket.

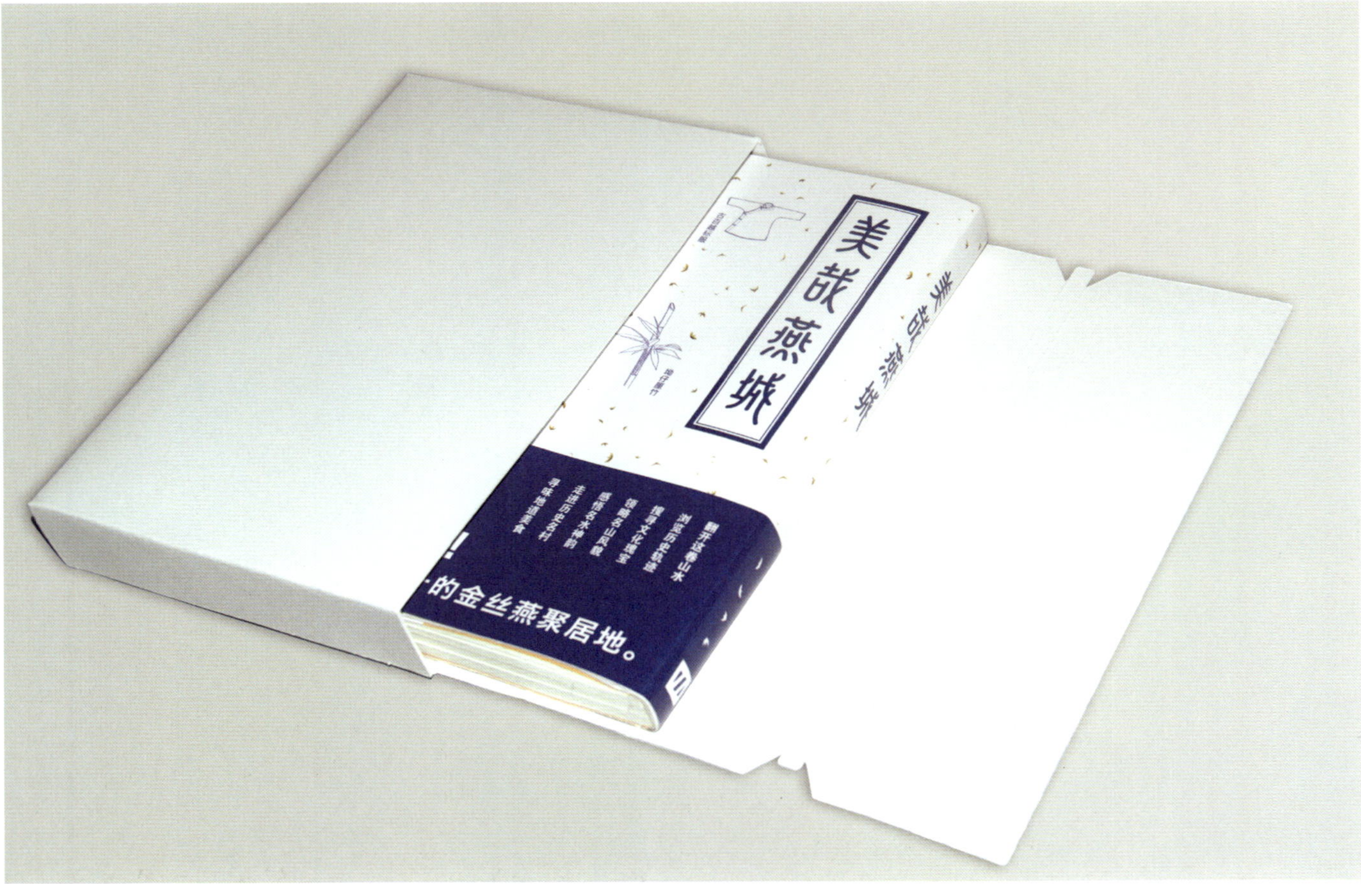

HERE/THERE

Embossing
UV coating
Lamination
Special binding

Paper Material: Linen, tracing paper, mixed cardstock
Size: 260mm X 280mm

Guangzhou Zhengdian Advertisement Co., Ltd. [China]

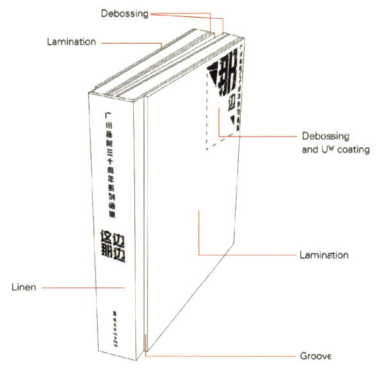

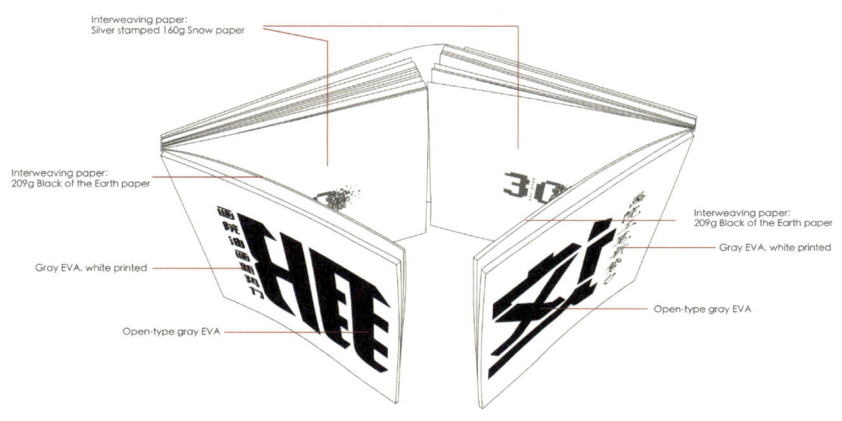

● This painting collection entitled *Here/There: New Waves of Fine Brushwork and Oil Paintings* is made up of two parts. The "Here" part covers fine brushwork, while the "There" focuses on oil paintings. The concept for this design aims to categorize and at the same time integrate the two genres in the same publication.

⁙ The packaging style of this book merges with the typography in a black and white design that references the aesthetic of contemporary art and design. Multiple materials were used including wood, flax, EVA and tallow paper.

CONTEMPORARY ART IN TURKEY (SERIES)

Special case
Inserts
Special jacket designs

Paper Material: Matte coated paper, uncoated paper
Size: 245mm × 190mm

Esen Karol Tasarım Ltd. [Turkey]

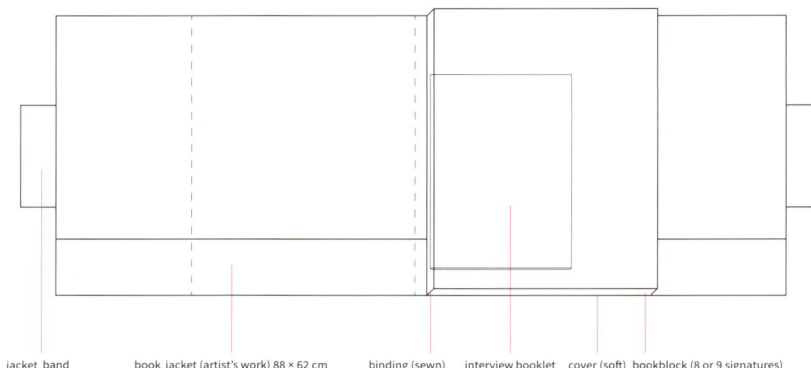

jacket band | book jacket (artist's work) 88 × 62 cm | binding (sewn) | interview booklet | cover (soft) | bookblock (8 or 9 signatures)

   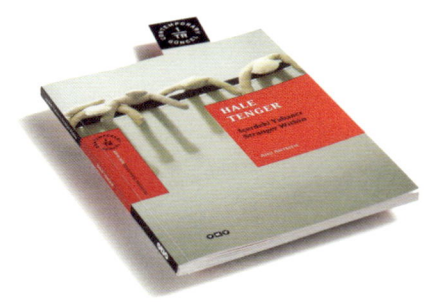

● Structure

● *Contemporary Art in Turkey* is a series of twelve books curated by René Block and published by Yapı Kredi between 2007 and 2011.

⁙ Each book features complete texts in both English and Turkish. Each book also features an interview with the artist and images of his/her works. Each book is wrapped in a special print prepared by the artist. The interviews appear in a booklet that is stitched to the book block.

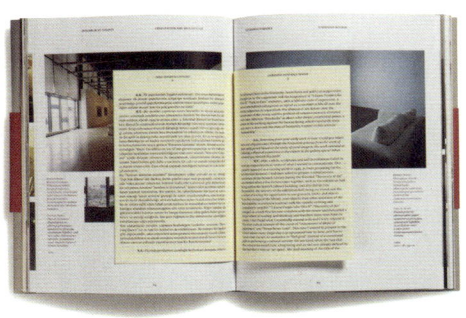

DLA THESIS

Open spine
Laser engraving

Paper Material: Offset paper
Size: 180mm x 260mm

Akos Polgardi [Hungary]

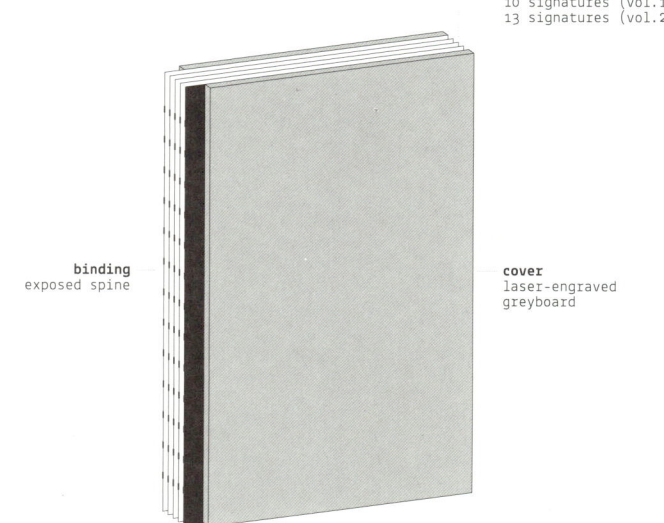

book block
10 signatures (vol.1)
13 signatures (vol.2)

binding
exposed spine

cover
laser-engraved greyboard

Structure

This is a book design for interior designer/architect Peter Szendro's D.L.A. (Doctor of Liberal Arts) thesis. The publication consists of two volumes: Vol. 1, the dissertation and Vol. 2, the portfolio.

The books feature an open-spine binding and laser-engraved greyboard covers.

DE BEST VORMGEGEVEN BOEKEN 2013

Unique cover
Unique materials

Paper Material: Recycled offset paper, cotton paper
Size: 163mm x 190mm

Stan Van Steendam [Belgium]

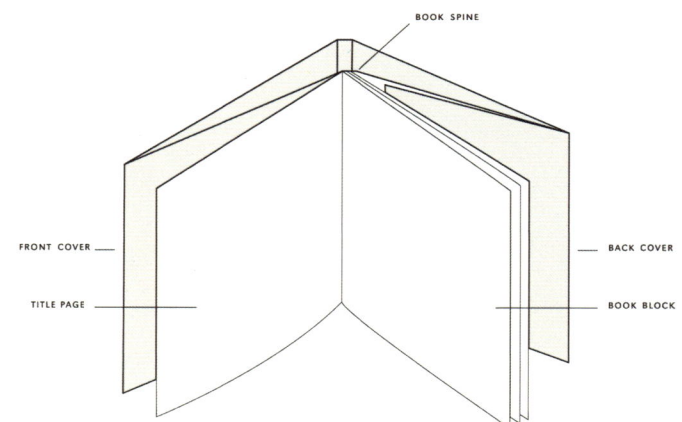

Structure

This book is a catalog for DE BEST VORMGEGEVEN BOEKEN. Recycled cardboard and cotton paper were used for the cover and the inside pages, giving the book a rough texture and appearance. This tactile approach creates a contrast with the clean and uniform look of the design.

The book is offset printed and bound with yarn. The cover is glued only to the back of the book block and is loose on the spine and front. The designer chose to create the book cover by folding the material over to create two layers, giving the cover added strength.

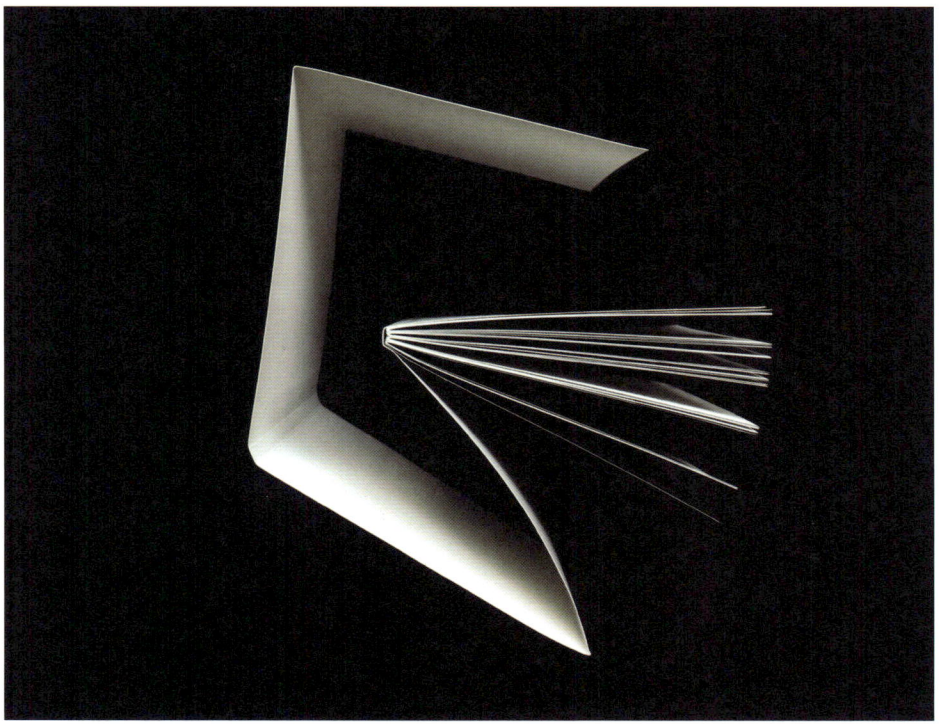

SLEEP

Special cover design
Multiple materials
Accordion binding

Paper Material: Book boards, Japanese fabric paper, marbled acrylic paper, charcoal paper, glossy card stock
Size: 217mm x 145mm

Joél Valdez [USA]

The evening hangs beneath the moon
A silver thread on darkened dune
With closing eyes and resting head
I know that sleep is coming soon

Upon my pillow, safe in bed
A thousand pictures fill my head
I cannot sleep, my mind's a-flight
And yet my limbs seem made of lead

If there are noises in the night
A frightening shadow, flickering light
Then I surrender unto sleep
Where clouds of dream give second sight

What dreams may come, both dark and deep
Of flying wings and soaring leap
As I surrender unto sleep,
As I surrender unto sleep.

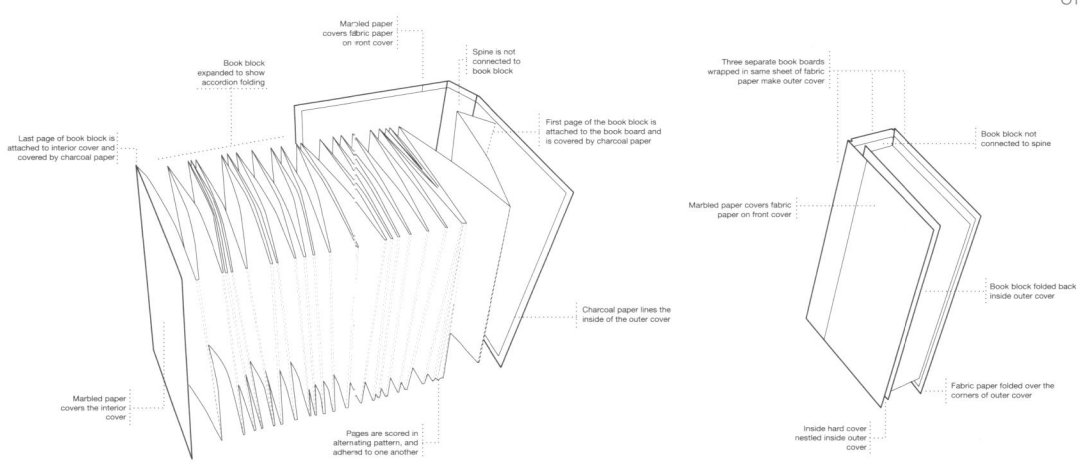

Structure

Sleep is a visual narrative. Its content is based on Charles Anthony Silvestri's poem "Sleep." It creates an alternate interpretation through photography and typography. The story follows a girl who wakes from sleep and takes a walk. As she ventures out, her subconscious begins to unravel. It is designed so that the reader can not differentiate dreams from reality.

The binding is wrapped in a dark blue Japanese fabric paper. The cover features a silver marbled paper with a pearly texture. The inside of the exterior binding is lined with black charcoal paper. The second cover is covered in a marbled acrylic paper. The pages of the book are inkjet printed on glossy cardstock. Each page is scored, folded in sequence, and adhered to the next one to form an accordion-like shape.

AS MEMORY FADES

Open spine
Linen cover
Screen printing
Inner pages in two colors

Paper Material: Gmund; Geese Papier
Size: 205mm x 290mm

Studio Sarah Schwarz   [Germany]

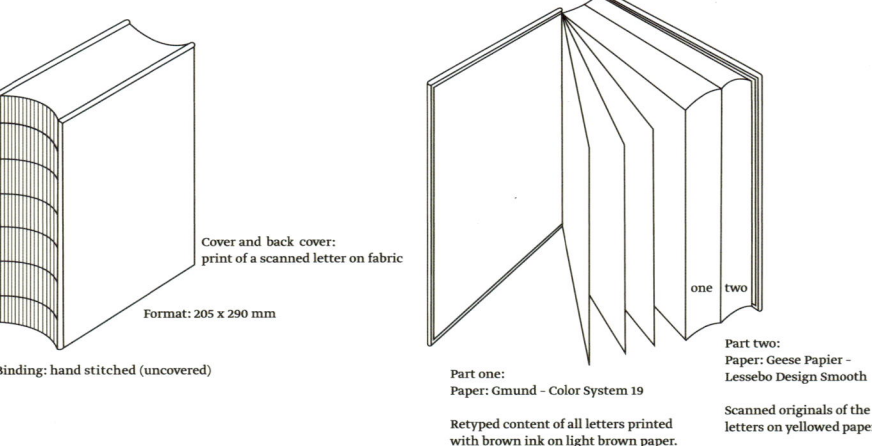

Cover and back cover:
print of a scanned letter on fabric

Format: 205 x 290 mm

Binding: hand stitched (uncovered)

Part one:
Paper: Gmund - Color System 19

Retyped content of all letters printed with brown ink on light brown paper. Text is interrupted by interview.

Part two:
Paper: Geese Papier – Lessebo Design Smooth

Scanned originals of the letters on yellowed paper.

Structure

This book design project documents a box of letters that belonged to the designer's grandmother. The letters were penned by fifteen different authors, including friends and lovers. The letters tell the story of her grandmother's life.

The book is divided into two parts. The first part shows the retyped content of all the letters, printed with brown ink on light brown paper. The second part of the text is made up of questions that the designer asked while her grandmother was reading the letters and her grandmother's responses. The second part also displays scanned originals of the letters on yellowed paper. The two parts are connected with the help of a double page style that enables readers to easily cross reference the text and images.

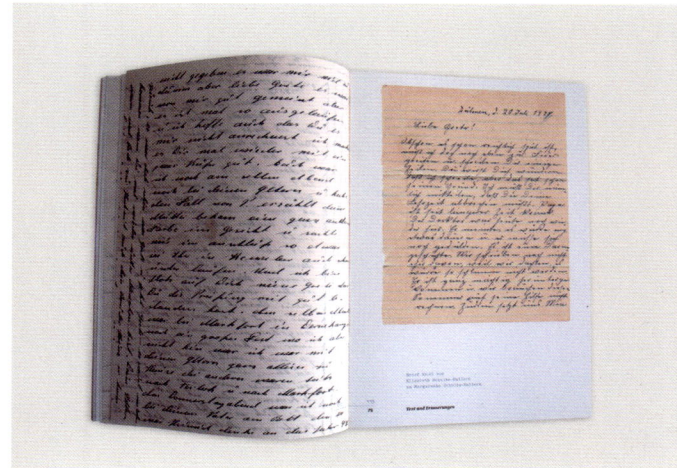
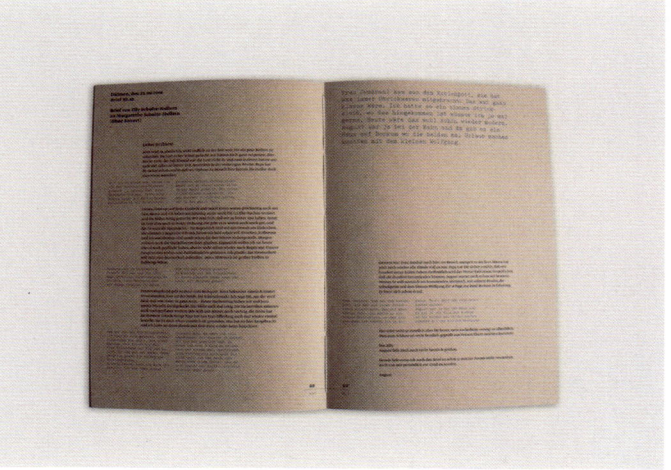

LINK UP: CREATIVE PROCESSES OF COUPLES IN DESIGN

Unique cover design

Contrasting paper textures

Paper Material: Munken Lynx Rough, Chromolux White, Chromolux White
Size: 260mm x 185mm

Sandra Weber Grafikdesign   [Germany]

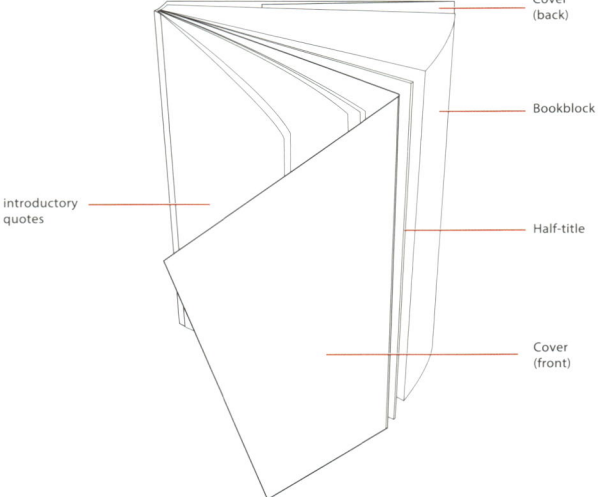

Cover (back)

Bookblock

introductory quotes

Half-title

Cover (front)

Structure

● This is a portrait of design couples that focuses on their cooperation and interaction during the creative process. The author queried the designing partners about what the key to their cooperation was and whether working with his/her partner makes the design process more efficient.

 The focus of LINK UP is contrasts. This focus is represented through the use of both coated and uncoated paper, contrasting color choices, and contrasts in the ways in which the couples' pictures are arranged. The cover itself features contrasts both in its design and material. The layout of the interior creates and plays with the notion of links through the visual representation of the interviews and the interview texts. In this way, the book is united.

87

20,000 LEGUAS DE VIAJE SUBMARINO

Special jacket

Antique finish

Paper Material: Cardboard, laid paper, Clariana
Size: 180mm x 250mm

Jess García [Spain]

The objective of the project was to develop a design for a special edition of the book *20,000 Leagues under the Sea*, a tale of grand adventures on the seas, explorations and discoveries of new worlds. Travel and adventure are the two central concepts of this novel, which are represented in the design and make this edition so special.

The book begins with interactions with the reader. The cover is designed with textures that give it a well-worn yet intriguing look, as if it is an old travel journal. Important chapters feature illustrations similar to the ones on the case. The printed cardboard case adds an additional layer of character to this publication.

Structure

CHOREOGRAM
—THE NEW LANGUAGE OF DANCE

Elongated format
Monochromatic design
Dropdown layout
Jacket band

Paper Material: Classic laid paper, cotton and spongy tact, grammage
Size: 105mm x 200mm

Alba Miralles Blanch [Spain]

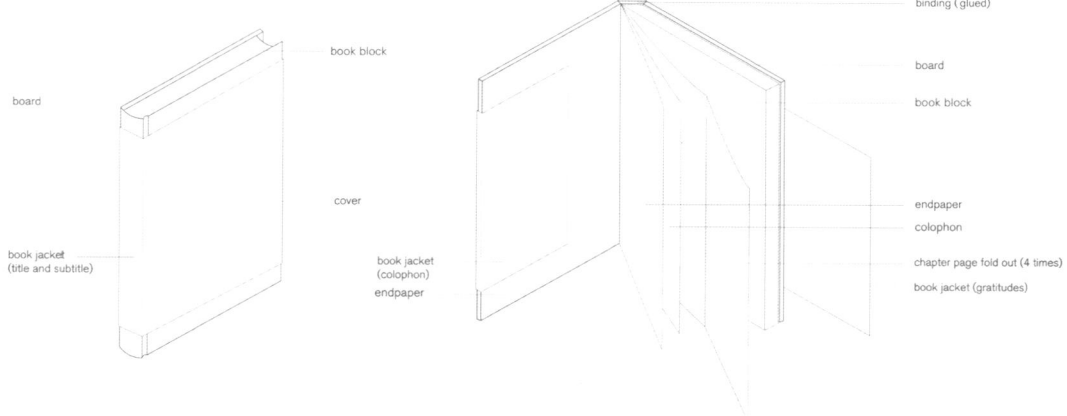

Structure

This design began with the objective of creating a publication on the topic of faith. The designer believed that the best way to do that was through dance, a common language. People have used dance to communicate emotional changes and facilitate relationships since they were babies. Music and dance can never be separated and *Choreogram* ("choreo-," in Greek means "to dance," and "-grama," "to write") aims to be an iconographic writing system for dance, a new universal language of dance built on the basic forms of graphic design. It uses the circle, triangle and square, which have similar aspects to musical language, but in the end create a more intuitive system. This method has special ways of communicating elements of dance, such as position, direction, shape, acceleration and pause, rhythm, time, reading sequence and movement.

The book's pages are adorned with black and white images of famous musicians and dancers in subtle poses. The chapters open with dropdown photographs, meant to create tension and emotion, as dance does. The book is handmade, with black cloth hardcovers and a jacket that wraps around with the title, subtitle and credits printed on it.

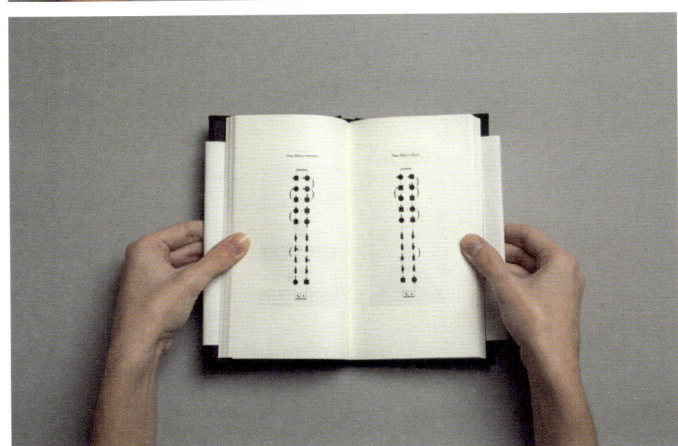

BICYCLE PORTRAITS

Special cover and binding
Foiling
Embossing
Ribbon bookmarkers

Paper Material: Matte coated paper, uncoated paper
Size: 300mm x 215mm

Gabrielle Guy   [South Africa]

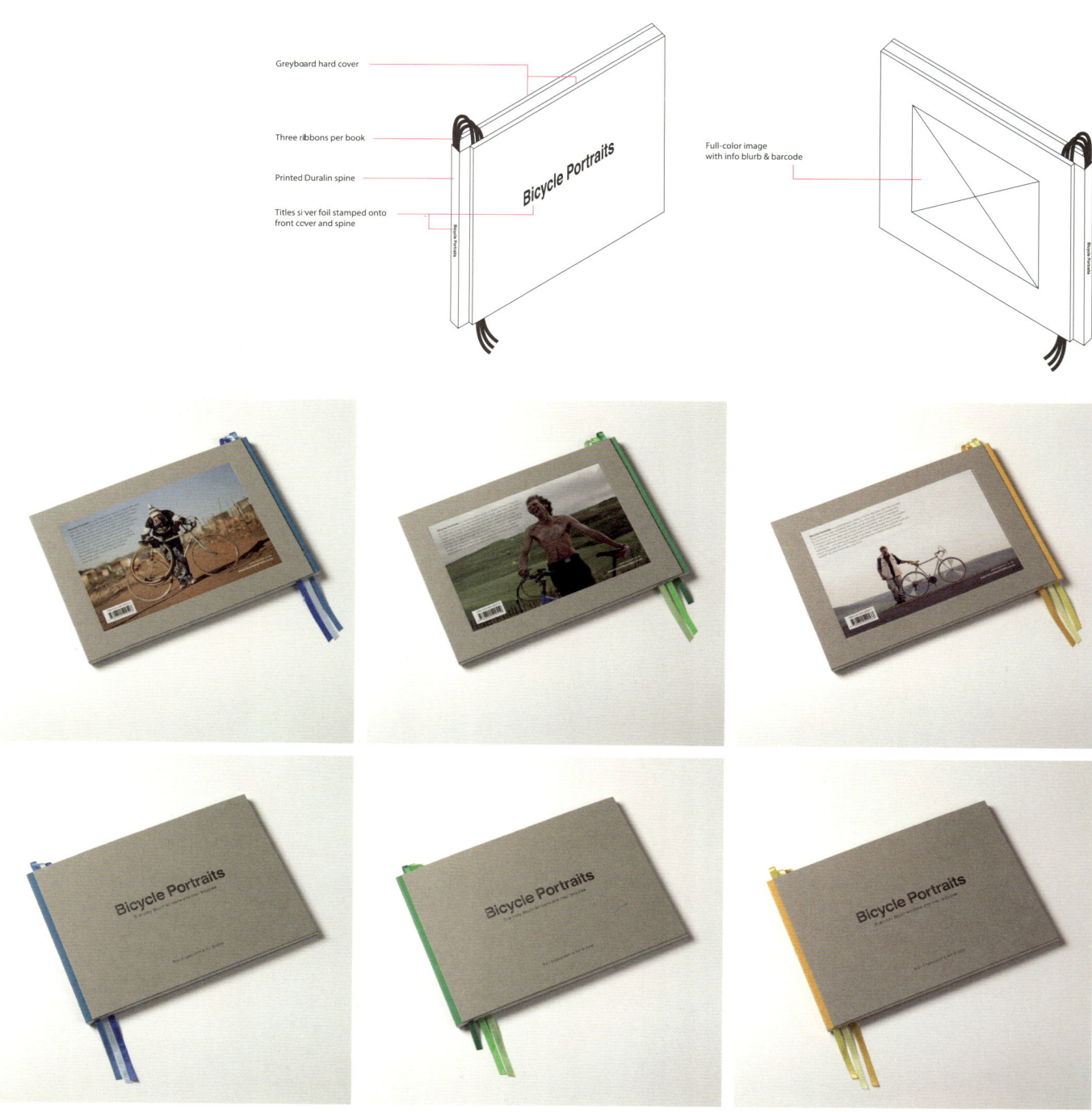

Structure

●
Bicycle Portraits by Stan Engelbrecht and Nic Grobler includes over 500 photographs and stories of individuals the photographers met on their bicycle journeys around South Africa. The designer decided to use 162 stories, and split them into 3 books. Dividing the material into three books instead of doing one very thick and heavy book made the resulting set more convenient for purchase and easier to transport.

Bright colors were chosen to be reminiscent of colorful bicycle paint. The silver foiling shines like silver chrome on a bicycle frame. The photos inside are printed on matte-coated paper, while the foreword (printed on the endpapers) and mini-essays (tipped-in to the center of each book) are printed on uncoated paper.

VONDELVERZEN: NIEUW MEUBILAIR VONDELPARK

Wire-o binding

Paper Material: Uncoated offset paper, matte coated offset paper
Size: 165mm x 210mm

Haller Brun   [The Netherlands]

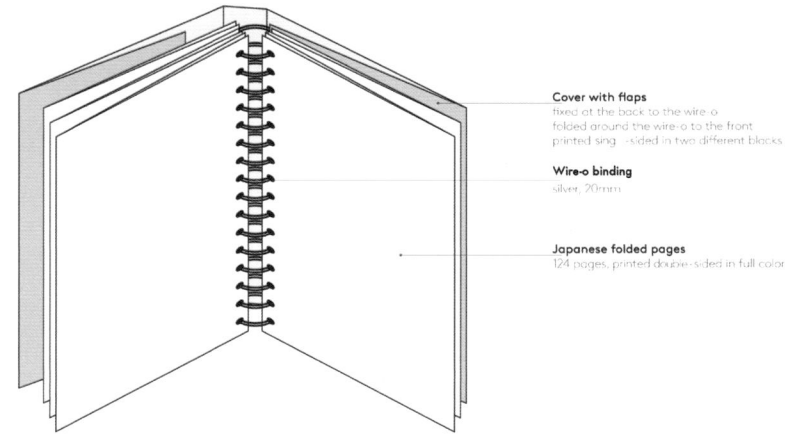

Cover with flaps
fixed at the back to the wire-o
folded around the wire-o to the front
printed single-sided in two different blacks

Wire-o binding
silver, 20mm

Japanese folded pages
124 pages, printed double-sided in full color

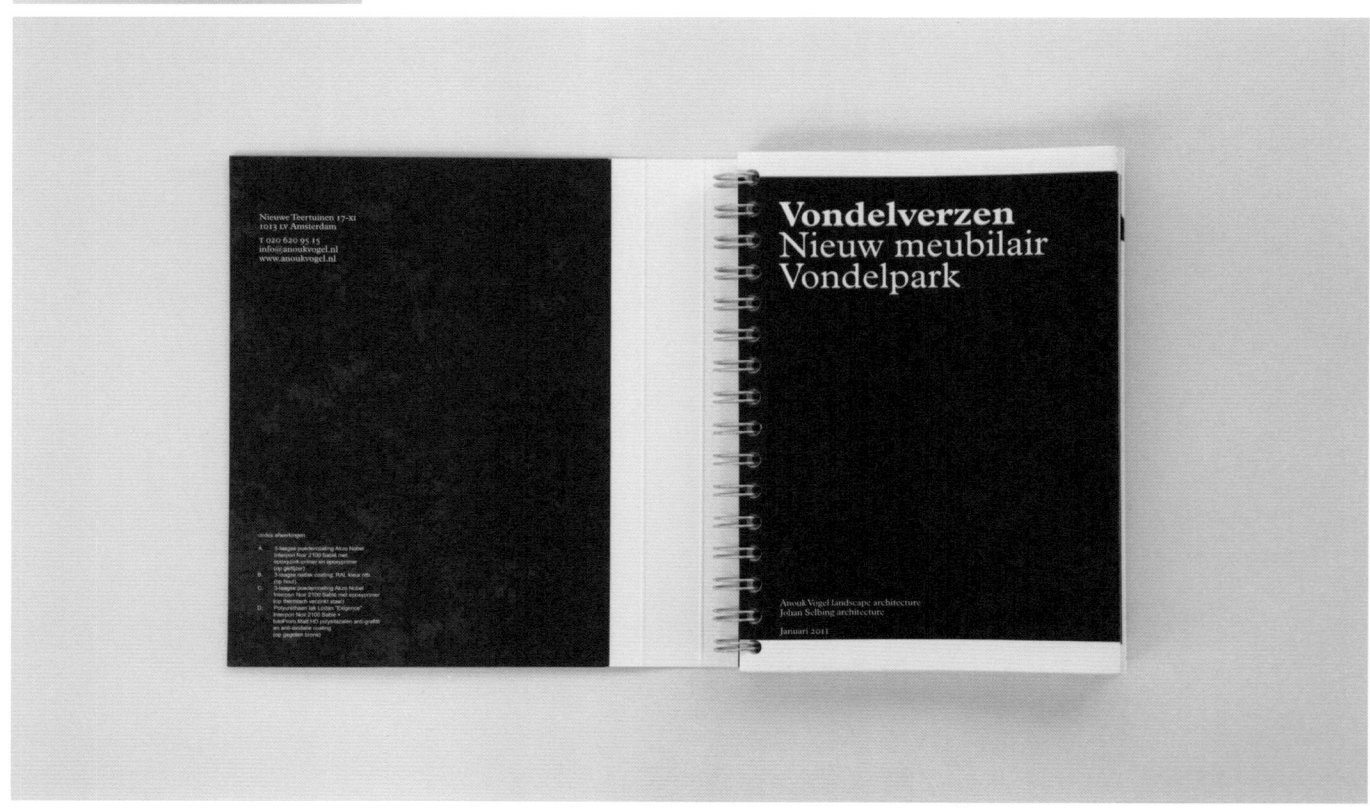

Structure

Vondelverzen is a book about the new designs for furniture for the Vondel park in Amsterdam. The book documents the design process with sketches, final drawings, renderings, and photos from production and of the finished products. The cover is printed in two different blacks, which fits with the design of the black furniture.

All of the chapters have a black register mark on the edge in the form of different tree leaves that can be found in the park. Together the register marks form evenly sized black squares on the cut edge of the pages. The book is wire-o bound, which fits with the content and helped to keep production costs down. To give it a chic finishing touch, the cover is attached in the back to the wire and is wrapped around the body of the book so that the binding is covered.

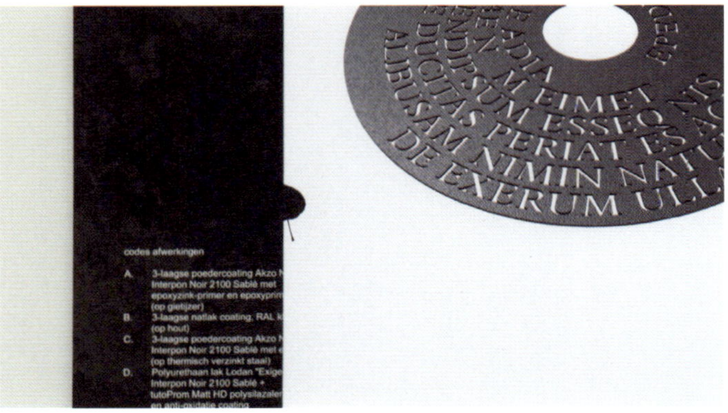

95

SURVIVAL OF THE PRETTIEST: THE SCIENCE OF BEAUTY

Unique cover design
Custom cutting
Metallic ink

Paper Material: Enviro
Size: 148mm × 210mm

Hanqingtang Design [China]

Survival of the Prettiest juxtaposes the beauty of men and women, to illustrate their compatibility and contrast, which is enforced by the design.

Structure

By enclosing the curtain on the cover, readers first see figures of beautiful men and women, and then come to content pages that have a "WM" (letters from "men" and "women") pattern throughout as an important visual element. The square and rounded corners also represent the differing beauty of the two genders.

MANIFESZTUM/PALASOVSZKY BOOK

Duotone
Double spine design
Hand-sewn binding

Paper Material: Tracing paper, Creative Rives paper
Size: 255mm x250mm

Balázs Klára [Hungary]

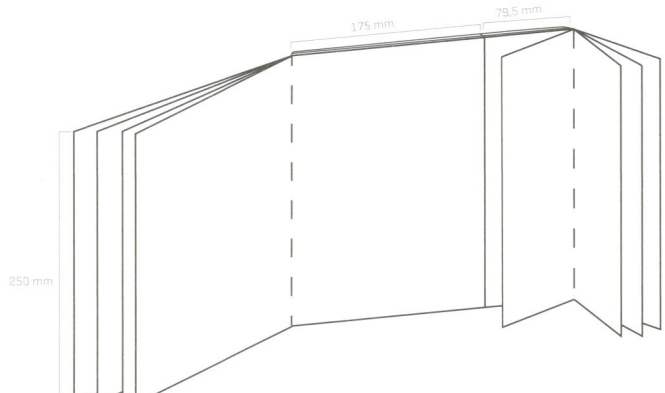

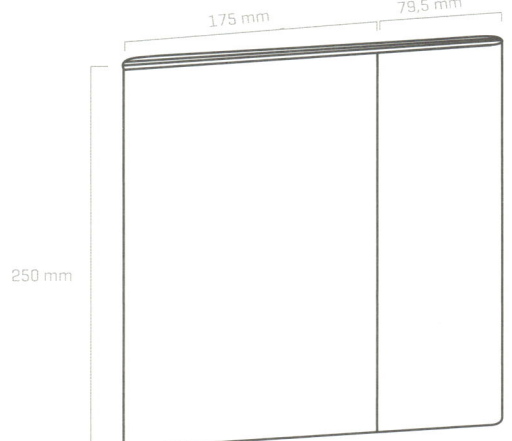

Structure

The poet Ödön Palasovsky is a major figure of the Hungarian avant-garde movement and activist theater. The volumes of work he produced caused a sensation within the literary circle of the period. His poetic volumes were less collections of poems, and more poetic texts composed in free verse. *Manifesztum's* design is based on a manifesto issued by Ödön Palasovszky and Iván Hevesy in 1922, arguing for collective art. This publication, with its particular form, design, word use, and radical approach, fits well in the genre of avant-garde manifestos. At the same time, it articulates a strong social critique: "the artist became dumb, the artist sold himself."

This book is organized in a way that allows each page to be read separately. The two spines allow the reader to turn the pages both right and left. This results in many possible page pairings. The careful graphic design evokes avant-garde art and Dadaist literature. Both red and black inks were used.

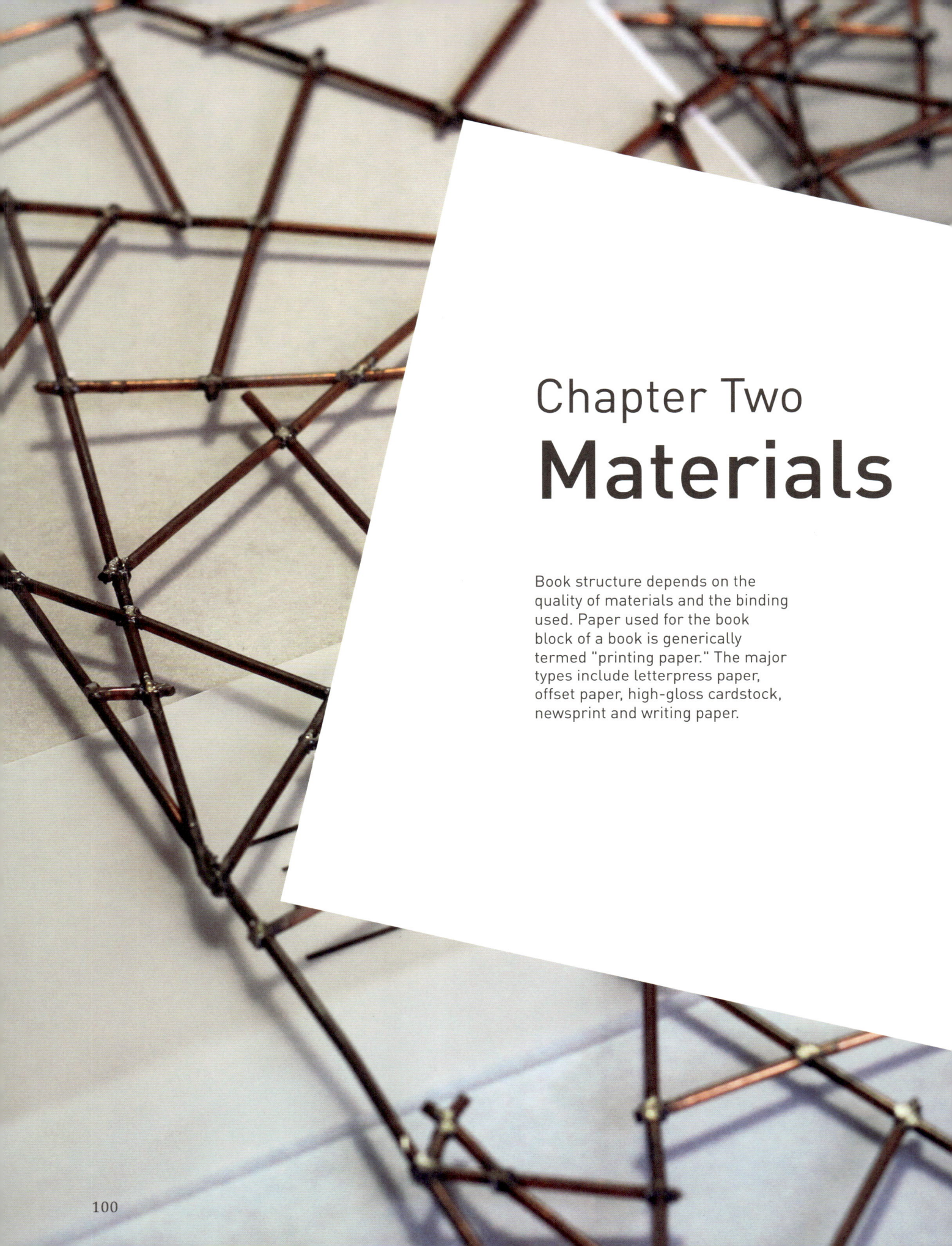

Chapter Two
Materials

Book structure depends on the quality of materials and the binding used. Paper used for the book block of a book is generically termed "printing paper." The major types include letterpress paper, offset paper, high-gloss cardstock, newsprint and writing paper.

Materials

Letterpress paper

P172~173

Offset paper

P94~95

Newsprint

P110~112

Common printing paper

Letterpress paper gets its name from its suitability for relief printing. It has a clean, smooth surface, even texture, good printing performance, high ink absorbency, an anti-drip property and is opaque. It has a smoother surface and is more waterproof than newspaper. It is also better at maintaining color purity and is not as absorbent, although it absorbs more evenly.

Offset paper, coated or uncoated, is generally web paper, or sometimes sheet paper, that features a strong surface strength and unusual breaking length (not less than 3000m), good ink-absorbency, a stable shape, does not easily crimp, and has an anti-drip property. It can be used in both lithography and offset printing and can be printed on both sides. Offset paper is a great choice for maintaining color purity.

Newsprint, or newspaper, is outstanding for its loose, elastic quality, which ensures the stability of printed ink. Furthermore, press polish treatment keeps it from dripping, which helps to preserve printed content. It is especially well suited to high-speed, revolving printing machines due to its strength and opacity.

Writing paper, as its name indicates, is paper that is good for writing. It is smooth, water-resistant and light-weight, making it the first choice for mass printing.

Specialty Papers and Materials

The materials mentioned above can serve basic printing needs, but higher standards of design demand the use of special paper or materials. Specialty paper is the result of processing multiple materials, like synthesized fiber and wood pulp compound. It can be decorated or treated with materials of other kinds, giving the paper various properties and making it suitable for a variety of uses. The result will be either visual or tactile specialty paper.

At the moment, the main types of visual specialty paper are transparent and colored paper. Transparent paper is usually vegetable parchment, sulfate or tracing paper which is made from thick paper of vegetable fibers and treated with sulfuric acid. Sulfate paper in modern design is usually used as endpaper or lining to enhance a theme or fit in with a modern design.

Iridescent paper, similar to common white paper, is created with a fiber base, filling and coating. The paper is made iridescent through the application of iridescent particles. These particles are susceptible to erosion and make it harder to apply ink to the paper. Its relatively high cost means that it is mostly reserved for the high-end printing market.

Tactile specialty paper mainly includes pressure laid paper and thermal paper. The former is created by exerting pressure on or crumpling paper to generate an uneven, patterned surface. This paper treatment technology has seen an increase in popularity in recent years. This process enhances the aesthetic value of the paper and adds value to the base paper. Meanwhile, thermal paper is created by applying a colored coat to the paper, the tint of which only shows when heat is added to its surface.

Both specialty paper and common printing paper can have various textures and visual effects, accommodating diverse printing needs. Besides quality, another important factor concerning the design process is paper weight, which is calculated on a per-square-meter basis. Inner pages tend to be lighter weight, ranging from 60g to 120g, while heavy paper is usually used for covers, at weights of 210g, 300g, 350g, 400g or above. It is an essential part of a designer's job to select the right paper weight to suit the printing specifications of a given project.

Modern technology has pushed the boundaries of modern book materials, which have been matched by the cutting-edge creations that those materials are used to design. Various media has been introduced into printing for inner pages, cases and covers like fabric, leather, wood and plastic to cater to an ever-changing market.

Transparent Paper

P130~131

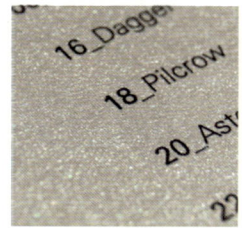

Iridescent Paper

P124~125

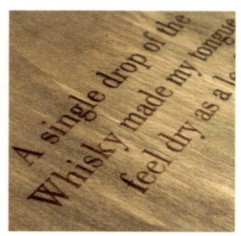

Wood

P122~123

Metal

P112~113

Materials

ASHLEY BICKERTON

> Special case
> Hand-carved edge
> Half-cloth binding

Paper Material: Natural and glossy paper
Size: 330mm x 280mm

Sagmeister & Walsh [Germany]

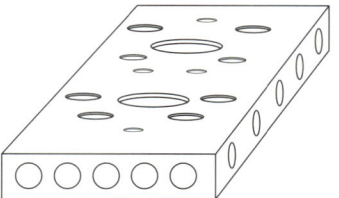

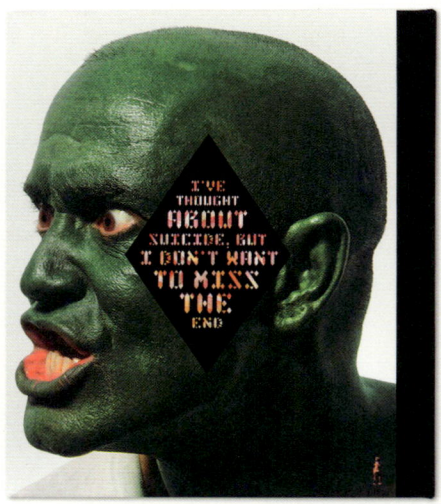
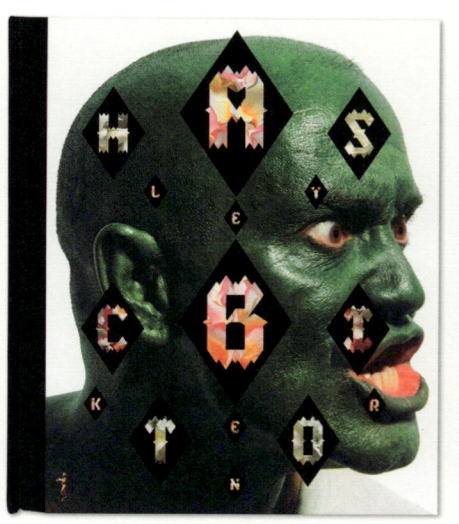

Materials

• This book is a monograph on Ashley Bickerton, who resides in Bali.

∴ The book is a visual journey through the artist's career. A customized typeface was designed, inspired by the mother-of-pearl inlays found in her works of art. In addition, for this limited edition, designers invented a carved fore-edge and a teak slipcase, which was handmade by Balinese artisans.

TOFU

Handmade paper

Wooden case

Minimalist layout design

Paper Material: Advocate Rough, handmade tofu paper, tracing paper, watercolor paper

Size: 300mm x 30mm (case), 285mm x 285mm (hardcover), 180mm x 280mm (softcover)

Chong Yee Cher Cheryl [Singapore]

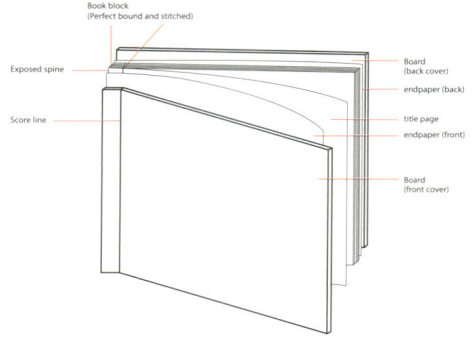
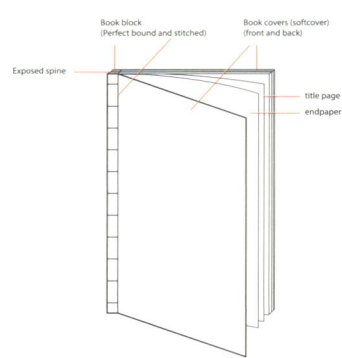

●

TOFU is a recipe book that aims to facilitate healthy eating and a wholesome lifestyle in a hectic modern world by using a common, healthy Asian food—tofu. The book features sections on purity, emptiness, Buddhist Zen and Daoist ideas.

Materials

The packaging is reminiscent of a traditional wooden tofu mold. The book is wrapped in cotton cloth, just like fresh tofu. A few textured pages are incorporated within sections of the book, reflecting different aspects of tofu. Layers of hand-torn paper represent the ripples created by stirring boiling soymilk and its gradual transformation into a smooth substance. A thin piece of tracing paper crushed and dyed with food coloring reminds readers of Yuba (tofu skin). The tofu paper was handmade with recycled paper and tofu so as "to express the intangible qualities of tofu through tangible materials."

 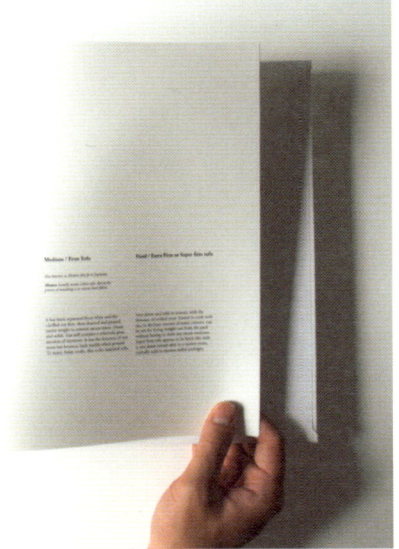

 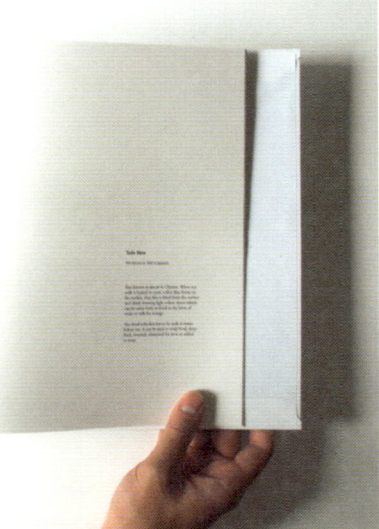

107

18 REALMS

Raffia string

Joss paper

Laser cutting

Paper Material: Joss paper, Antalis Conqueror Crema
Size: 290mm x 188mm

Derrick Li Hua [Malaysia]

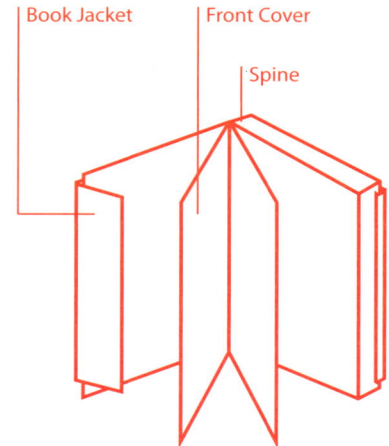
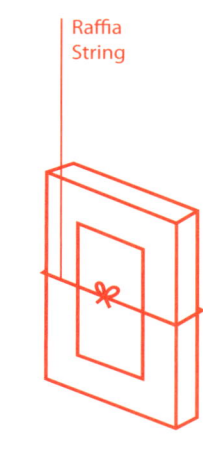

18 Realms is a self-initiated project that brings readers into the realm of dead or hell in Chinese mythology. 18 Realms is depicted as an underground maze with various levels and chambers where souls are taken after death to atone for the sins that they have committed. Illustration is one of the major elements used to present the scene of underground realms.

A Raffia string is used to bind the joss paper book jacket, giving the readers an experience similar to untying a traditional stack of notes for the dead. The book structure looks similar to a "Hell Note," a form of joss paper printed to resemble bank notes and burned for the deceased in China.

STRANGE CASE OF DR JEKYLL AND MR HYDE

Sleeve with a mirror

Tear-open cover

Paper Material: Offenbach Bible paper, Redeem paper, recycled paper, newsprint paper, glossy photo paper, mirror paper and offset paper
Size: 125mm x 190mm

Alberto Hernández [UK]

This interpretation of *The Strange Case of Dr. Jekyll and Mr. Hide* tries to take a new look at the story by adding playful graphic devices to the original novel, engaging readers in a more dynamic narrative experience and at the same time helping them to understand the story more easily. The publication is printed on a wide range of white and peach colored stocks to communicate the idea that homosexuality is hidden in the story.

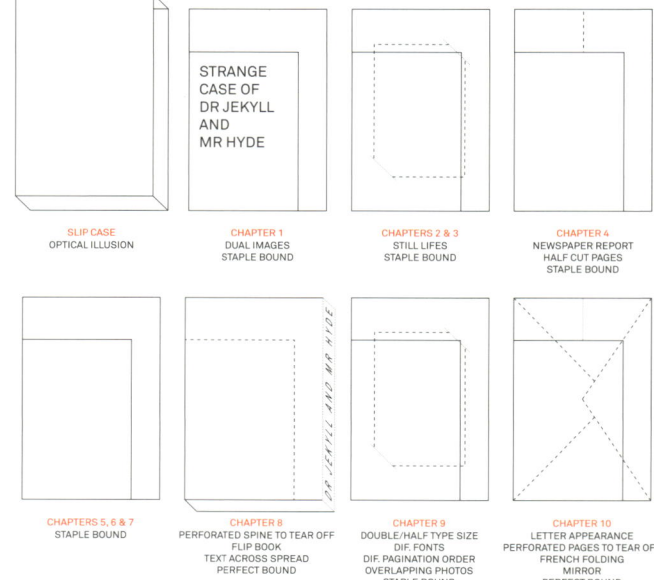

SLIP CASE
OPTICAL ILLUSION

CHAPTER 1
DUAL IMAGES
STAPLE BOUND

CHAPTERS 2 & 3
STILL LIFES
STAPLE BOUND

CHAPTER 4
NEWSPAPER REPORT
HALF CUT PAGES
STAPLE BOUND

CHAPTERS 5, 6 & 7
STAPLE BOUND

CHAPTER 8
PERFORATED SPINE TO TEAR OFF
FLIP BOOK
TEXT ACROSS SPREAD
PERFECT BOUND

CHAPTER 9
DOUBLE/HALF TYPE SIZE
DIF. FONTS
DIF. PAGINATION ORDER
OVERLAPPING PHOTOS
STAPLE BOUND

CHAPTER 10
LETTER APPEARANCE
PERFORATED PAGES TO TEAR OFF
FRENCH FOLDING
MIRROR
PERFECT BOUND

This book is divided into different booklets which are staple bound and perfect bound. The booklets are united in a slipcase featuring a stripe pattern and a mirror on the inside. This creates an optical illusion that reminds readers of one of the main themes in the story. Another of the most important features of this reiteration is found on the last double page spread, it hides a mirror in which the reader sees the reflection of him/herself. Seeing his/her reflection distorted conveys the idea that everybody has a Mr. Hyde inside.

* The mirror

Welded case

Translucent paper

Paper Material: Grain paper, tracing paper
Size: 240mm x 180mm

Dan Lawrence [UK]

ANTONY GORMLEY

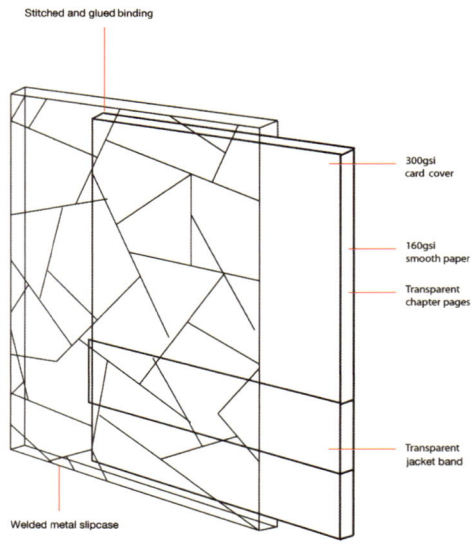

Stitched and glued binding
300gsi card cover
160gsi smooth paper
Transparent chapter pages
Transparent jacket band
Welded metal slipcase

•

This is a project that was created to help the reader learn and discover more about book binding as well as structure and identity. The book has been split into chapters based on materials ranging from concrete to copper, with the opening pages of each chapter featuring a full-page spread depicting a material and a semitransparent page bearing the opening paragraph. The design throughout the book complements Gormely's work, instead of overpowering the minimalist, classic photography. For the designer, the binding of the book was a great learning process in understanding the craft, passion and time that goes into every book.

Materials

The designer set out to make a piece of art out of the book itself. The welded metal cover is the art while the book acts as the stage. The spot wielded case was made to be the central part of the book, in which the reader can have their own piece to feel and experience.

113

THE SOUTHERN IMAGES

French binding
Hand-sewn binding

Paper Material: Rice paper
Size: 235mm x 170mm

Shenzhen Huathink Design Company
[China]

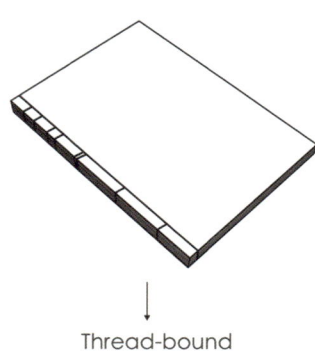
Thread-bound

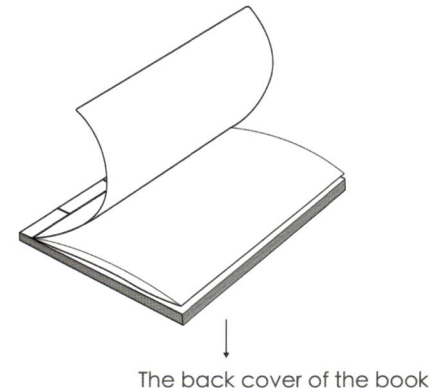
The back cover of the book

Materials

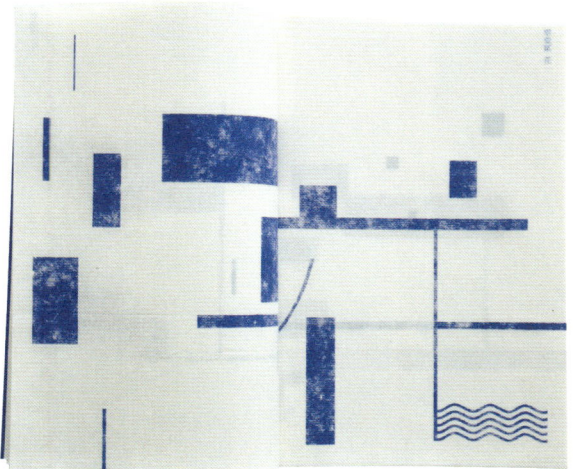

The Southern Images is an experimental book by Liu Yong-qing, creative director of Huthink. It collects Chinese poetry (from the Jiangnan region) on rice paper pages. As the famous Chinese poem "Memory of Jiangnan" goes: "Like always in the dreams, as a veiled picture it unfolds. Flowery flames against sunrise, Spring and rippling water in dyes. Never could I mislay such good memories. "

This book features silkcreen printing and thread binding.

Special binding

Paper Material: light-weight paper
Size: 130mm x 185mm

United Design Lab　[China]

《英俊》ハンサム

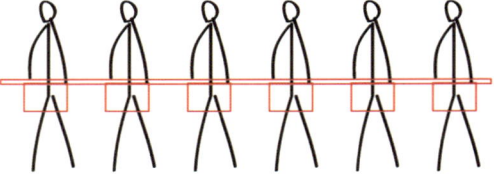

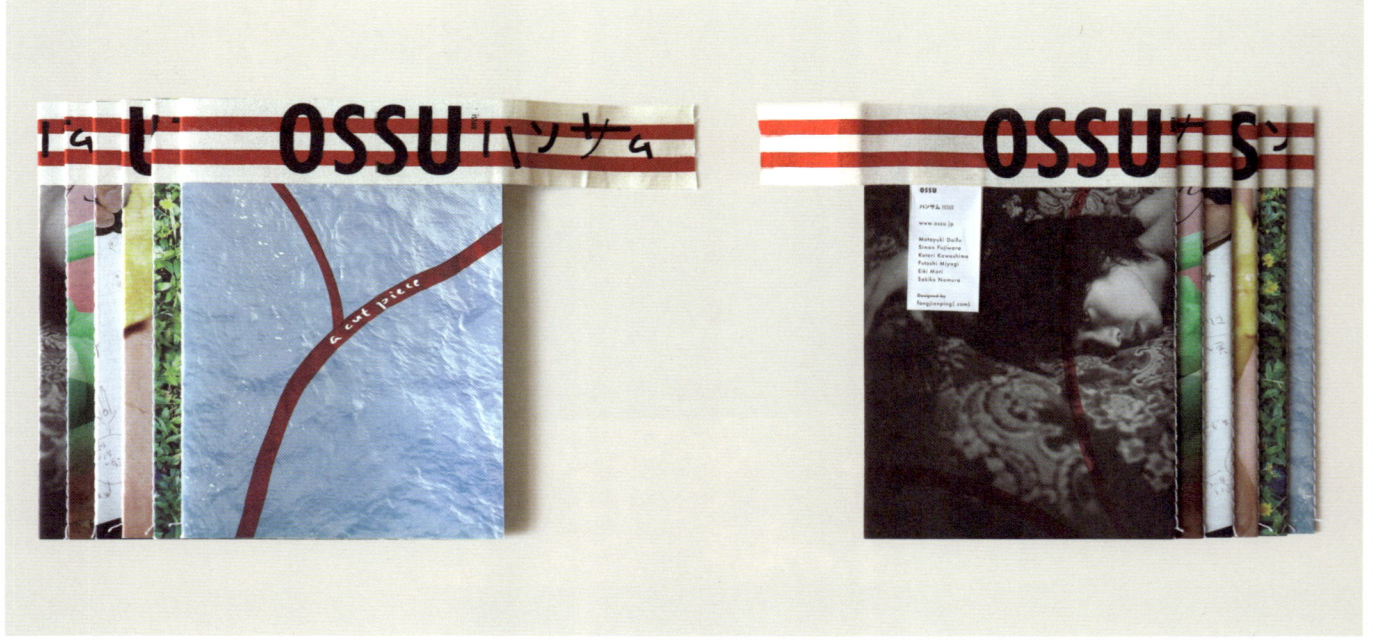

Materials

This is a magazine designed for a Japanese OSSU design group of six people.

The team's design takes a look at Japanese boys. For this issue, the topic is "handsome," which records the real life of young boys. For this book the designers created six books that resemble male underwear to represent six types of personalities.

MUCH MORE THAN A BOOK!

Cardboard box design

Paper Material: Carton board, raw kraft paper
Size: 400mm x 400mm

Sibyl Cherry Lai   [Hong Kong, China]

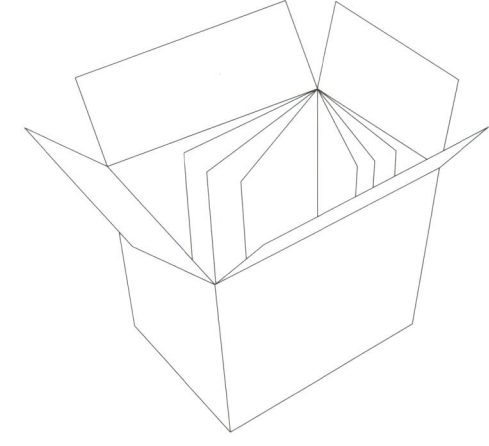

Materials

● This book was designed for Eloisa Cartonera, a Buenos-Aires-based publishing group. The motto for the design is "much more than a book!"

 This carton is ready-made to transform into a book. Reading and standing the book up for display are easily achieved by unfolding the carton. Eloisa Cartonera has continued the tradition of making book covers with materials that could have been discarded, but instead has turned trash into a part of the finished book.

DEEP FOCUS

Velvet cover

Special binding

Paper Material: Coated paper
Size: 250mm x 150mm

Karolien Pauly [Belgium]

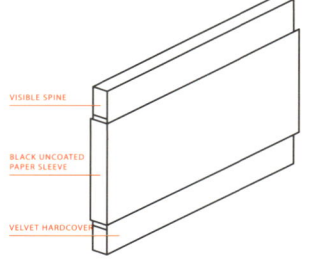
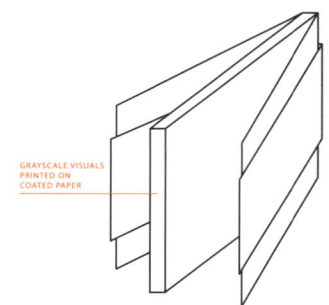

● Every movie can be analyzed on three levels: the narrative, the cinematic approach and the symbolism. These three layers are generally interwoven and aren't perceptible on their own; they form one single entity. The intention of this project is to break through this entity and to study the three layers separately.

∴ The designer used a velvet cover because velvet curtains bear a special significance in movies. Using this element connects the book with film as a medium. The spine is visible for a practical reason, which is that the book needs to open easily. The pages are attached loosely, so that the book does not tear apart when the reader tries to open the book.

THE WATER OF LIFE: A BOOK ABOUT THE MANLIEST DRINK

Wooden case

Laser cutting

Paper Material: Watercolor paper
Size: 210mm x 330mm

Christer Dahlslett [Norway]

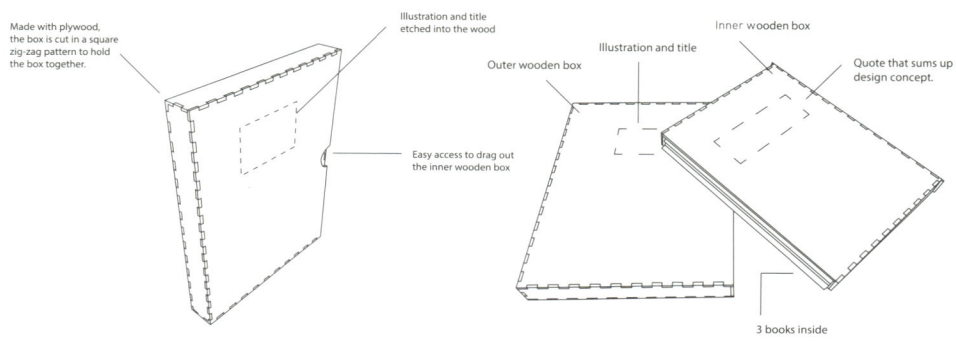

Materials

This design began with the aim to "create something about something that is interesting." This goal was applied to the topic of whiskey, which is a drink that is associated with manliness throughout the world. The design process drew on the designer's concept of manliness, and resulted in a book divided into three parts. This division is an attempt to visualize different ways of looking at whisky.

The first book features hand-drawn illustrations and traditional etchings, giving it a rough look. The second is slightly more polished and features watercolors. The last utilizes clean vector infographics for a sophisticated look. The cover was handmade from plywood that was laser cut, dyed and then assembled. It was inspired by the wooden casks in which whisky matures.

 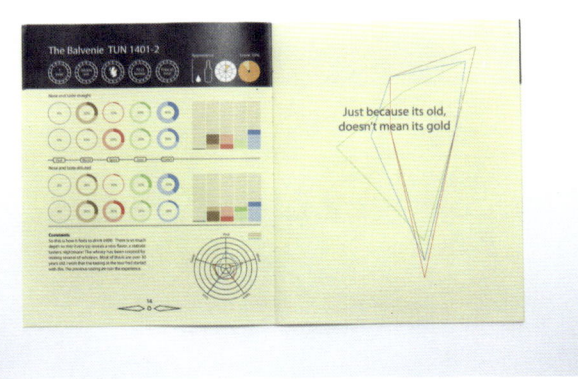

A PUNCTUATED HISTORY

Hand-stitching

Monochromatic printing

Paper Material: Metallic Silver, black paper
Size: 200mm x 290mm

Oliver Ward   [New Zealand]

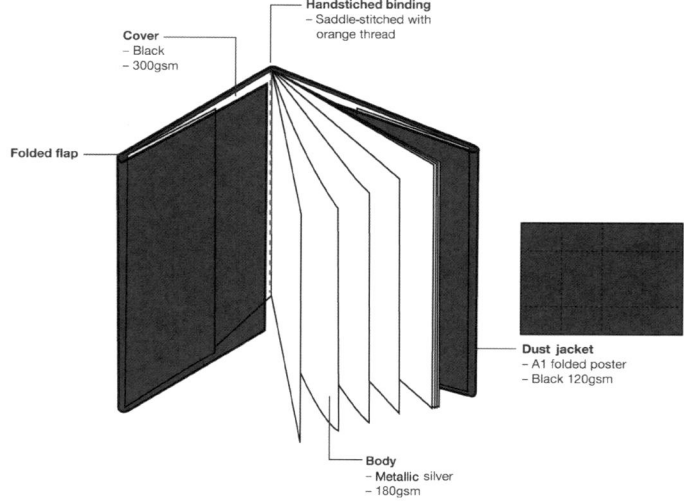

Materials

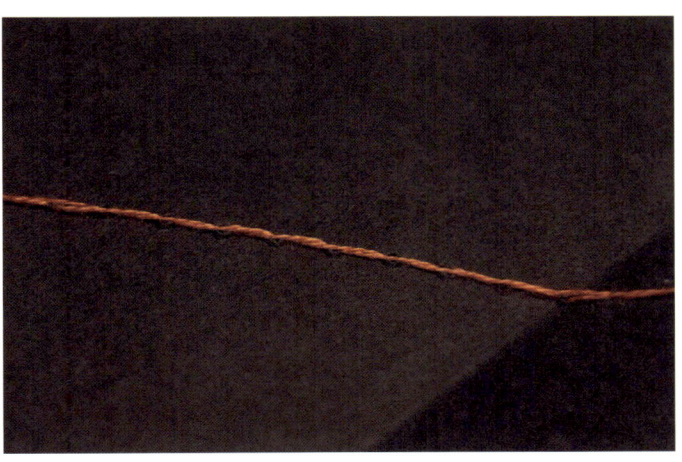

This book contains an essay on the history of typography written by Ellen Lupton & J. Abbott Miller. A selection of glyphs and an explanation of the history of glyphs are also included.

The booklet is printed in black and white on silver paper. The dust jacket is a black print on black paper, with a hand-stitched ampersand that matches the orange thread of the hand-stitched binding. The dust jacket unfolds to form a poster.

JADE CLARK LOOKBOOK

Vinyl cover
Coptic binding

Paper Material: White Silk Paper
Size: 148mm x 105mm

Danielle Muntyan [UK]

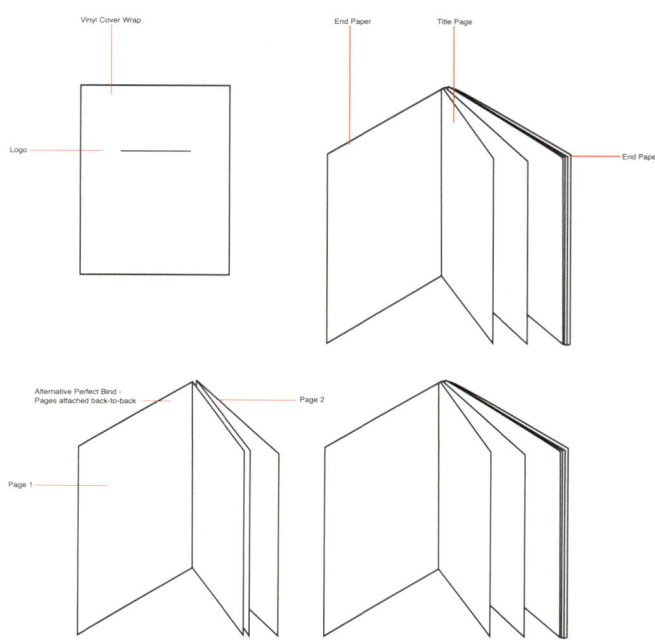

Materials

 Fashion designer Jade Clark approached the designer and asked her to design four lookbooks for her 2011 graduate collection and freelance works to date. Her work is high-end, bespoke and bold.

 In keeping with Jade's personality and her vibrant color choices, holographic imagery and vinyl were used. The cover is made entirely out of vinyl, reflecting the main material used by Jade in her over-the-top yet wonderful works of wearable art.

A BOOK ON DECOMPOSITION

Fluorescent ink

Tracing paper

Foldouts

Paper Material: Matte inkjet paper, matte acetate, grey paper
Size: 240mm x 160mm

Carolina Vargas [Colombia]

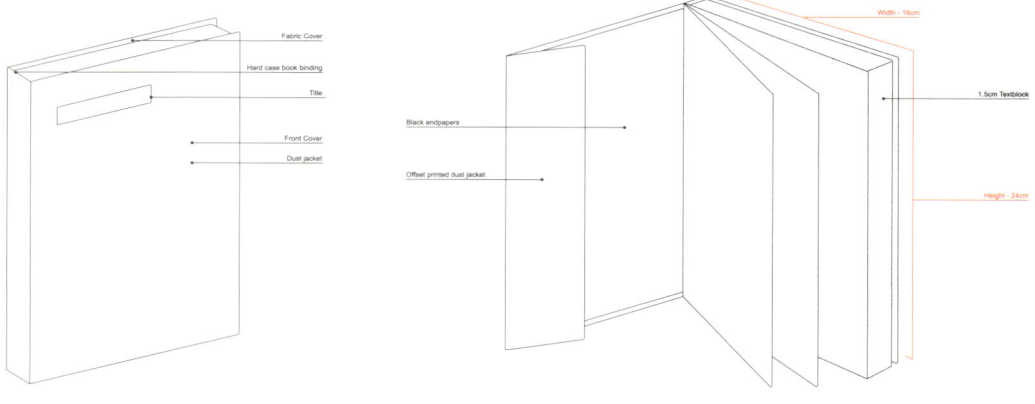

Materials

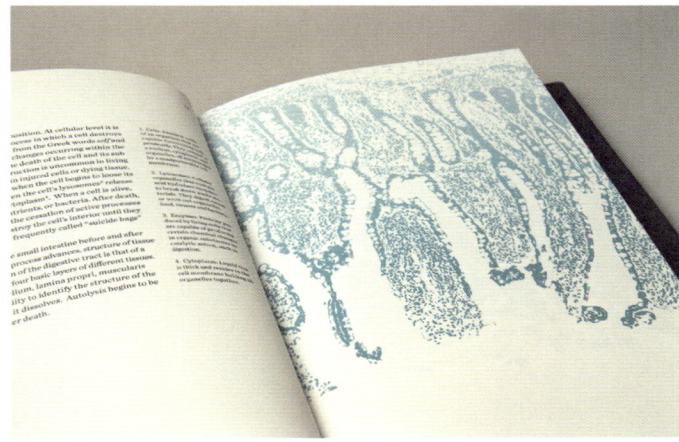

What happens after death? The question of a spiritual afterlife is a contentious one, since it is falls outside the realm of science. Physically however, cadavers undergo dramatic changes immediately following death. This is an essential part of nature's recycling process, which transforms a dead life form into a new life form.

In five steps, the book blends an informative scientific commentary with illustrations and infographics that exhibit the beauty and complexity of this natural phenomenon. The illustrations explore the microscopic world of nature, where rich textures create amazing images while the infographics present the technical and quantitative information. The book is case bound, with a printed dust jacket attached to the cover. The book also contains foldouts and inserts that elaborate on the main body of text.

SELF-PROMOTION PACKAGE

Special size
Card set

Paper Material: Vellum; color cardstock paper; white presentation paper
Size: 200mm x 240mm

Mina Zarfsaz [USA]

 Materials

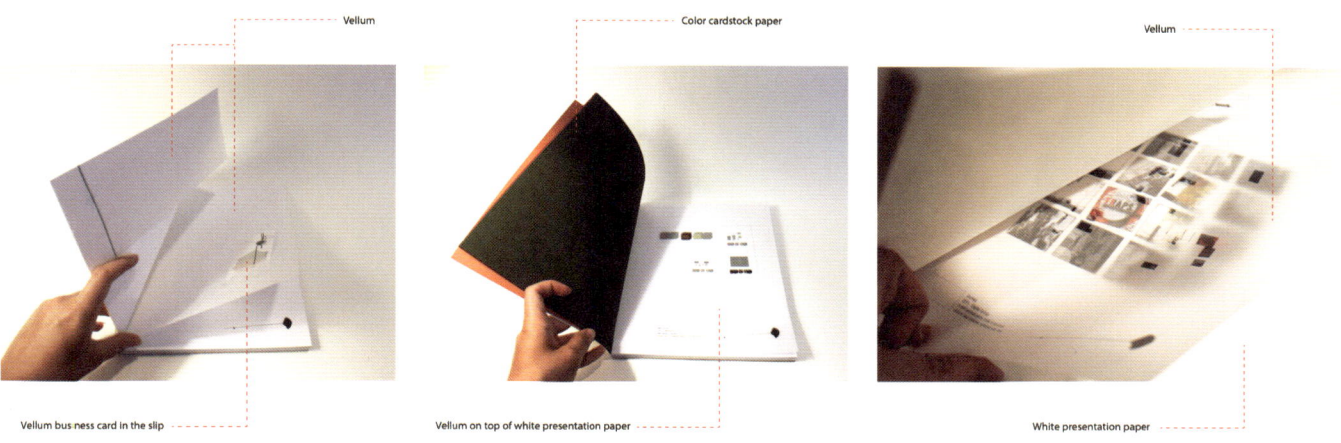

- This is a self-promotional package. The theme of the presentation is "echo," which is incorporated into the design, layout, and even the paper used in the book.

- Among the highlights of the book are the inserted translucent pages with subtle details of the artwork transposed on them, echoing the actual work on the next page. These "echo pages" lie on top of the actual image of the work, "echoing" them.

WONDERFUL

Wood cover

Open spine

Laser-cut title

Paper Material: Wood board, grandeur zen white, kishu color paper, enviro white
Size: 170mm x 240mm

Jooey Lek [Singapore]

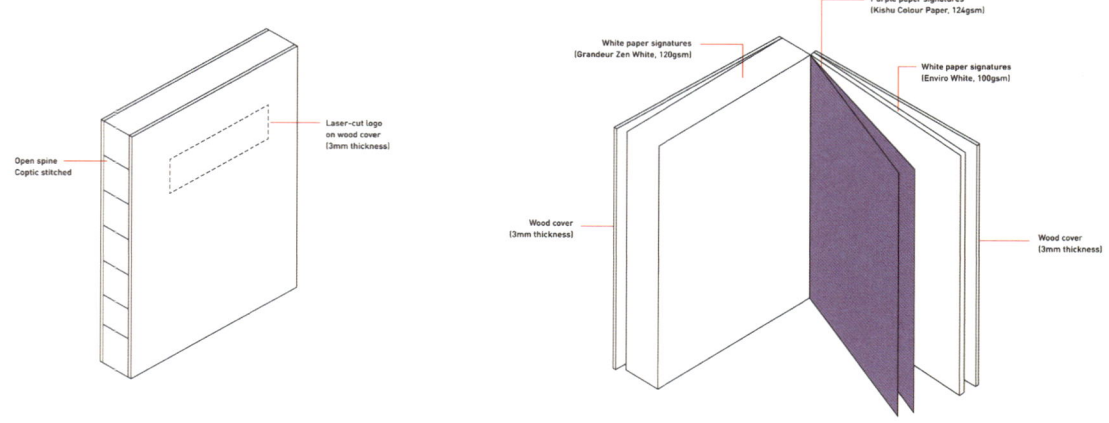

132

Materials

● The book *Wonderful* takes a peek into the wonderful studios of creatives. Looking at designers and illustrators, it captures the personal experiences, insights and work processes of these artistic people. The spaces included depict 4 types of emphasis: personalization, comfort, communication and efficacy.

Wood was chosen as the material for the cover as it has always been a construction material for furniture. With the logo laser-cut on the cover, it creates a raw and honest experience for the reader holding it. The Coptic bound spine reveals the intimate side of the dynamic working process of design creatives.

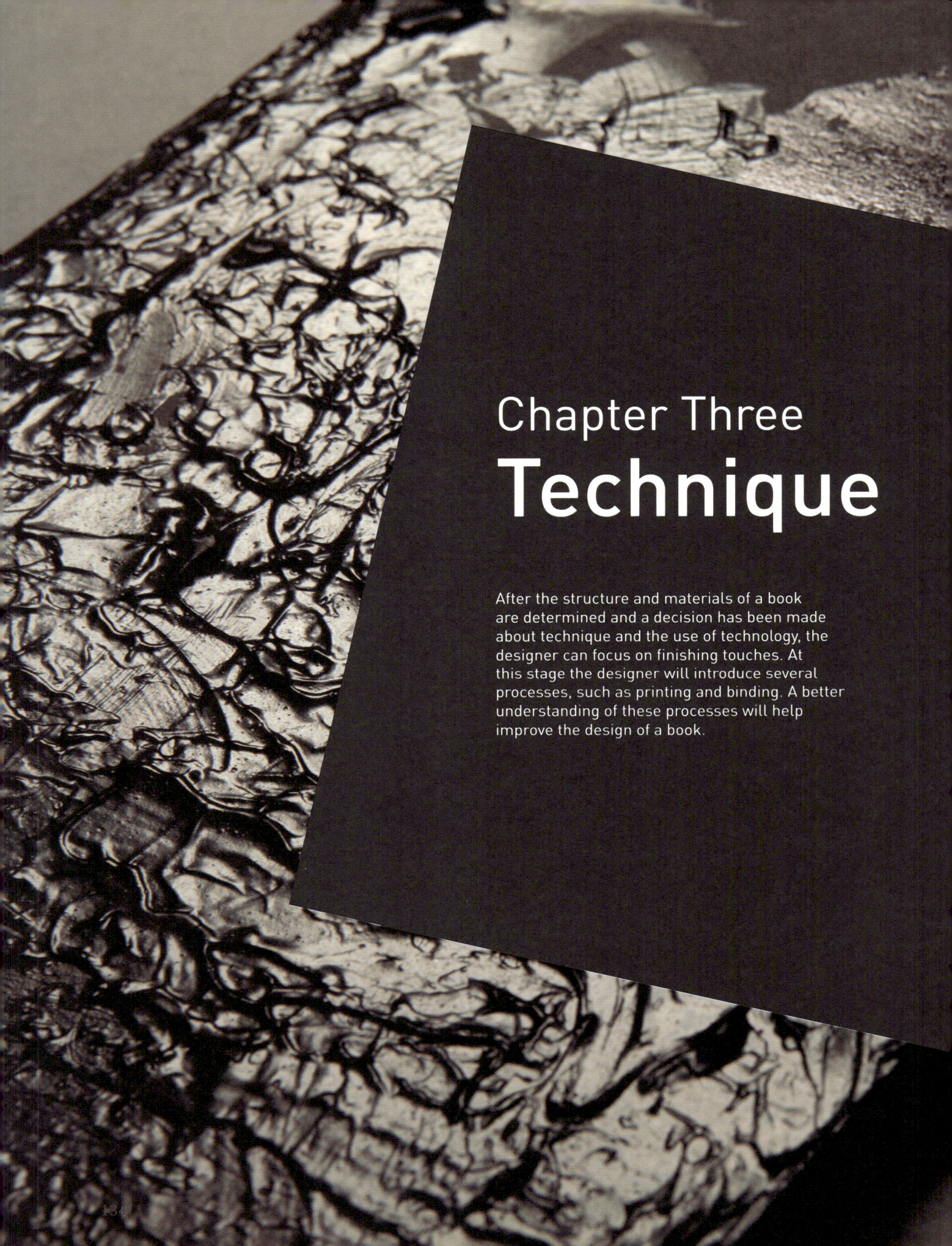

Chapter Three
Technique

After the structure and materials of a book are determined and a decision has been made about technique and the use of technology, the designer can focus on finishing touches. At this stage the designer will introduce several processes, such as printing and binding. A better understanding of these processes will help improve the design of a book.

Printing

The major types of printing we use today are letterpress printing, intaglio printing, lithography, and screen printing.

Letterpress printing is a type of relief printing achieved through the use of a printing press. In the process of letterpress printing, a worker composes and locks movable type into the bed of a press, inks it, and presses paper against it to transfer the ink from the type, which creates an impression on the paper. This type of printing results in good ink performance and can also be adopted to generate foiling and embossing.

Intaglio is a printing technique that involves incising an image into a copper or zinc plate. Ink is then applied applied to the plate and tarlatan cloth is used to remove the ink left on the surface of the plate, leaving the ink in the incision. Paper is placed on the plate and pressure is exerted from the printing press to force the ink onto the paper.

Lithography is the most commonly used printing method at present and it is based on the principle that oil and water do not mix. It is used on a smooth surface like a stone (lithographic limestone) or a metal plate. In the initial stage, it uses an image drawn with oil, fat, or wax on the surface of a smooth, level lithographic limestone plate. The stone is treated with a mixture of acid and gum arabic. The mixture only affects the portions of the stone that are not protected by oil, fat, or wax. When the stone is subsequently moistened, the treated areas retain water and an oil-based ink can be applied and will stick only to the areas that haven't been treated with acid and gum arabic, that is, the original drawing. The ink is finally transferred to a blank paper sheet, producing a printed page.

Screen printing is a printing technique that was developed in China. Ink or other printable materials, a screen plate with an ink-blocking stencil, a fill blade or squeegee and a substrate are the basic tools. Ink or other printable materials are pressed through the screen plate with the use of a squeegee to achieve the desired image on the substrate. Due to the ease, simplicity, effectiveness, and low cost of the technique, screen printing is widely used in graphic design, the clothing industry and even metalworking.

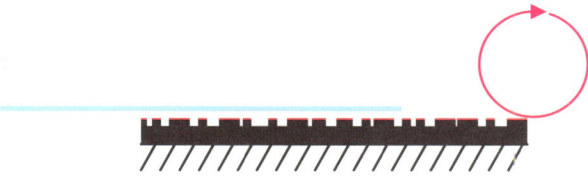

Letterpress printing

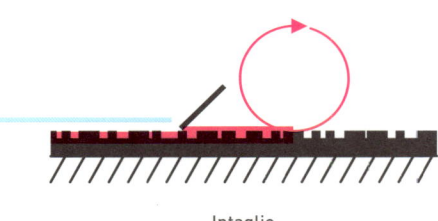

Intaglio

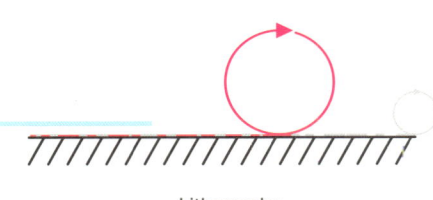

Lithography

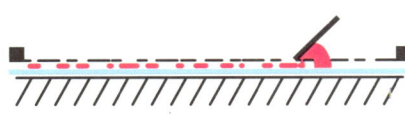

Screen printing

Color

Color printing can be categorized into single color and multicolor printing.

Single color printing uses only one plate and one ink. It can be matched color, selected color, flat color and spot color.

Spot color refers to color that is designed to be printed alone, rather than blended with other inks on the paper to produce various hues and shades. Generally, it has a specific formulation, the range of which, much like paint, is nearly unlimited, and much more varied than colors that can be produced by four-color-process printing, ranging from subtle pastels to intense fluorescents to reflective metallics.

Meanwhile multi-color printing is based on an additive color mixing process, by breaking original colors into primary colors and then using a subtractive color mixing process to overlap such inks on the paper. The most commonly used are the CMYK color model and Hexachrome printing.

CMYK, probably the most used color printing model, gets its name from the initials of cyan, magenta, yellow, and key (black). Those four colors are mixed to achieve full-color printing. Hexachrome printing, also called six-color process printing, adds orange and green to the CMYK system, which gives the process the name of CMYKOG, for a larger and more vibrant color range. However, such alternate color systems still rely on color separation, halftoning and lithography to produce printed images.

Other printing techniques

Besides common printing needs, sometimes special printing techniques are utilized to achieve exceptional effects. Modern technologies are simplifying these processes, which include embossing, debossing, stamping, UV, die cutting, creasing, laminating and laser cutting.

Embossing
P8~9

Debossing
P192~193

UV printing
P156~157

Die cutting
P178~179

Creasing
P182~183

Laser cutting
P140~141

Binding

The most commonly seen page orientations in books are portrait and landscape. There are, however, other innovations like roll-shaped, triangular, multi-faceted, or circular books. Typically though, book binding takes into consideration reader convenience and protective function. Based on these considerations, we divide books into paperback and hardcover.

Paperback is the binding solution used for common publications, and has the advantages of being a simple procedure and inexpensive. It can be further classified into categories based on the techniques used such as thread stitching, saddle stitching, flat stitching, and perfect binding etc.

Thread stitching is used to sew signatures at the fold line, and is good for binding thick books.

Saddle Stitching refers to the binding method in which folded sheets are gathered together one inside the other and then are stapled through the fold line with wire staples. The staples pass through the folded crease from the outside and are clinched between the centermost pages. Two staples are commonly used but larger books may require more staples along the spine.

Flat stitching is a method of sewing stitches in which individual stitches are made without crossing or looping the thread. It is not done along the crease, but instead on the margin.

Perfect binding uses only glue, without thread or wire. Perfect-bound books are known for their majestic look, low cost, high printing efficiency and reader convenience. It is the most widely used binding technique today, especially for thick books.

Hardcover books date back to the sixteenth century. These books are characterized by their firm covers and more diversified surface decoration. Hardcover books are more costly to produce, making them suitable for large or higher value books. Hardcovers can be rigid or semi-hard and can be circular-backed, square-backed or soft-covered in form.

Circular-backed binding results in a round spine with staggered signatures.

Square-backed is square at the back, as its name indicates, and is usually a solution when a paperback needs to be converted into hardcover or when single pages are the basic binding unit.

Soft cover is made to cut down on book weight by changing the hard front board into soft board, as seen in tool book binding.

Thread stitching
P238~239

Saddle stitching
P8~9

Flat stitching
P220~221

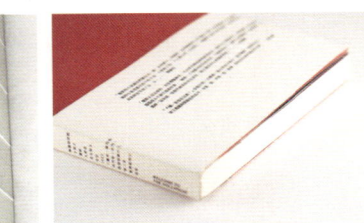

Perfect binding
P176~177

Circular-backed
P242~243

Square-backed
P158~159

Soft cover
P60~61

FOR BROWSING ONLY

Raw material

Paper Material: Recycled paper
Size: 380mm x 300mm

A Beautiful Design [Singapore]

The "Browsing Copy" project focuses on unloved books that remained unsold on the shelves of local bookstores. Designers from around the world are invited to use them as canvases to express their creativity to give those books a second life. Part of the project is to document the "befores and afters."

This is an on-going project and 20 to 25 designers are invited for each series. Two series are already being exhibited online. A 300-page catalog was printed to feature both series, and only 300 copies were printed, circulated and exhibited around the world's finest bookstores, shops and design studios. The catalogs are not for sale; they will be collected back after a period of time and passed on to the next line of shops. The condition of the catalogs and the places they have been will be documented on the project's website.

Technique

ADCN SINCE 2012

Unique cover design
Laser cutting
Laser engraving

Paper Material: Sulfate Cardboard, Arctic Volum White, recycled paper
Size: 300mm x 300mm

Autobahn [The Netherlands]

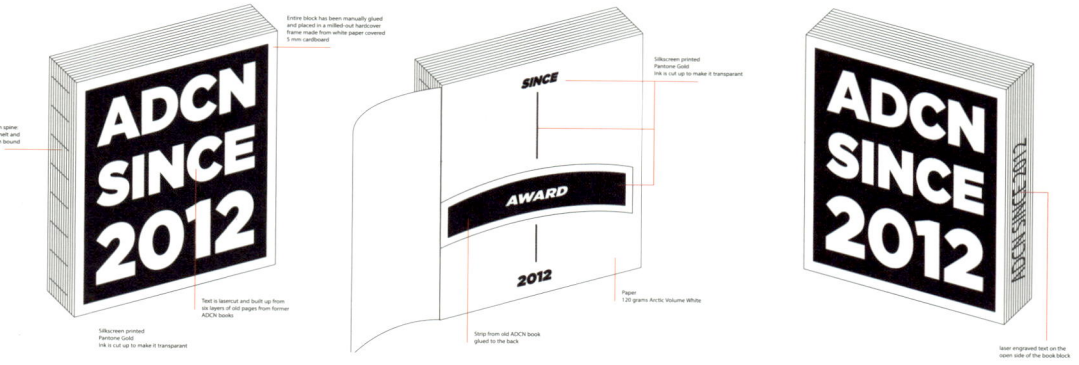

Technique

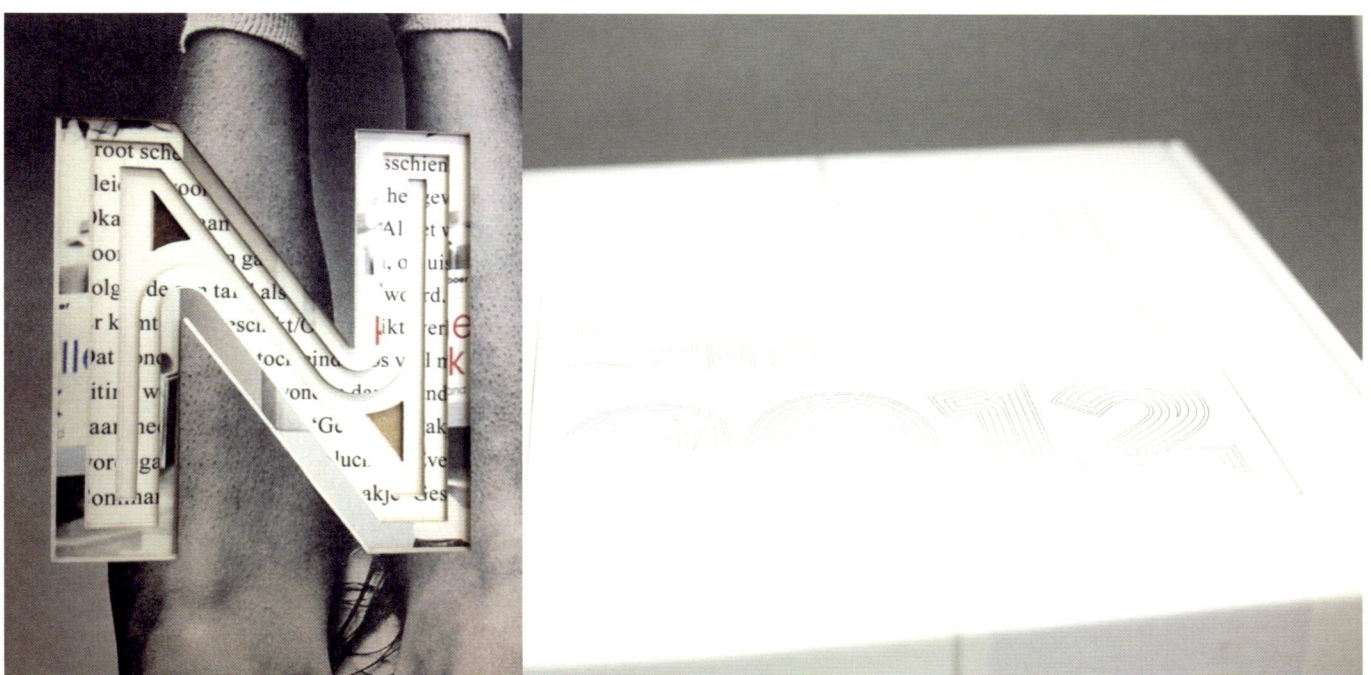

This yearbook for the Dutch Art Directors Guild is made from 45 generations of yearbooks from the dusty archives of the ADCN. They were collected, dismantled and cut into raw materials to create this unique book.

The laser-cut title is made from six layers of old pages from former ADCN books.

141

MUNT PARK

Envelope
Scratch coating
Guilder
Sewing

Paper Material: Sulfaatkarton, Arctic Volume
Size: 210mm x 297mm

Autobahn [The Netherlands]

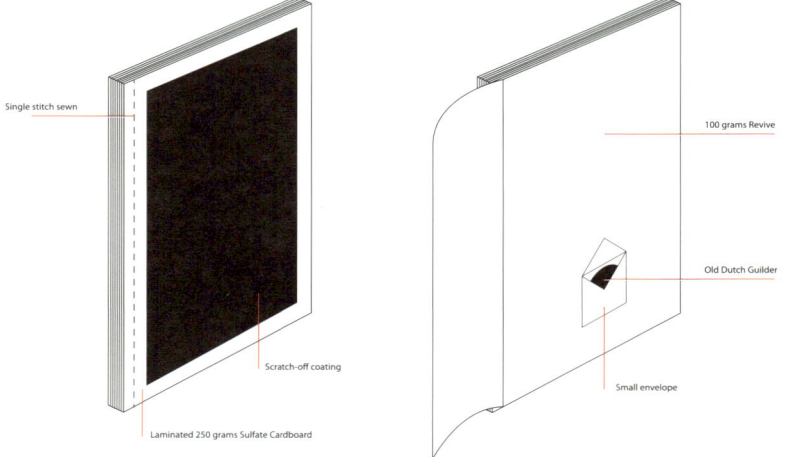

Technique

● Autobahn designed the publication to celebrate the Munt Region in Utrecht, The Netherlands, which gets its name from its famous Munt Coin Museum ("munt" means coin in Dutch) where the Dutch Guilders (the money used in Holland before the Euro) used to be minted. The area is a hidden treasure full of opportunities.

✦ The book starts with a scratch coating on the cover. The inside cover has a little paper envelope with an old Guilder that can be used to reveal the hidden landscape on the cover. In order to discover the Munt area landscape, you need to get the coin out of the pocket and scratch off the coating to find the hidden treasure!

TRANSVERSAL

Hand-made binding
Silhouette
Screen Printing

Paper Material: Cardboard, Fedrigoni Arcoprint, Curius translucents
Size: 170mm x 230mm

Buenos días [Spain]

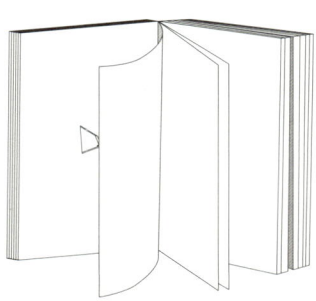 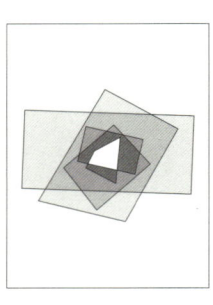 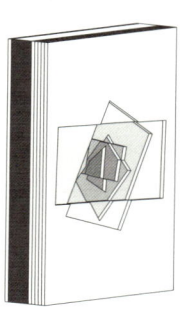 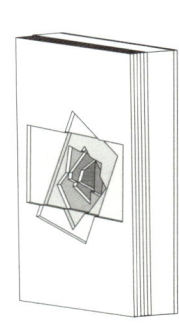

○ Technique

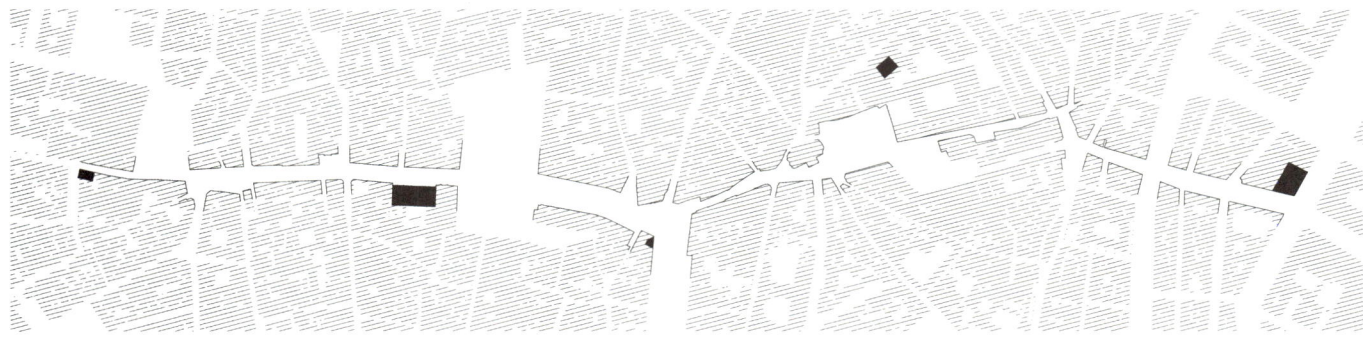

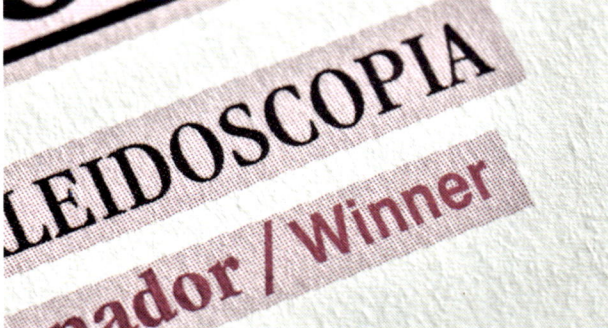

This bilingual book compiles Universidad de Sevilla's submissions to the Transverse contest of the BIACS3-YOUniverse (the third edition of the Biennial show of Contemporary Art of Seville). It covers a tour of 5 areas in the city of Sevilla. The works included are arranged following the itinerary westward, through a historical part of the city. This publication is about embodying the urban transverse tour in Sevilla. The book explores the capacity for the transformation of daily spaces.

The quality of the materials stands out from the very beginning, starting with the cover, which is actually the aggregation of five pages of silhouettes of controlled spaces. The silhouettes imitate the shapes of building fronts and courts mentioned in the book. The shapes were brought to the same scale by die cutting and were then glued together, oriented to show the embedded book title. The content is arranged in a similar style: a tracing sheet, followed by a map of Sevilla with intervention spots representing the five locations, followed by maps of the areas. The spine of the book is wrapped in black fabric. The title of the book was silkscreened onto the the spine. The books are all hand-bound.

BE MYSELF

Packaging
Hand sewing
Cutting

Paper Material: Wood-free paper, semi-woodfree paper
Size: 210mm x 280mm

DEPT. OF VISUAL COMMUNICATION DESIGN, K.S.U./MIXED MEDIA STUDIO
[Taiwan, China]

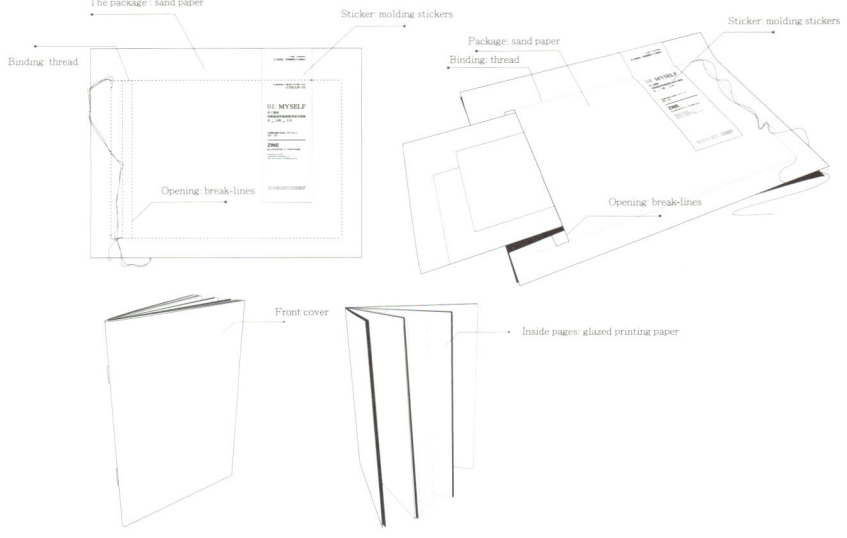

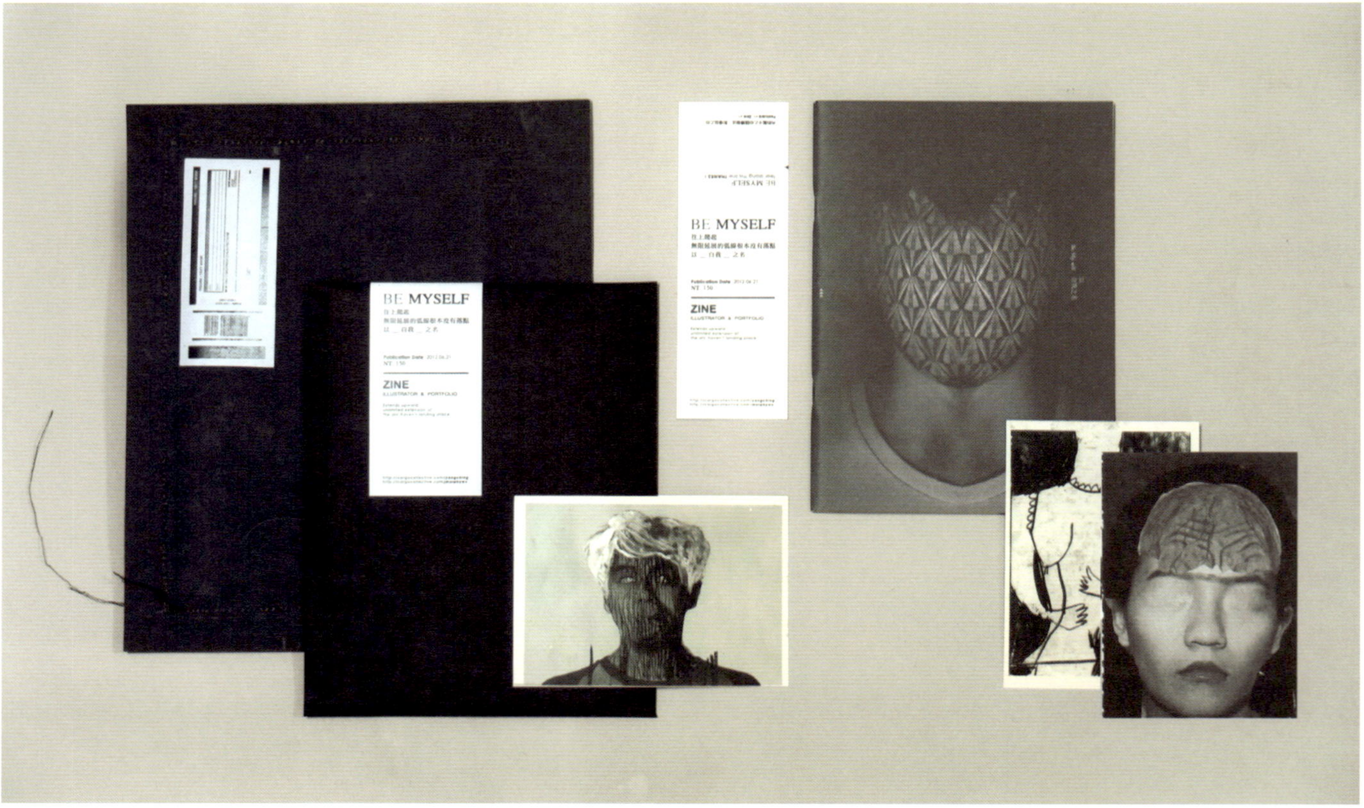

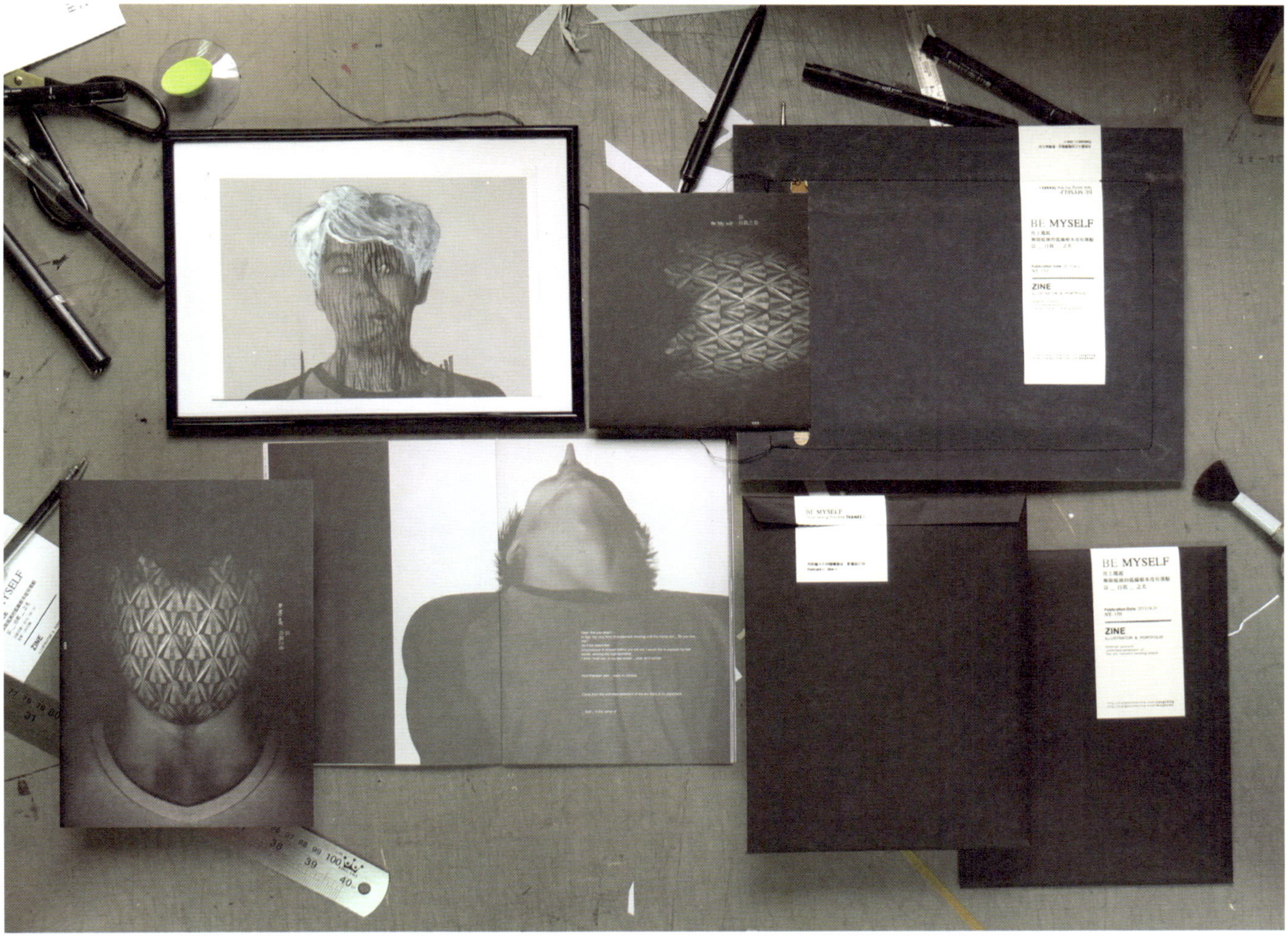

○ *Technique*

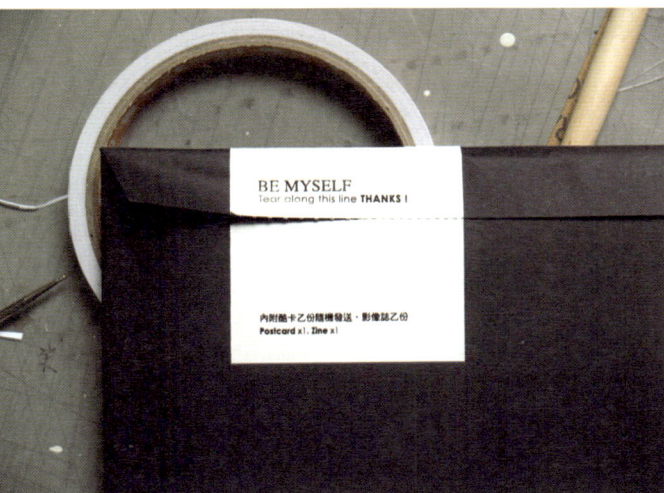

● *Be Myself* is a piece of self-expression that symbolizes every conscious being in this world. It attempts to delve into human psychology and individual consciousness, as exhibited via gestures, language, expressions and emotional reactions.

 Be Myself does not use complex binding to stand out, but instead focuses on the packaging. Compared with traditional packaging of small-sized books, this project is more complex and costly. But this is exactly what the designer wanted: to make the package a visual shock even at a quick glance, and to create a piece of art to keep for a lifetime along with the book inside.

147

MANIPULATED INSPIRATION

Double print
UV printing
Fluorescent ink

Paper Material: Mixed paper stock
Size: 210mm × 297mm

David Newman [UK]

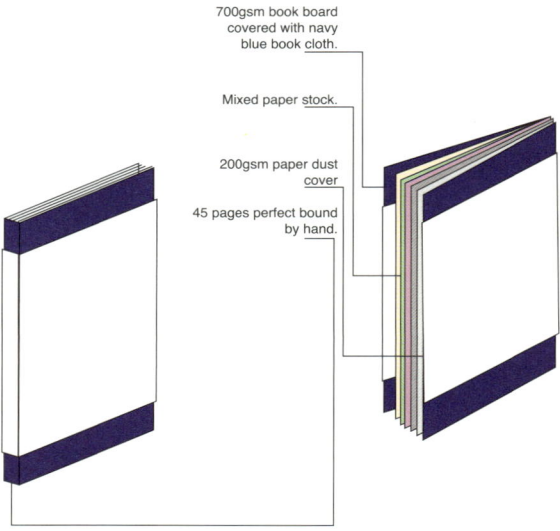

Technique

 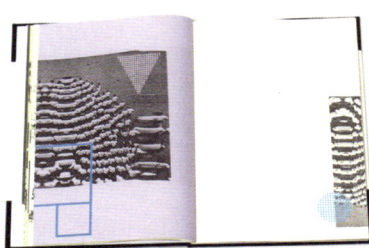

This book is a visual journey surrounding the artists that inspired the designer. These artists helped to shape his creative mind. The book is a tribute to them and their work.

To create the book the designer photocopied pages from design, art and photography books. He then discovered pieces of paper left on the floor and printed over these pages. He printed and double printed onto the different paper stocks to create a unique composition for this book. The book consists of only 34 pages, perfect bound by hand, inkjet printed on mixed paper stocks. The colored pages were printed with UV reactive luminous acrylic ink and various colors were used to highlight his favorite pieces of work.

 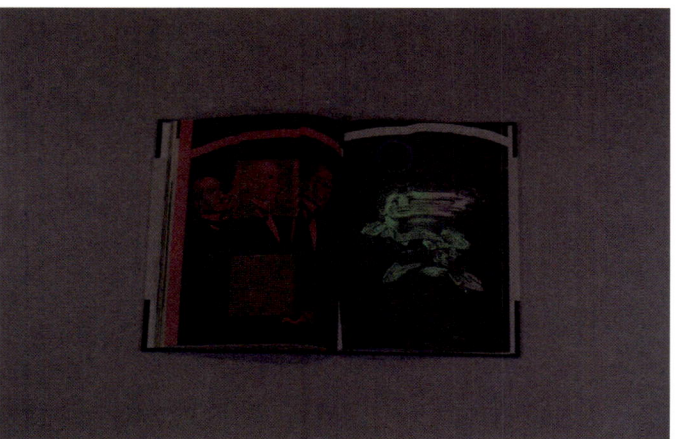

Offset printing

Open spine

UV ink

Paper Material: Cyclus Offset, Eksa Board, Cyclus Offset, Holmen Book White
Size: 172mm x 230mm

Marton Borzak [Denmark]

P.S. – SECRETS OF THE BARGUZIN SKELETON

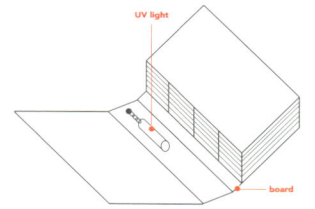

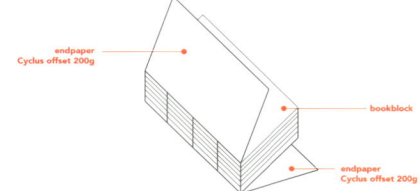
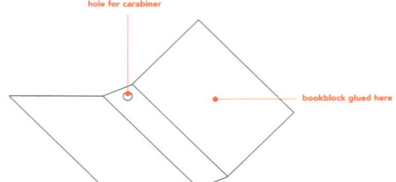
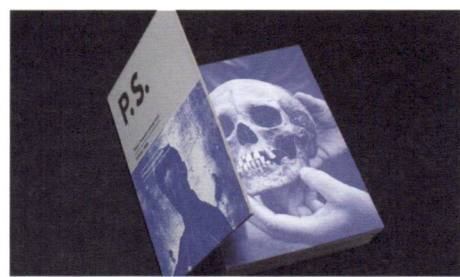

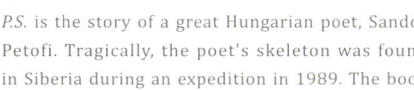 Technique

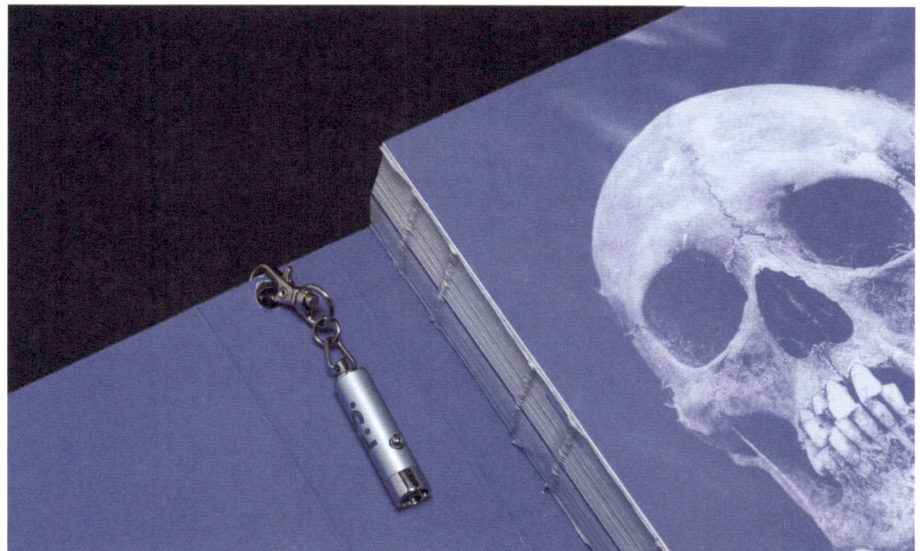

P.S. is the story of a great Hungarian poet, Sandor Petofi. Tragically, the poet's skeleton was found in Siberia during an expedition in 1989. The book presents facts and documents about the expedition.

The book was designed to reflect on secrets of the story. Commentary, explanations and annotations by the author are printed in UV ink, which is only visible under UV the designer wanted the light, since reader to have the experience of searching for secrets. The book consists of several layers: the actual story, article inserts from 1989, and the UV layer mentioned above. The binding is designed such that the included UV lamp fits inside, but can easily be removed.

MN-LOOK BOOK 1&4

Painted covers (Books 1&4)
Open spine (Book 1)
Painted edges (Book 1)
Special binding (Book 1)

Paper Material: RJ Sirio Nero, Cyclus Offset
Size: 240mm x 150mm (book 1), 215mm x 150mm (book 4)

Somewhere Else [Singapore]

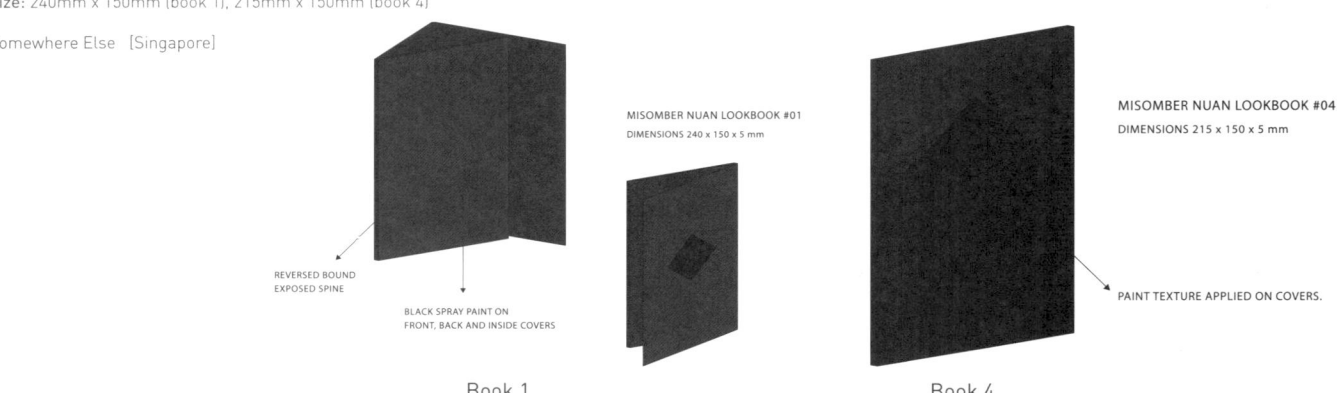

Book 1 — MISOMBER NUAN LOOKBOOK #01, DIMENSIONS 240 x 150 x 5 mm — REVERSED BOUND EXPOSED SPINE; BLACK SPRAY PAINT ON FRONT, BACK AND INSIDE COVERS

Book 4 — MISOMBER NUAN LOOKBOOK #04, DIMENSIONS 215 x 150 x 5 mm — PAINT TEXTURE APPLIED ON COVERS.

Composed mainly of black materials, Misomber Nuan's collections are reflections of emptiness and voids, the promise of happenings and emotions with the intention of touching others through their experimental creations. The various promotional literatures created for Misomber Nuan are all directed at expressing their experimental approach towards materials.

Book 1

○ *Technique*

Book 1

Book 4

These lookbooks are mainly characterized by a paint texture that is applied as a finishing effect to dramatize the reading experience, to turn it into an intriguing experience that involves touch.

153

NUS—DID 2012

Tinted edges
Screen printing

Paper Material: Greyboard, Olin
Size: 260mm x 210mm

Somewhere Else [Singapore]

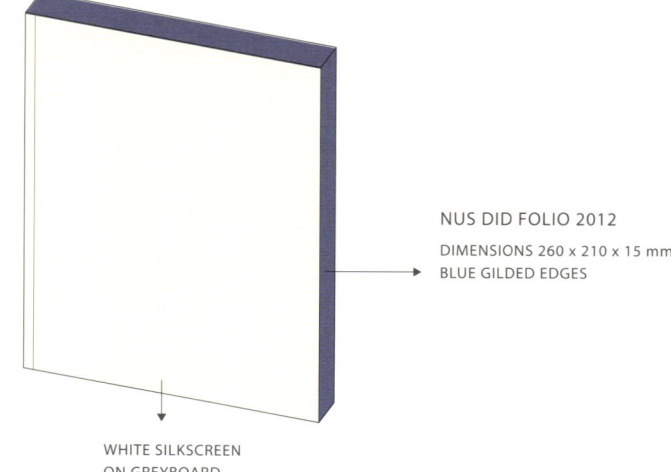

NUS DID FOLIO 2012
DIMENSIONS 260 x 210 x 15 mm
BLUE GILDED EDGES

WHITE SILKSCREEN
ON GREYBOARD

This book is a yearly compilation of National University of Singapore's graduates' work. The publication includes information about the school's programs and curricula.

○ *Technique*

The cover is screen-printed white on a light grey board. This process creates an unusual texture and leads to a slight surprise when the book is flipped open to reveal the bare grey board. A simple photo story of environmental portraits is used to lead the reader into the book before proceeding to the works. Unlike most books of this nature, the layout of each spread in this publication is completely customized depending on the types of images collected. Dividers and sections related to the university are highlighted in technical blue and, to further complete the book, this blue is applied around all the edges.

BLACK WHITE GRAY
—GRAPHIC DESIGN

Tinted edge
UV printing
Screen Printing
Printed fore-edge

Paper Material: Coated paper
Size: 280mm x 215mm

SendPoints Publishing [China]

- *Black & White & Gray Graphic Design* displays outstanding graphic designs that are based on these three basic colors. Designers share their insights on the use of these raw and honest colors in notes that are included with the book.

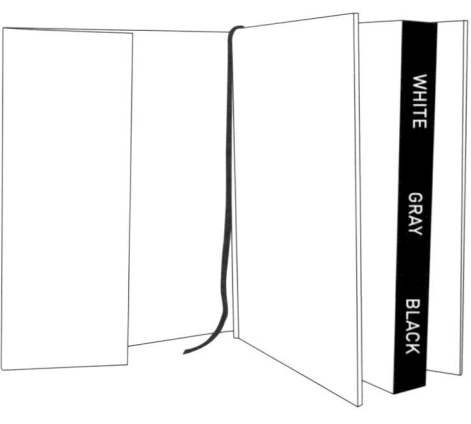

Technique

This book comes with a jacket, wrapped in black fabric paper that has been screen printed with white and UV ink. To enforce the gradational elements of the impression, the fore-edge was then tinted with black ink, leaving space for the caption to be reiterated in white. The design resonantly speaks for the theme—simplicity, contrast and impact.

NOT THE END OF PRINT

Foiling
Gold edging

Paper Material: Curious Touch Wet, Munken Lynx
Size: 120mm x 160mm

Isabel Seiffert [Switzerland]

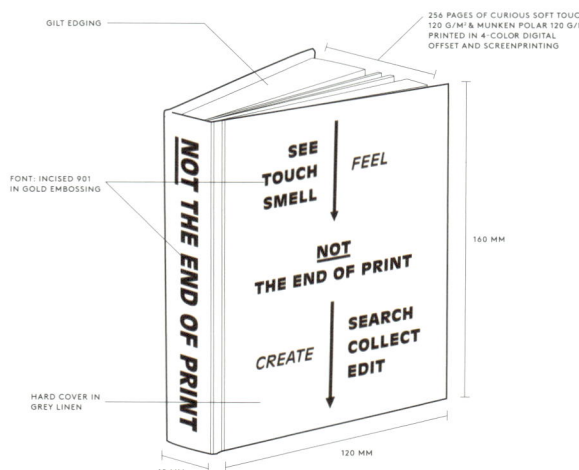

Technique

Designers develop and publish magazines and books in order to create a platform for self-initiated projects and experiments with their visual language. They want to be able to work autonomously and have complete control over the content, purpose and message of a project. *Not the End of Print* not only contains a theoretical investigation concerning this matter but explores the print medium in the form of a book. It looks at the book's sensual impression as well as the creative process of a designer. The Bible was the inspiration for this book's form.

The gold embossing is a metaphor for the increasing value of the print medium. In times of fast-spreading and disposable digital information, the purchase of a book seems like a decision for relative eternity—it becomes a valuable object. This book deals with the creative process of a designer on the one hand and the sensual perception of the viewer of a print medium on the other hand. To experiment with contemporary and traditional printing techniques, *Not the End of Print* was partly produced in screen print and partly with a digital printing machine.

EXPREIENCE FASHION STORES

Black stamping
Fabric cover wrapping

Paper Material: Coated paper, matte paper
Size: 230mm × 300mm

SendPoints Publishing [China]

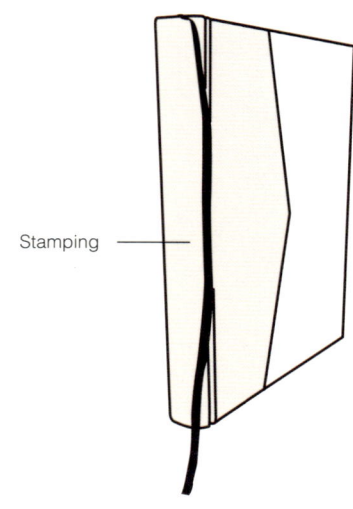
Stamping

• *Experience Fashion Stores* features store designs by LOHAS styles, the Ladies' World, and the Gentlemen's Kingdom. Each of the stores has a style of its own, but all stand out with exemplary creativity in the fields of interior design, architecture and fashion.

To start with, the fabric used on the cover references the topic of fashion. The cover is made unique with the special shape caused by the die-cut wrapping. The internal text was hot stamped in black ink.

Technique

BRANDING ELEMENT —LOGOS 3

Tinted edge

Matte UV

Paper Material: Coated paper
Size: 260mm x 210mm

SendPoints Publishing [China]

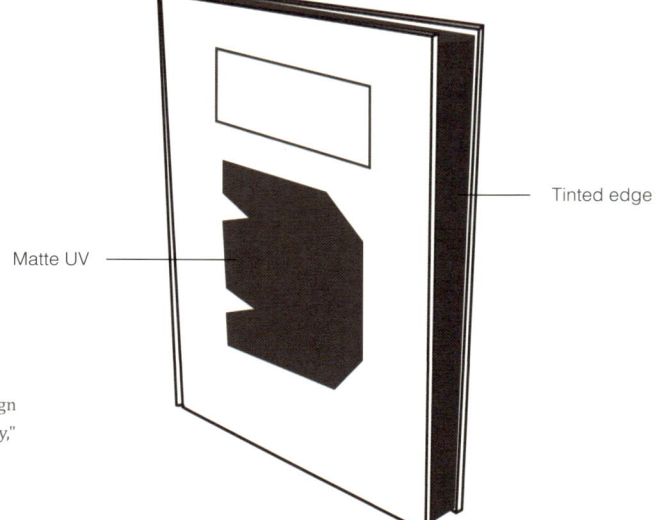

Tinted edge

Matte UV

• *Branding Element—Logos 3* is a compilation of over 200 recent works of logo design paired with applications for promotional materials. The sections include "Typography," "Animal," "Plant" and "Geometry."

○ Technique

This book stands out for the techniques used—the printed blue edges tie the book block and the exquisite case together. The matte UV printing on the cover completes the layered visual and tactile experience.

SYNAESTHESIA

Hand sewing

Dust jacket

Paper Material: Naturalis Vanilla Matte; tracing paper; malmero mango orange; efalin (f/linen) orange
Size: 175mm x 230mm

Mak Yu Jing [Singapore]

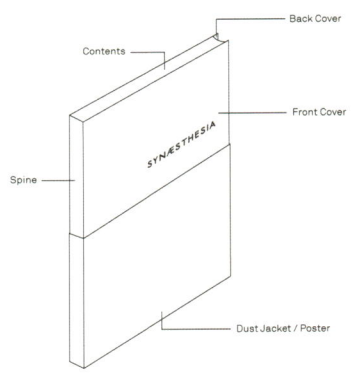

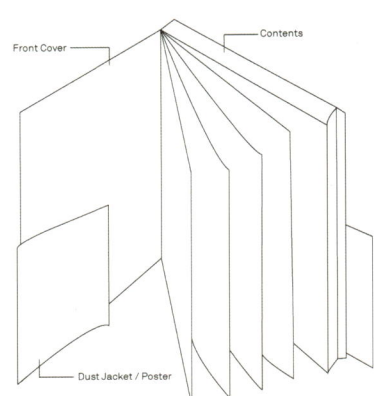

This publication is about Synaesthesia, a rare neurological trait in which activity in one sensory modality, such as vision or hearing, evokes automatic and involuntary perceptual experiences of another type, due to "cross-talking" between sensory pathways in the brain. This self-generated publication aims to raise awareness about this unusual and thought-provoking phenomenon. It provides an insight on Synesthesia as well as its relation to art and design.

To emphasize the intertwined sensual evocations of Synaesthesia, there is a page inside in which threads cross each other to add a dramatic effect to the content. One out of the many forms of Synaesthesia is the "touch-emotion." The designer added a few textured materials like plastic, wood, paper and cotton cloth to enhance interest in the content of that specific topic.

Technique

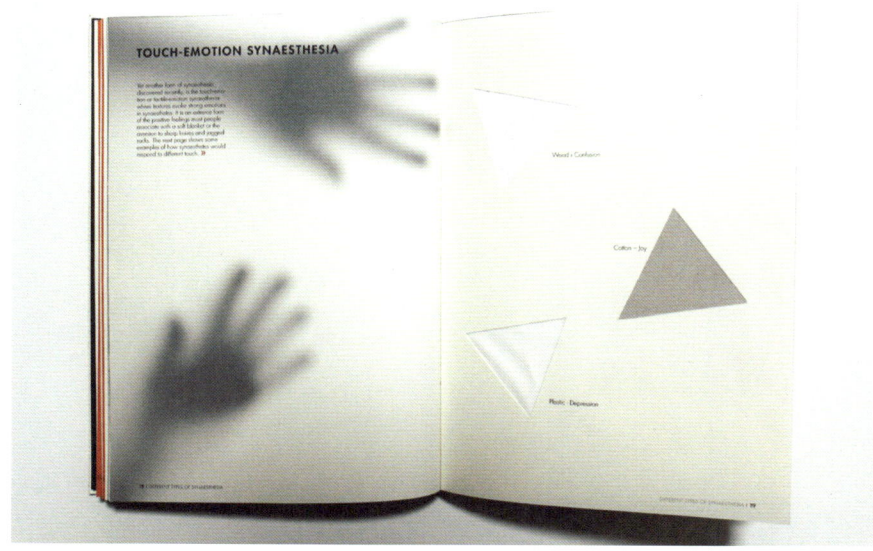

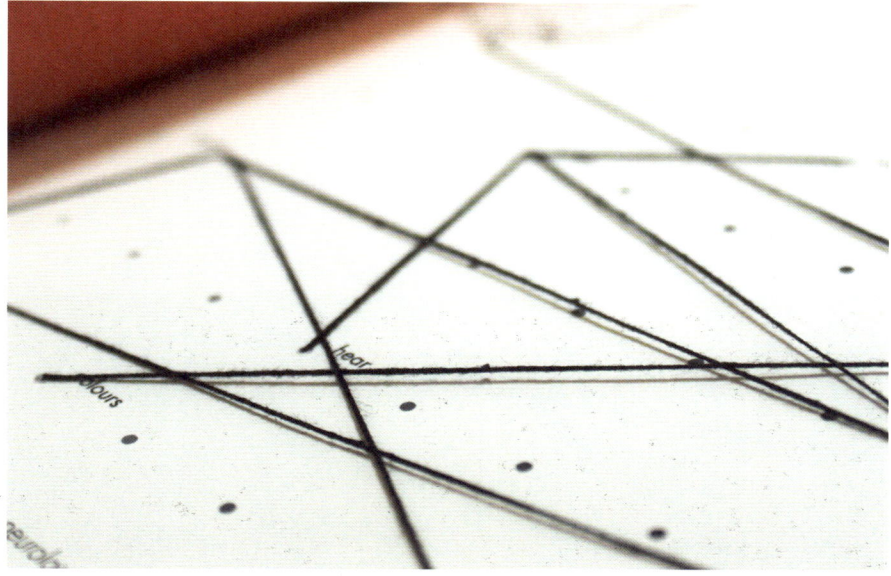

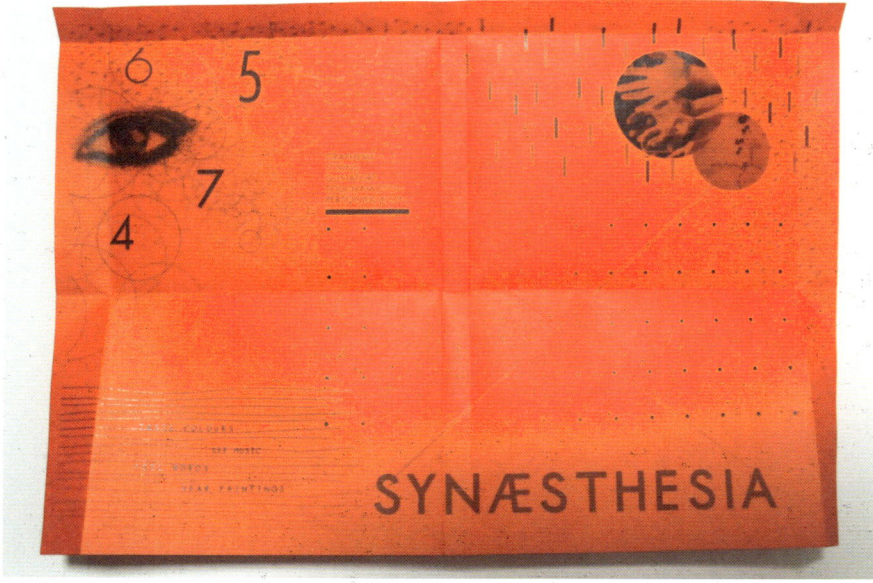

ROM 13

Embossing
Metallic printing

Paper Material: Scandia 2000 white
Size: 250mm x 360mm

Work in Progress [Norway]

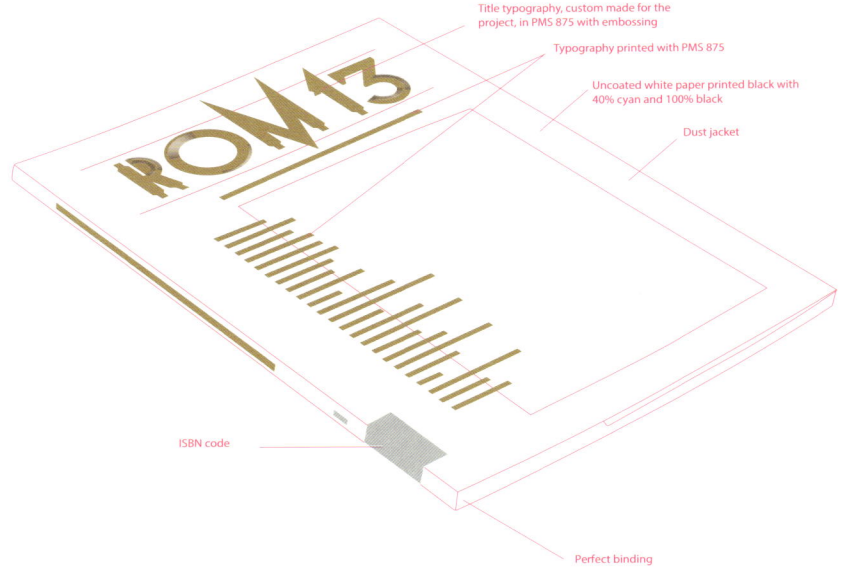

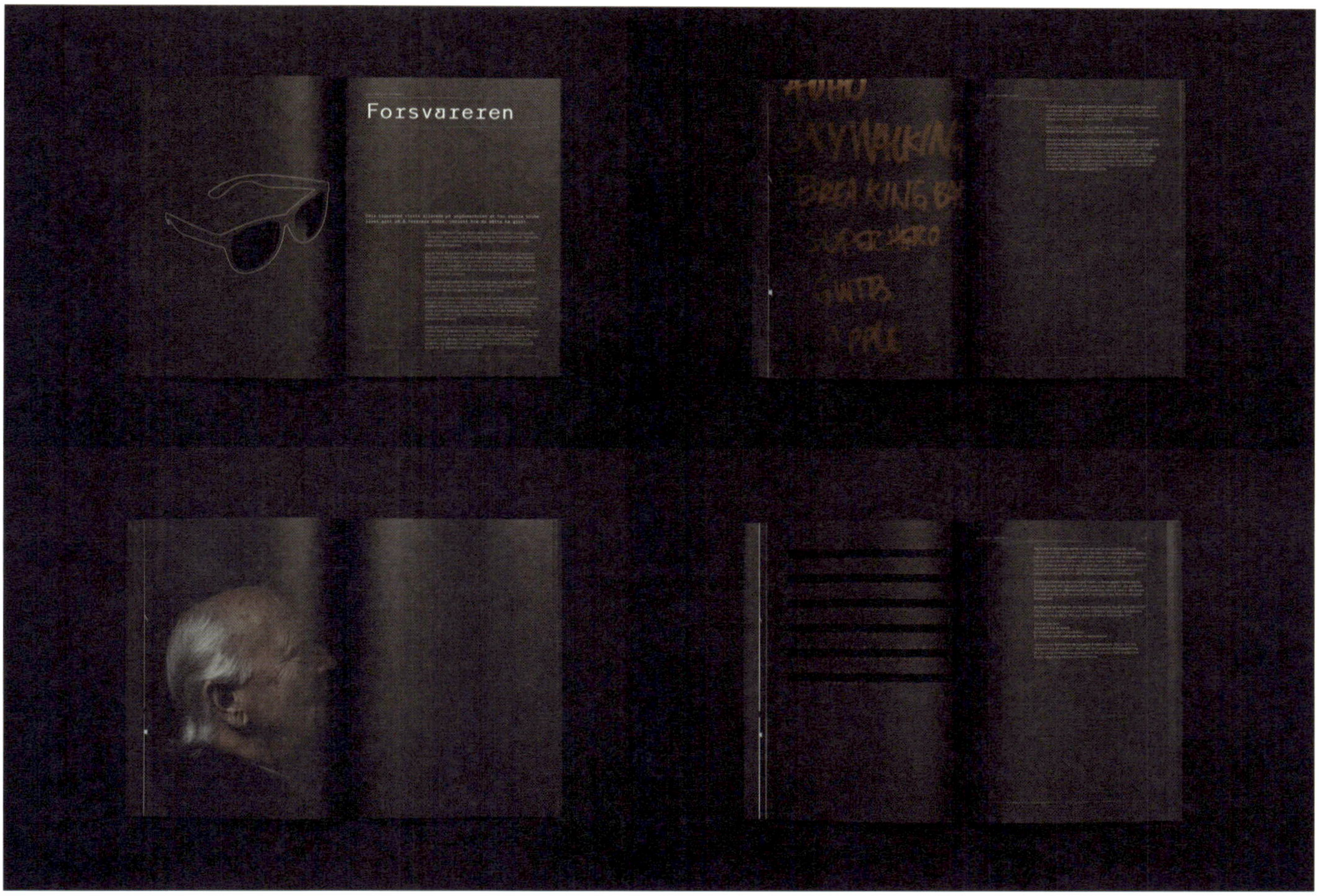

Technique

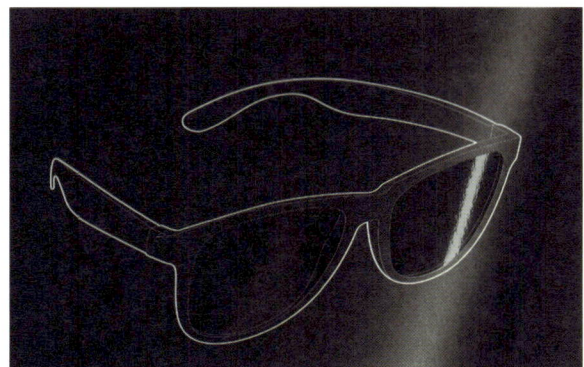

What is the one important choice that changed your life? *Rom 13* (Room 13) sets out to ask celebrities and former criminals that very question. The book begins with an introduction by the president of the Norwegian Red Cross and a short synopsis by Jonas Forsang. Photographer Marcel Leliënhof shot all the participants in one 30m hotel room. All proceeds from the sale of the books will go directly to a Red Cross organization that rehabilitates former criminals.

The book pages are printed in 40% cyan and 100% black for a rich color. It is a paperback with the title typography printed in metallic ink and embossed on both dust jacket and cover. The book also uses metallic and spot varnish on selected pages. The binding relates to art books and magazines, with bold titles and short introductions. The angular construction of the custom typography for the title of the book reflected the architecture of the warehouse, Shed 13, where the project was first displayed and photographs from the book were also exhibited.

N°3 - OBLIQUE

Debossing
Gold and black foiling
Gold pantone ink
Varnish
Hand-engraving

Paper Material: Pop'set ultra red; Mat Périgord Infinity
Size: 280mm x 230mm

Aris Zenone Studio [Switzerland]

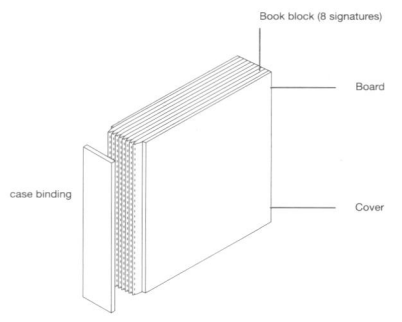
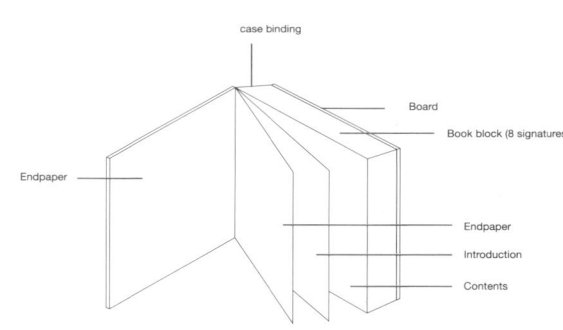

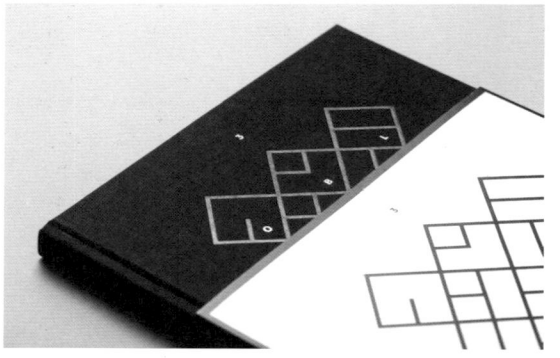

•

N°3 is the third publication by OBLIQUE. It is something between a magazine and a book. The content covers art, illustration, design and architecture. It presents works from Ariane Goetz, Lilo Baur, Blaise Sahy, Sibylle Stoeckli, Catherine Gfeller and Aris Zenone.

 Technique

This volume is a canvas hardcover with gold foil and black debossed foil print, encased in a white cardboard case.
For the interior, two paper types were used, one coated and another red offset printed in gold 2X Pantone to create a distinctive effect. The last section's offset plate style was hand-engraved with a paintbrush using plate corrector gel and Iris printed, which means that every copy of this book is different.

SGDA MEMBERS ANNUAL 2012-2013

Metallic ink printing
Foiling
Gilded fore-edge
Embossing

Paper Material: Coated paper
Size: 190mm x 260mm

Shenzhen Huathink Design Company
[China]

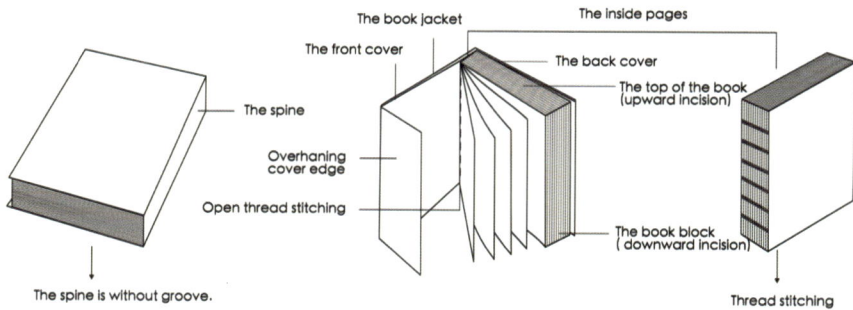

● *The SGDA (Shenzhen Graphic Design Association) Members' Annual 2012-2013*, was produced to record the achievements of the association, present new works and introduce new members, It serves as a testament to the development of the Chinese graphic industry.

 It features a soft cover and four-color printing. Other printing technologies used include foiling and stamping.

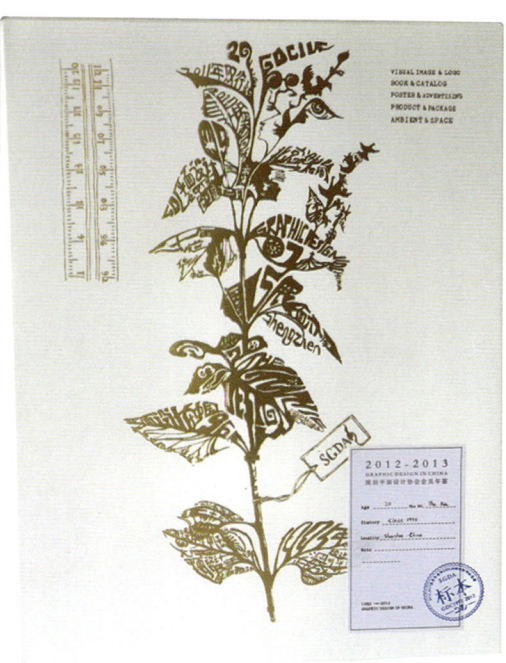

RECOLLECTION

Spot color

Embossing

Foil blocking

Paper Material: Color stamping paper, tracing paper, offset paper
Size: 170mm x 230 mm

ACST Design [Norway]

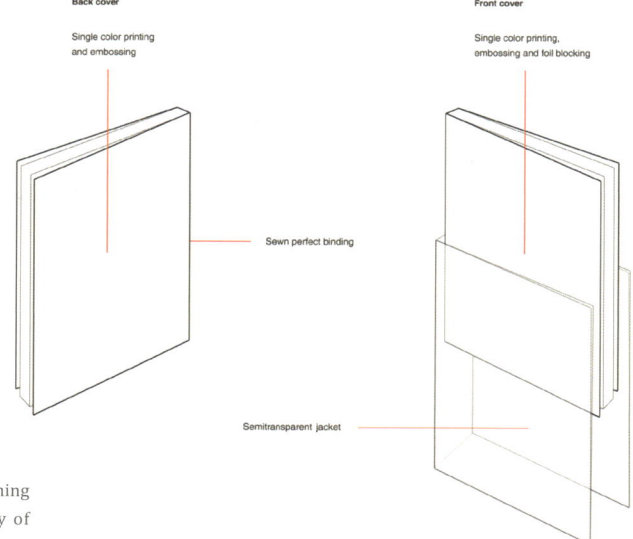

- *Recollection* is a special issue featuring the achievements of a Taiwanese e-learning and digital archives program run by the Institute of History and Philology of Academia Sinica, Taiwan.

Technique

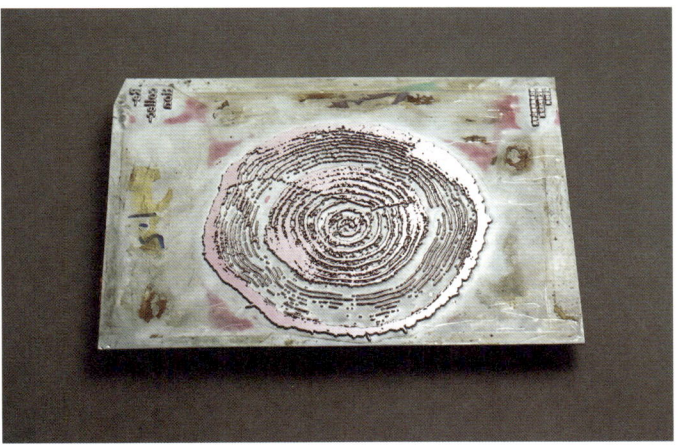
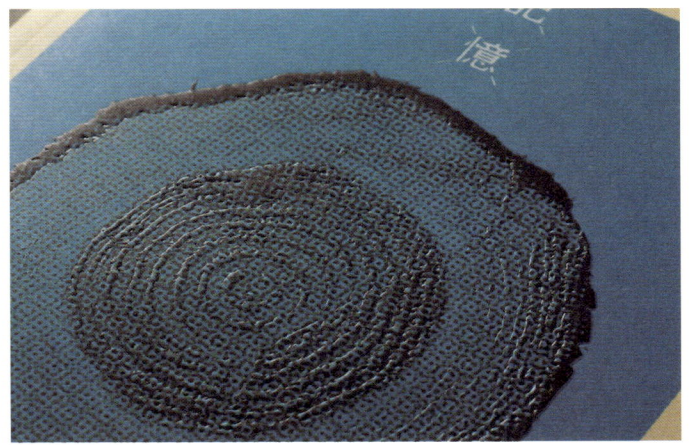

This set consists of a collection of projects and information on research along with a jacket poster and a manga booklet. The imagery of embossed tree growth rings on both front and back covers not only symbolizes the program's achievements over the past ten years, but reflects the title and emphasizes that every project and piece of research in the book are memorable parts of the whole program. The jacket poster shows the program's achievements concisely (in English) and in order to visually enhance the diversity of the research projects, tracing paper was used as a printing material to give the poster a changing appearance when placed against different backgrounds.

Die cutting
Coptic binding

Paper Material: Matte Off-White
Size: 140mm x 210mm

Jiani Lu [Canada]

VISUAL LANGUAGE

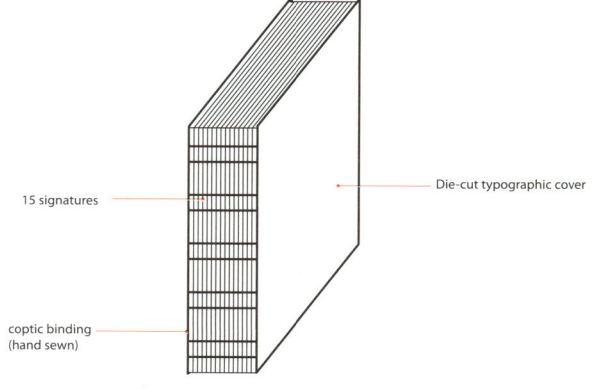

15 signatures

Die-cut typographic cover

coptic binding
(hand sewn)

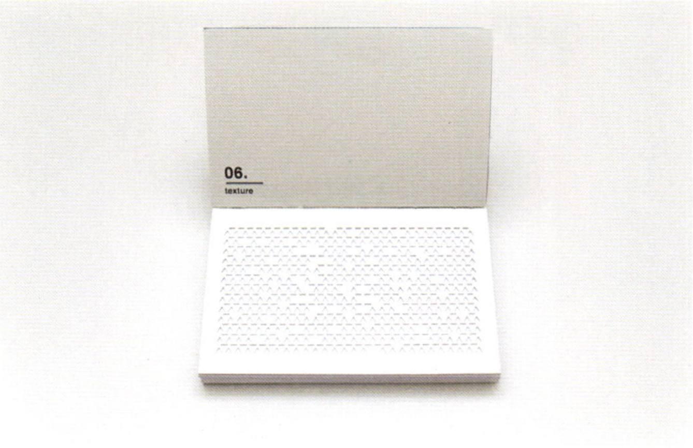

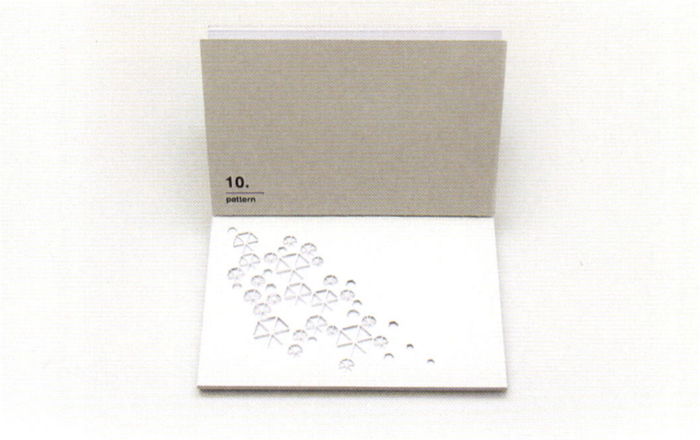

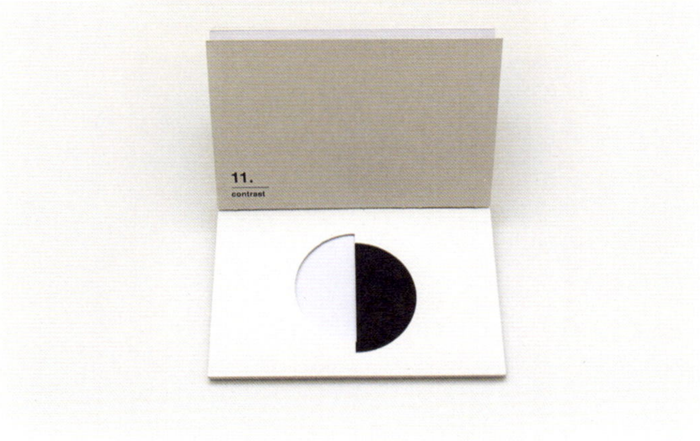

◯ *Technique*

Visual Language explores the founding principles and elements of design in the interactive and tactile format of a hand-bound book. The project approaches each element and principle through a restricted palette and the use of elementary shapes and forms.

The book features tactile die-cut designs and invites participation and interaction. The binding allows the book to lay flat and gives the book a raw feel.

175

WELCOME TO THE DOLLHOUSE

Offset printing

Die Cutting

Perfect binding

Paper Material: Coronado paper
Size: 147mm X 210 mm

ACST Design [Norway]

This design is for the talented Taiwanese writer Li-chun Huang's novel *Welcome to the Dollhouse*.

The vivid red front cover and the black composition inside convey the strange, imaginative yet absorbing moods of the book. The design of a half-open door revealed on the cover alludes to the scenery the main character sees in the story. When opening the cover, the reader discovers an upside-down scenery with text to visually present the story.

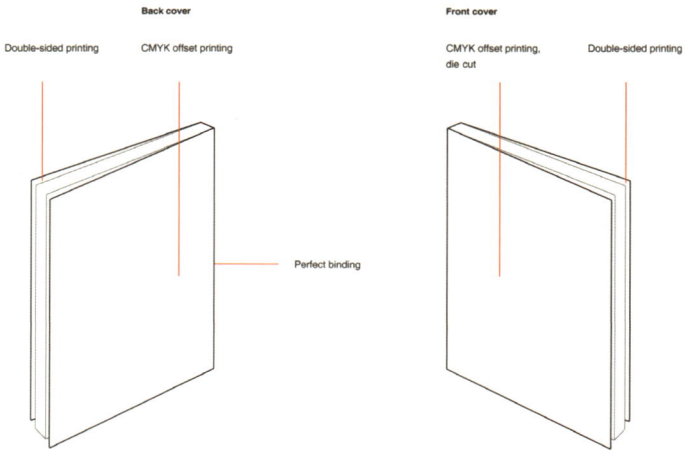

Technique

海邊的房間

WHAT'S NEXT

Die cutting

Cutting

UV printing

Paper Material: Coronado SST, Sundance Felt, Sundance Ultra, Classic Linen, Coronado SST Cover, Mohawk Superfine
Size: 185mm x 240mm

carmentrino & Zafir Pri/Emir hakim Design
[Indonesia]

● The biggest misconception about recycling is that people perceive it as the "in" thing. In fact, whenever a new life begins, so does the process of recycling. We keep on recycling our life through options until one day, everything returns to where it once started, and then proceeds to its next journey, which is exactly the essence of recycling. So recycling is not a one-time process, rather, it's an on-going one.

 The binding for this book is side stitch binding. The most outstanding feature of the book is the die cut technique that can be found on both the cover and inside pages. It is a publication celebrating smarter paper choices through the use of different printing techniques, a campaign to raise awareness on future ideas and action plans.

178

Technique

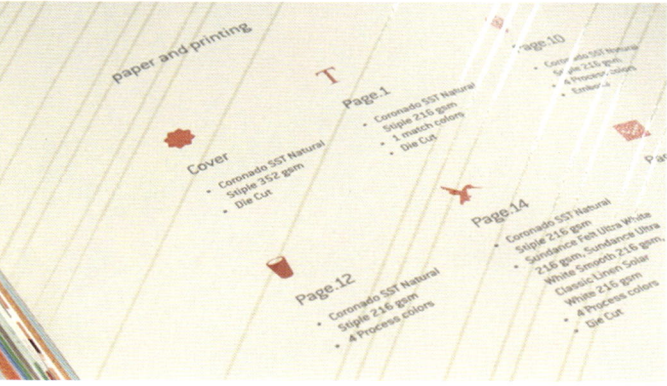

TRI—DÉ KNIHA

Pop-up design
Hand-gluing

Paper Material: White paper
Size: 148mm X 210mm

Robert Urban [Slovak Republic]

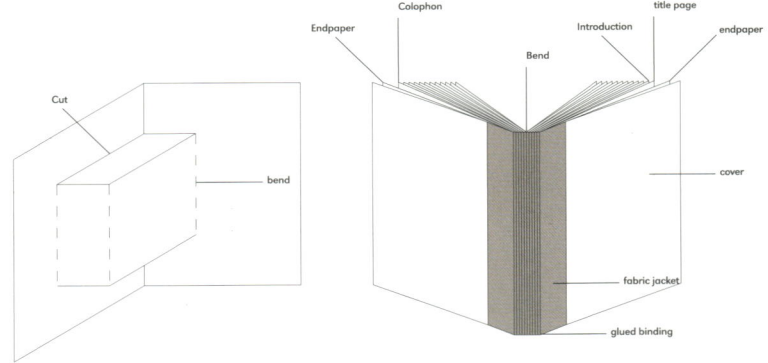

• This book is a result of the designer's contemplations on the connection between people and the classical medium of the printed book in an age when digital mediums are beginning to dominate but may be failing to generate that genuine feeling that paper provides. In addition, traditional books have a special feeling and it is the goal of this publication to highlight the feelings that are created and experienced by the user of traditional publications.

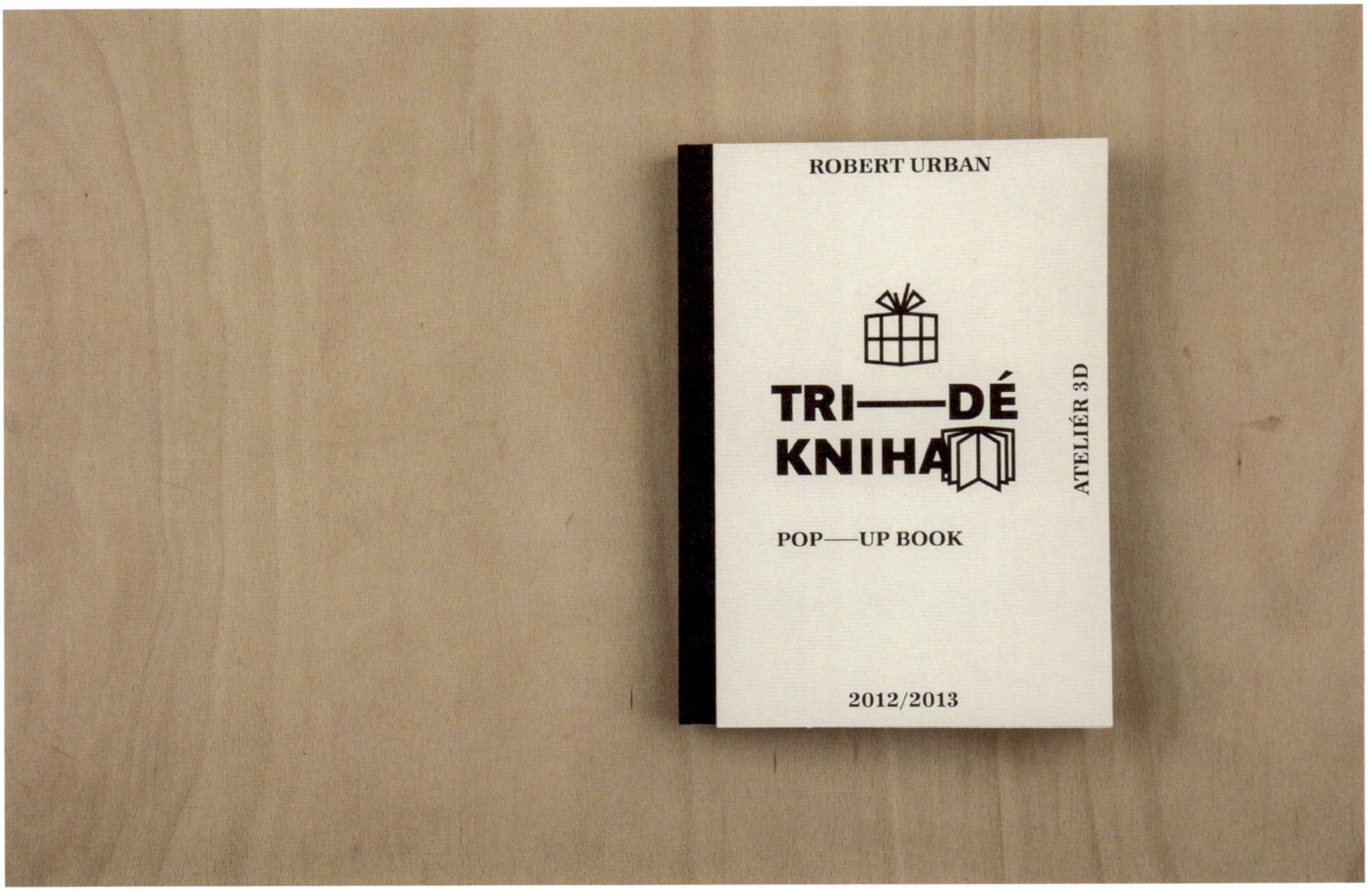

 Tri-dé kniha is about paper techniques, pop-up experiments and exploration of possibilities. Each spread possesses a dual nature and features a flat sheet and a pop-up system, which can only be discovered via reader interaction. It combines classical book design techniques and paper engineering, based on the designer's previous works. In addition, the meticulous typographic layout helps to boost the visual impact. Some segments of the contents and the jacket were hand-glued by the artist himself.

DZHARYLGACH ISLAND

Special binding
Debossing
Tinted fore-edge
Hot-stamping

Paper Material: Munken pure paper, cardboard, tracing paper, Nettuno camoscio
Size: 140mm x 210 mm

Roman Dzyvulskyi [Ukraine]

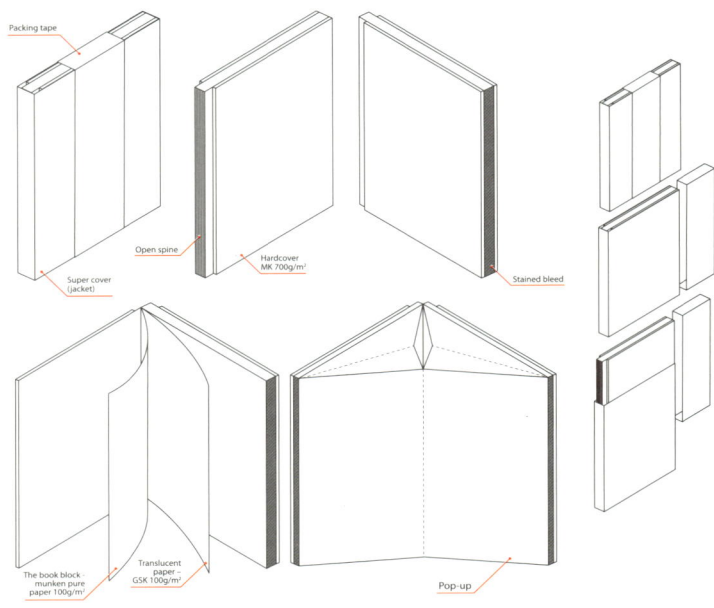

182

○ Technique

The book conveys the tenderness and instability of the easily eroded sand island by using different types of paper. It is a hardcover with an open spine. Outstanding printing characteristics include offset printing, hot stamping, a stained bleed, creasing, gluing, cutting and printing on translucent materials.

●

Dzharylgach Island has an international importance for migratory birds which flock to and take possession of the island during migratory seasons, many of which are recorded in the "Red Book." The author of the book *Dzharylgach Island* intended to convey the importance of this corner of the earth in relation to the entire planet. The goal was to direct the focus to the environment of the island with the help of design elements. The designer hopes that this publication will draw public attention to the ecological problems of Dzharylgach Island and encourage people to support the careful management of nature.

SECRET: BETWEEN HIDING AND REVEALING

Laser cutting
Perforation
Embossing
Creasing
Swiss brochure folding
Unique dust jacket design
Stamping
Screen printing

Paper Material: Papyrus PlanoPlus, Neusiedler Mondi Color Copy, Xerox Translucent
Size: 210mm x 297mm

Katharina Schiessler [Germany]

Keeping secrets is a phenomenon with major social relevance, which is largely unappreciated. This work is meant to generate public awareness about secrets and their scope and relevance to our social coexistence. It combines theoretical considerations by significant scientists with short, illustrative stories to establish their relevance to the reader.

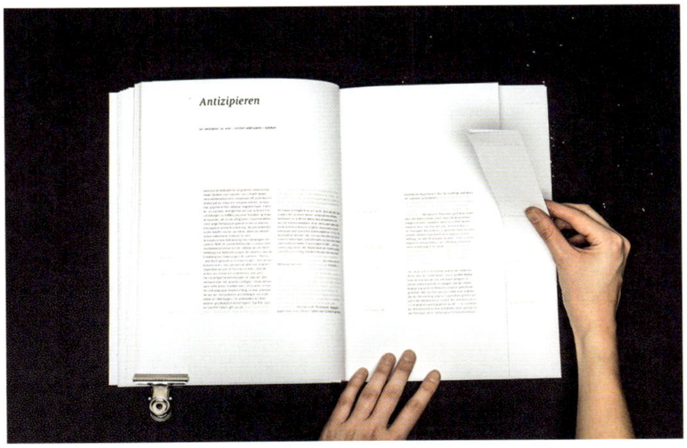

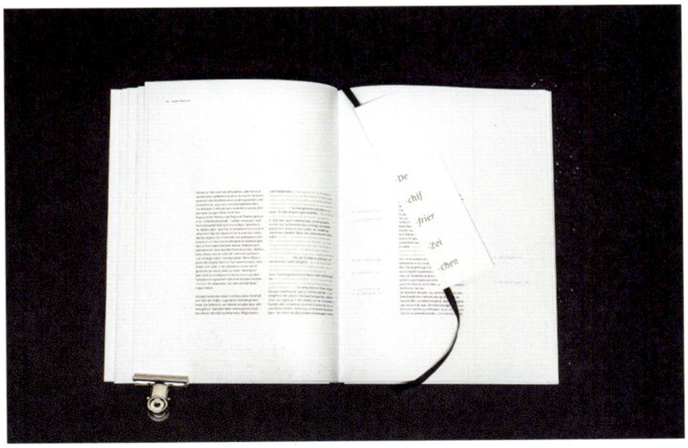

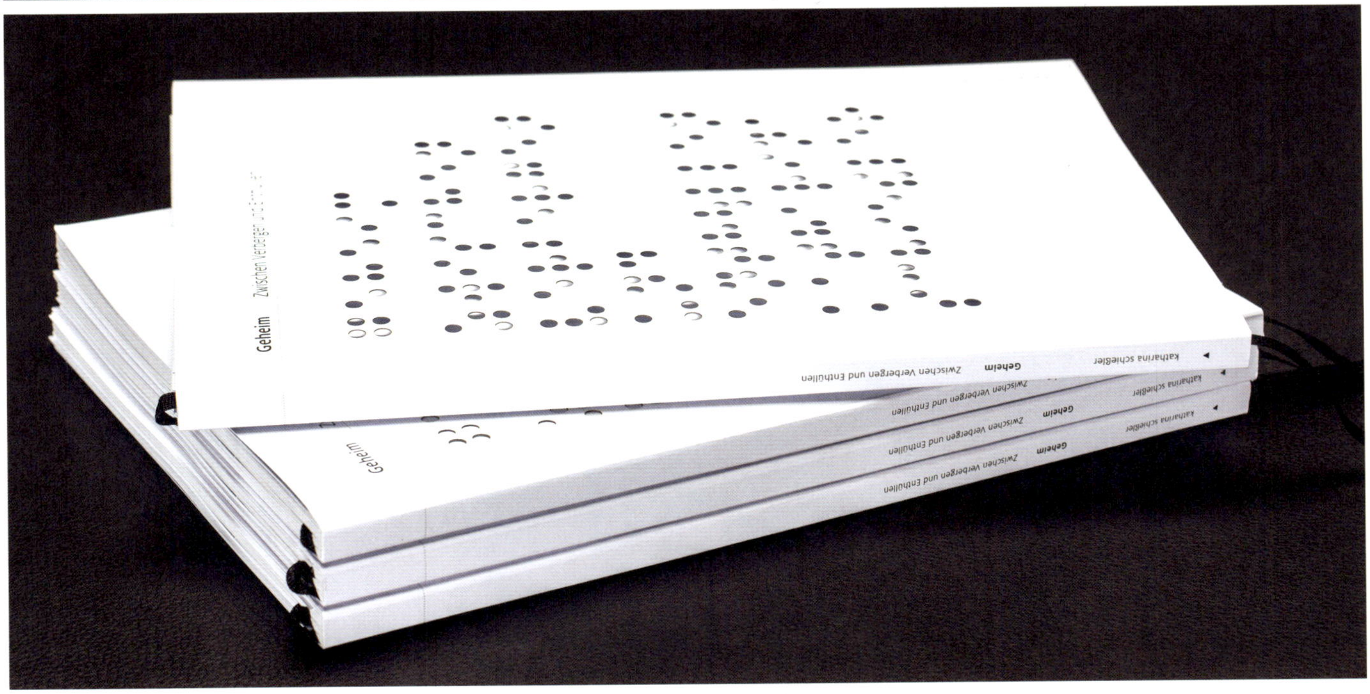

The form of this book allows the reader to directly confront the subject—secrets, by interactively revealing hidden content. The reader is constantly faced with the excitement and danger of revealing something unknown, especially when tearing apart perforated pages is required—an act that means destroying the book irreversibly. The result is a prototype to show that human life is a process of constantly weighing, deciding and finding balances between concealing things and revealing them.

UV printing
Photochromic Paper
Thermochromic Paper
French Binding
Silhouette

Paper Material: Sketch paper Fabriano, cardboard
Size: 263mm x 188mm

Yolaine Codjovi [Canada]

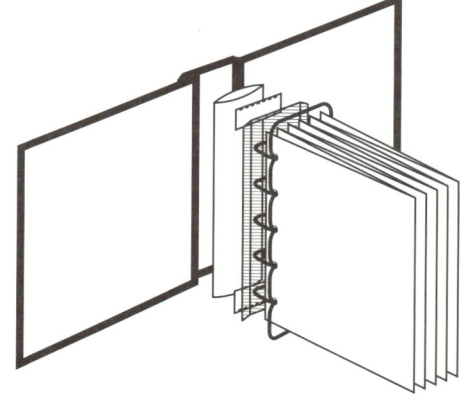

• This project is based on the theme of secrets. But what is more secret than the story of someone's life? This book follows the story of a character and the mysteries surrounding his life.

∴ The book is highlighted by two variables, thermo-reactive elements and UV, which are complemented by typographic elements that have been silkscreened with thermochromic and photochromic inks. Various forms of cryptography and steganography are traceable through the pages, cover and spine. If the reader wants to know the whole story, he must be involved in this adventure of hidden secrets. Inspired by designs of old books, the grid of the book is based on the "division by 9" by Villard de Honnecourt. The final hardcover binding uses "à la française" bookbinding to give the book a more traditional aesthetic.

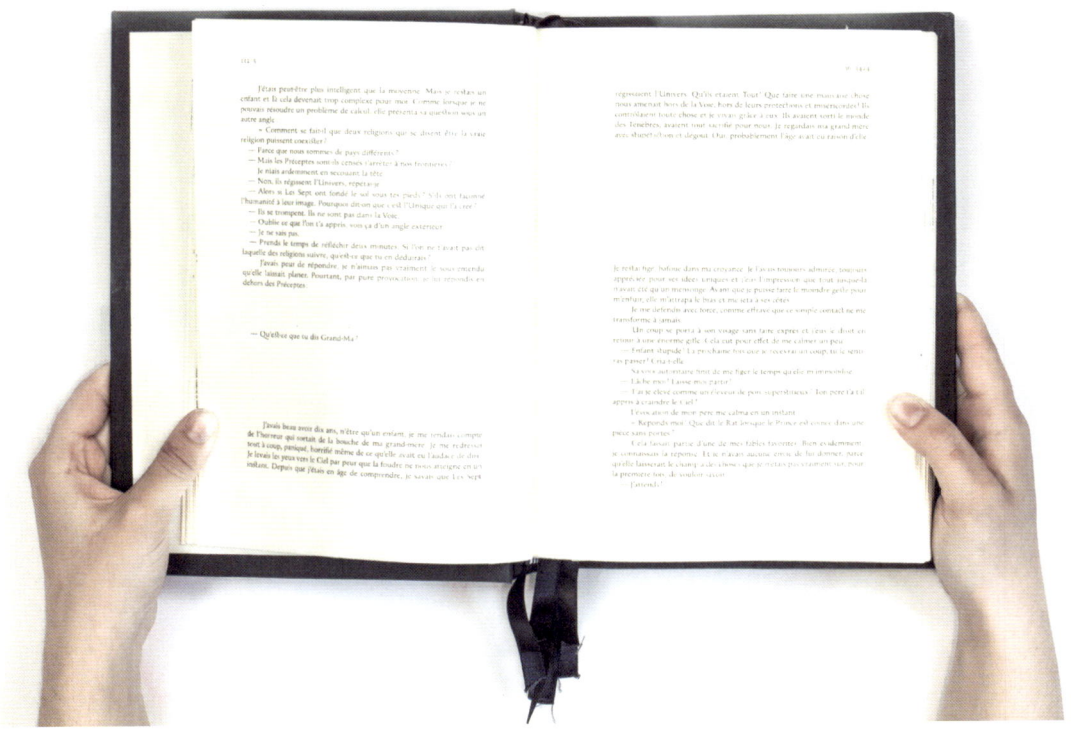

Technique

LOS BRAVO BROTHERS

Screen printing
Spot color
Open spine

Paper Material: Rives paper, orange tracing paper, black paper
Size: 225mm x 160mm

José Luís Sousa Dias   [Portugal]

○ *Technique*

 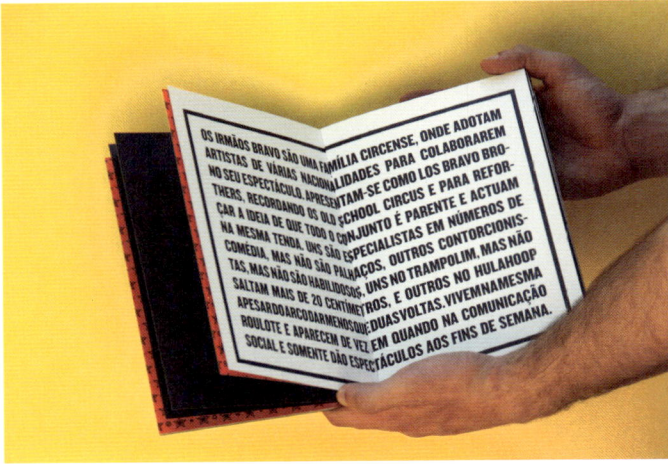

● The Bravo Brothers is a circus family that adopts artists of various nationalities to collaborate on their show. They bill themselves as Los Bravo Brothers to call to mind the traditional circus and to reinforce the idea that the whole family is related and acts in the same tent. Some are experts at comedy, but are not jokers, others are contortionists that are not skilled, others jump on the trampoline, but do not bounce higher than 20 centimeters, and others focus on the hula hoop in spite of not being able to spin it more than twice. They live in the same caravan and appear from time to time in the media while only giving performances on weekends.

 The book cover and back is silkscreen printed with florescent orange descriptions on black Plike paper that resembles rubber. This allows the color to stand out. The whole book is digitally printed on Rives Paper (Rives Tradition). This simulates an offset print and accentuates the color of the illustrations. The separators are also digitally printed on an orange tracing paper, which allows the names of the characters to appear on both sides of the paper. The idea is to enable reading the strange names of the characters from both sides.

EVENTI LETTERARI PROGRAMME GUIDE

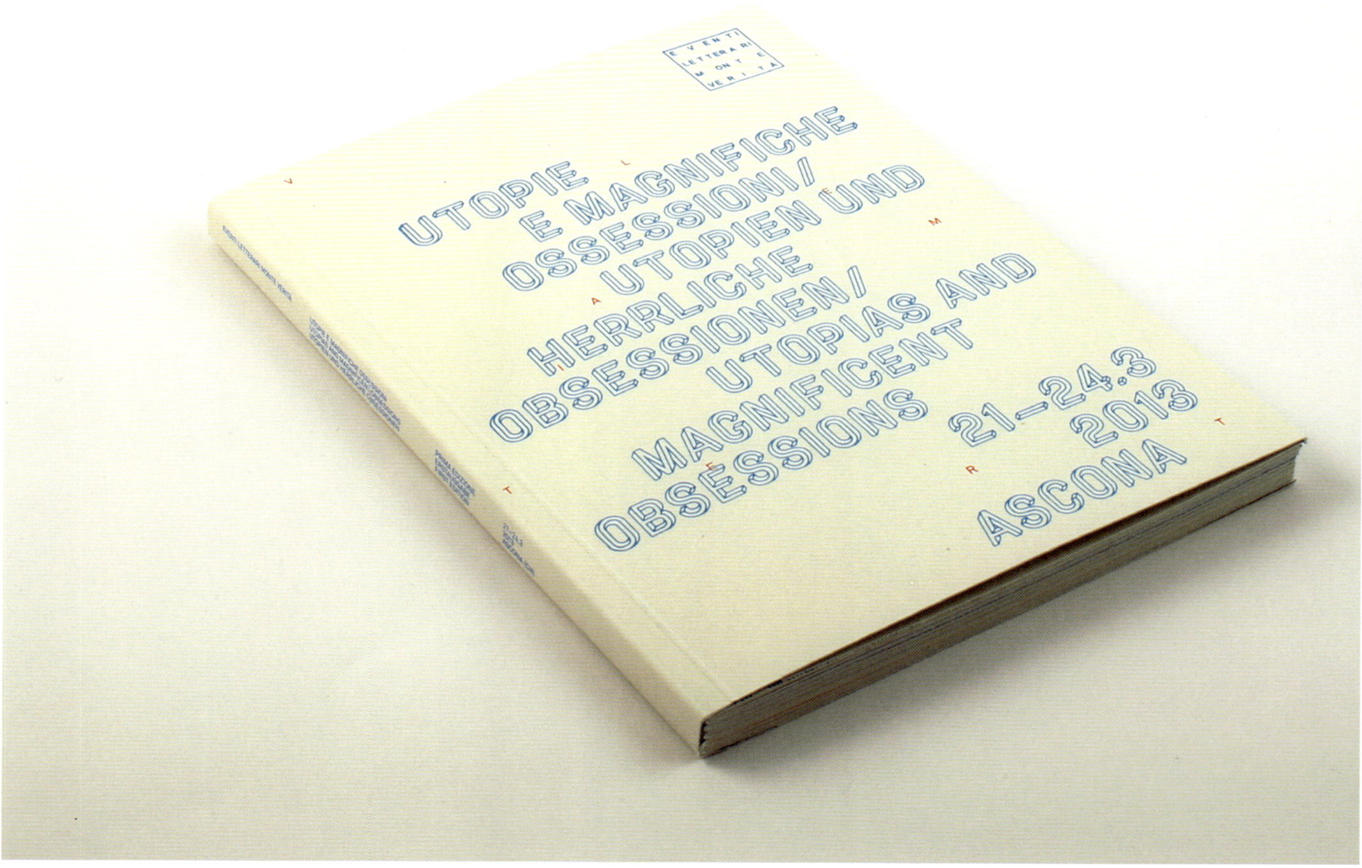

Monochromatic printing

Unique layout design

Paper Material: Recycled paper Cyclus White

Size: 150mm x 210mm

RM&CO [Switzerland]

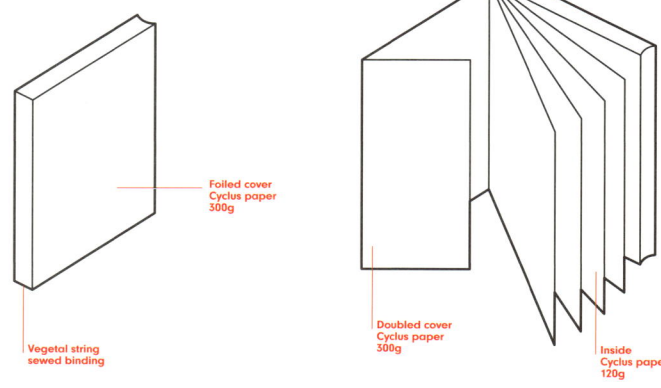

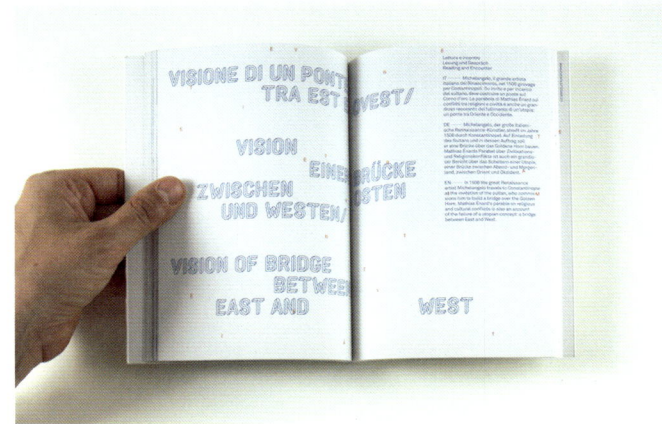

● This program guide uses a bespoke typeface Utopie, which was designed as part of the overall graphic system and identity for Eventi Letterari, a festival of Literary Events in Monte Verità Switzerland. This place has served as a meeting place for artists, anarchists, philosophers and thinkers since the beginning of the twentieth century.

 The material chosen for the book is 100% recycled paper, 300g for the cover and 120g for the interior. The book is sewed with vegetable string and employs offset printing, except for the cover, which is partially foiled.

FOOD. CHOCOLATE. DESIGN.

Four Pantone Colors

Embossing

Open spine

Paper Material: Centaure Naturale, Selena New Ivory
Size: 190mm x 260mm

Happycentro [Italy]

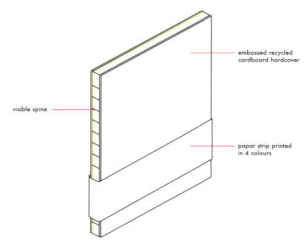 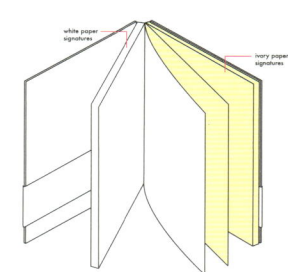

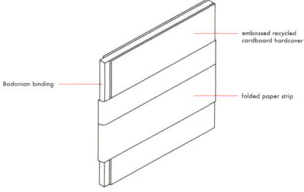 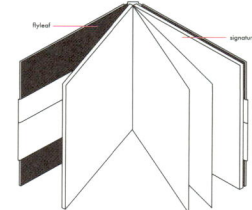

● This book was designed for the 2013 Pitti's Taste Fair in Florence, an event that involved chocolatier, Simone Sabaini-Sabadì, 9 top Italian food artisans, 8 food bloggers and 16 designers.

Technique

 The designers used four Pantone colors to create the color scheme for this project. Brown is the link with the ground and with chocolate; yellow for the sun and Cyan for water since they are sources of life. Red stands for passion, a common feeling shared by food makers, designers and food bloggers. The book preserves the memory of the works exhibited in the fair and the whole event in a tiny but remarkable volume.

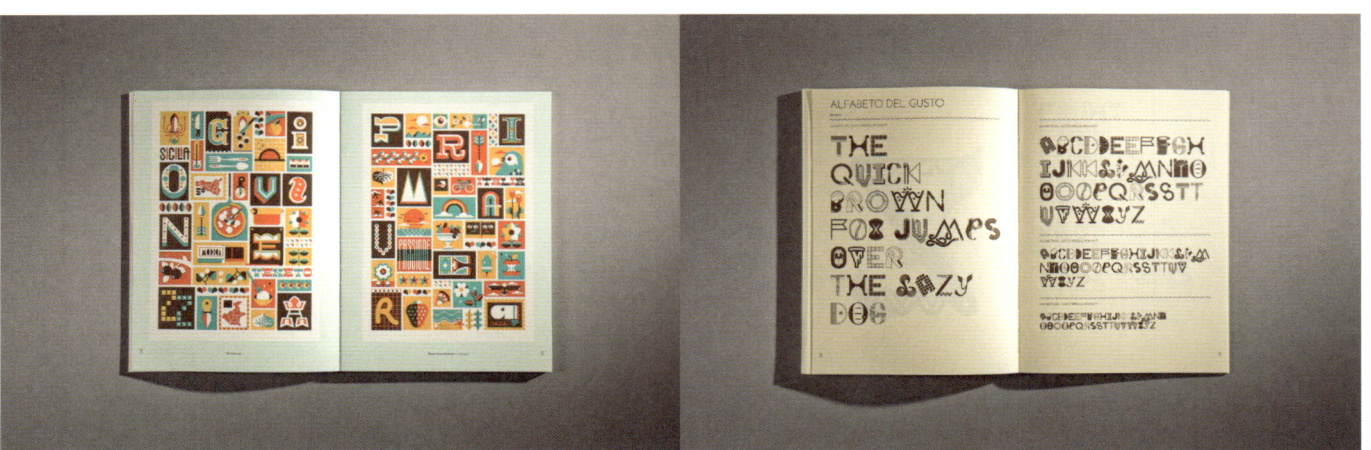

CREATE CHANGE

Fluorescent colors
Silver foiling
Bleeding

Paper Material: Cougar Cover, Endurance Gloss Book, Wausau Exact Brights, Wausau Opaque Colors, Wausau Astrobrights, Domtar Colors Opaque
Size: 650mm x 925mm

Design Office, Art Center College of Design [USA]

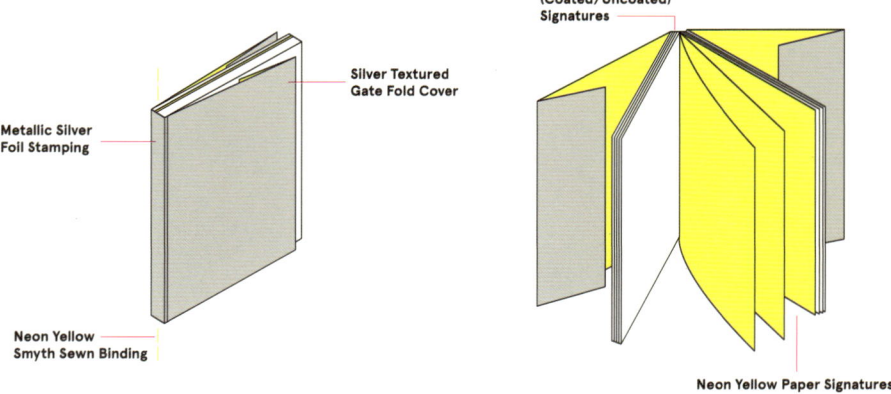

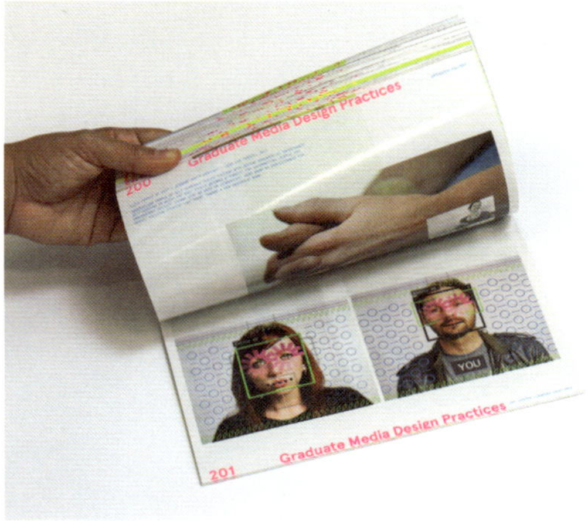

○ Technique

●
The Art Center's 2013-14 viewbook features a textured silver cover with gatefold edges set back from the fore-edge of the book, allowing the words "Art Center" to appear in fluorescent magenta when the book is closed. The page numbers are also visible, serving as navigators through the book. This visual effect is enhanced when the book is fanned open.

A C1S (coated on one side) stock normally used for bottle labels was used for the bulk of the book, resulting in spreads with alternating gloss coated and uncoated surfaces. An information section printed on yellow paper separates the front half of the book, which is comprised of an introduction and descriptions of undergraduate programs, from the last part, which features descriptions of graduate programs. The graduate section is rotated 90°, further differentiating it from the preceding sections.

THE MIRACLE OF THE GOLDEN PEARL

Gold foiling

UV printing

Offset printing

Paper Material: coated paper, translucent paper
Size: 300mm x 300mm

Milan Janic [France]

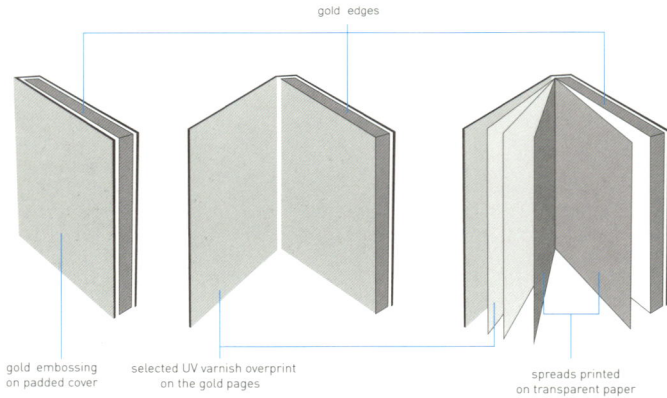

gold edges

gold embossing on padded cover

selected UV varnish overprint on the gold pages

spreads printed on transparent paper

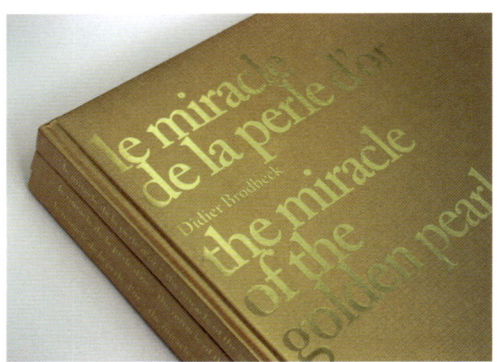

Technique

The Miracle of the Golden Pearl is a book created for Jewelmer, a leading farmer of golden pearls in the Philippines. These special pearls are considered a miracle and a gift from the sea. The goal of this book is to showcase the work of the most prestigious jewelry brands, including Chanel, Chopard, and Cartier among others, that features these pure pearls. The qualities of the lustrous surface of a golden pearl were the inspiration for this golden jewel box, which houses magnificent examples of the art created using golden pearls.

This book is divided into 5 chapters that explain the process of forming pearls. Jewelry spreads are categorized by brand and separated by photographs of the sea. They are printed on transparent paper for contrast. The book was offset printed, with a golden tone. Selected UV varnish overprint is used on golden pages featuring maps of over 7,000 Philippine islands. The book's cover is golden, as are the paper edges.

197

EATING IN YANGCHOW

> Unique jacket design
> Foiling
> Open spine
> Cutting
> Metallic ink
> Gilded edge

Paper Material: Light-weight paper
Size: 140mm × 203mm

Hangqingtang Design   [China]

●

Eating in Yangchow starts with a pair of chopsticks and goes on to highlight exquisite design details in a way that is reminiscent of the faint, delicate fragrance of cuisine in the city and the larger Jiangnan region.

Based on the Chinese dinner tray pattern, every chapter is layered with stylish food imagery and precise text arrangement to form a grid system in a shape that resembles a southern Chinese garden. The book includes a stint of southern humor while investigating the possibility of creativity beyond text.

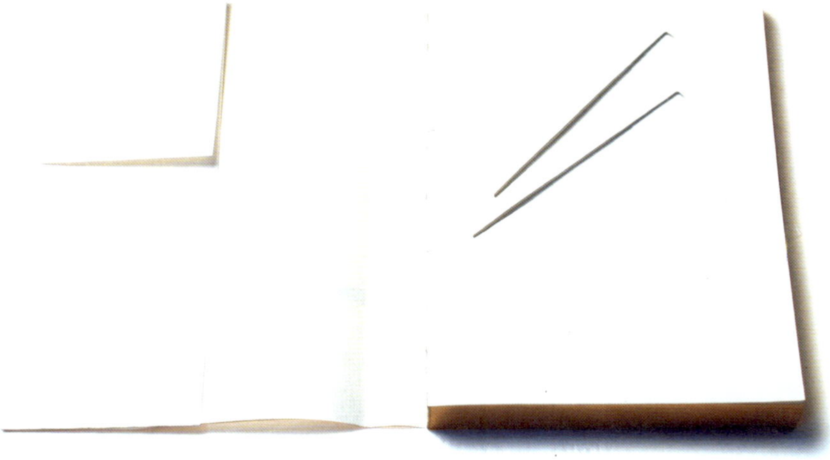

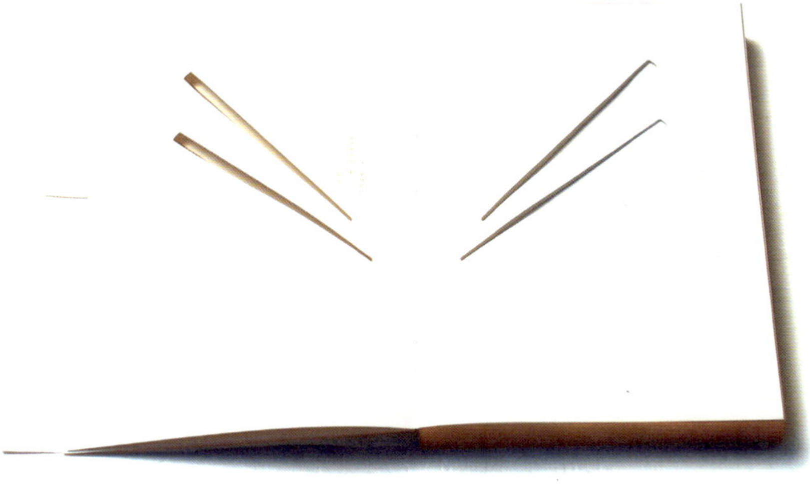

SOLAR ENERGY DEVELOPMENT

Cutting

Metallic ink

Paper Material: Enviro
Size: 190mm × 260mm

Hangqingtang Design [China]

• Although it can be a challenge, the designer of Solar Energy Development makes this dry, scientific reading material "come alive." This book emphasizes the importance of human cognition with regards to tapping solar energy. Topics include light, energy, spots, rays, and rings caused by the sun.

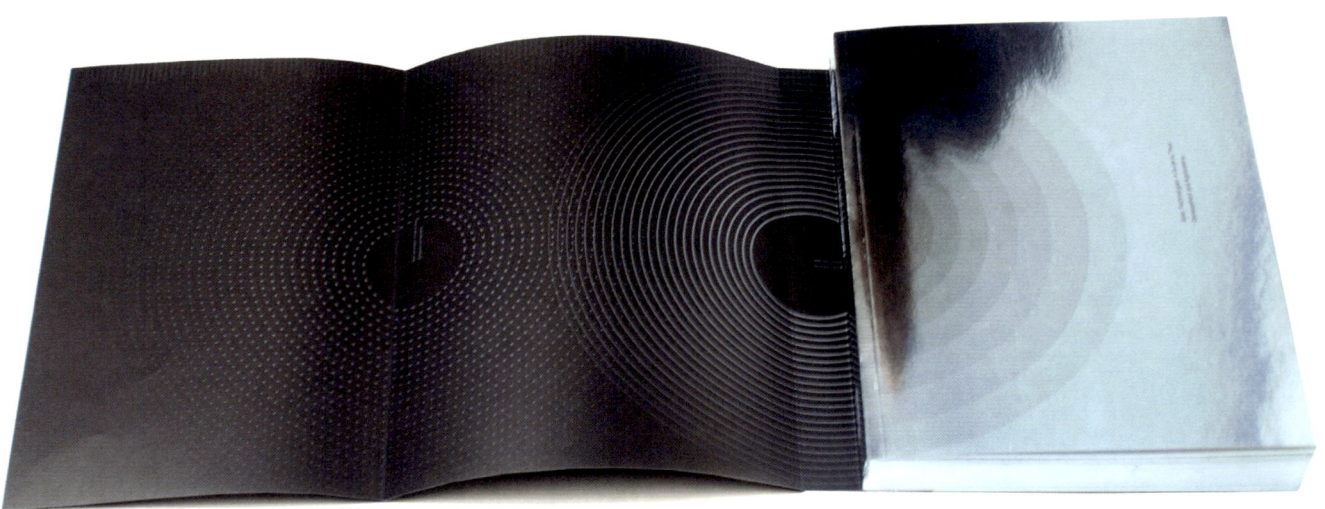

○ Technique

The layout is based on a diagonal grid system to imitate slanting sun rays. The semi-circular page design acts as a transition between chapters while the fluid lines entwined with the text remind the reader of the way the sunlight is entwined with life on this planet. Metallic ink was added to represent the role of technology and for reading convenience. Additionally, different colored paper is used for different chapters.

Debossing

Open spine

Purple stamping

Paper Material: Cardboard; offset plain paper; matt kunstdruck paper
Size: 170mm x 238mm

Metaklinika [Serbia]

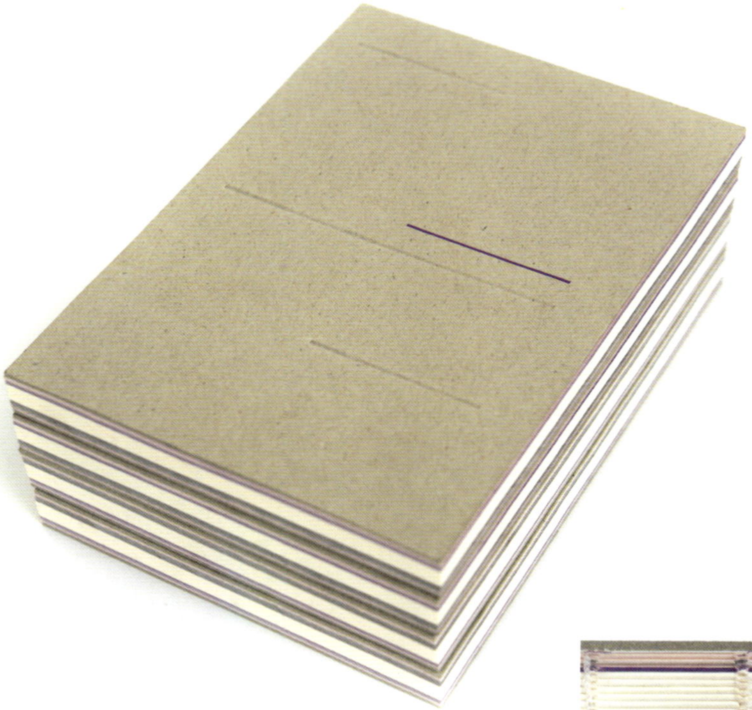

LASER SUMMIT: UNTIL THE END

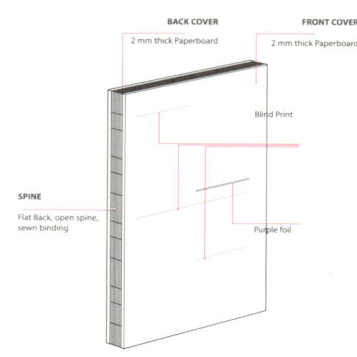
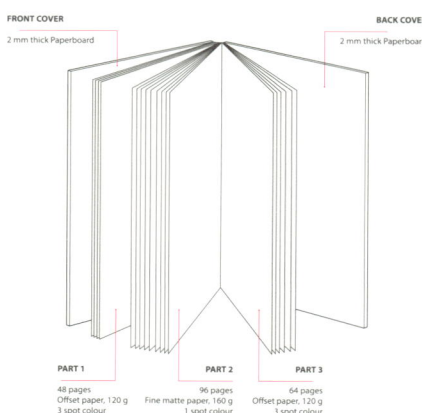

Technique

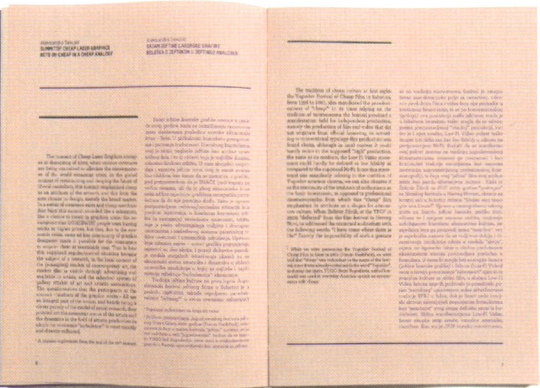

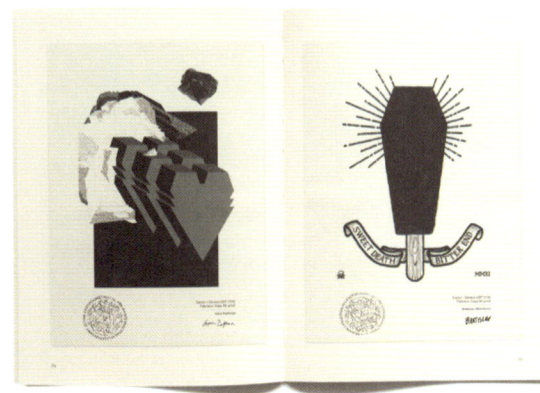
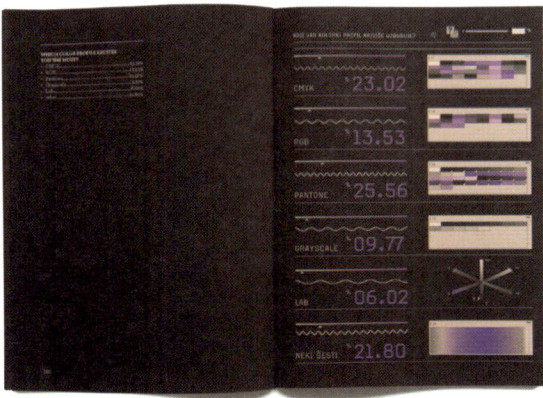

The book *Laser Summit: Until the End* is a collection of works presented at the Spring Summit of Cheap Laser Graphics in 2011 at the Center for Cultural Decontamination, Belgrade. The book is a logical continuation of the book *By Force* the testimony of the sustainability of the designers' event. The book consists of three parts. The first contains texts dedicated to the event itself followed by photos. The second is a collection of the works exhibited in the event, and at the end are infographics that illustrate the answers to questionnaires completed by the artists.

The book has been done in offset mono printing, in two tones. On the cover there is golden foil print and blind print. The book is a combination of raw materials. A fine matte kunstdruck paper was used for the depictions of the artists' works. The layout is designed to bring the content to the forefront. Purity and minimalism give the book its striking design. Some of the artists developed infographics to display data collected from over 130 questionnaires.

Gradient color
Layout

Paper Material: Uncoated paper, Glossy coated paper
Size: 250mm x 210mm

Raw Color [The Netherlands]

THE ESSENCE OF LIGHT

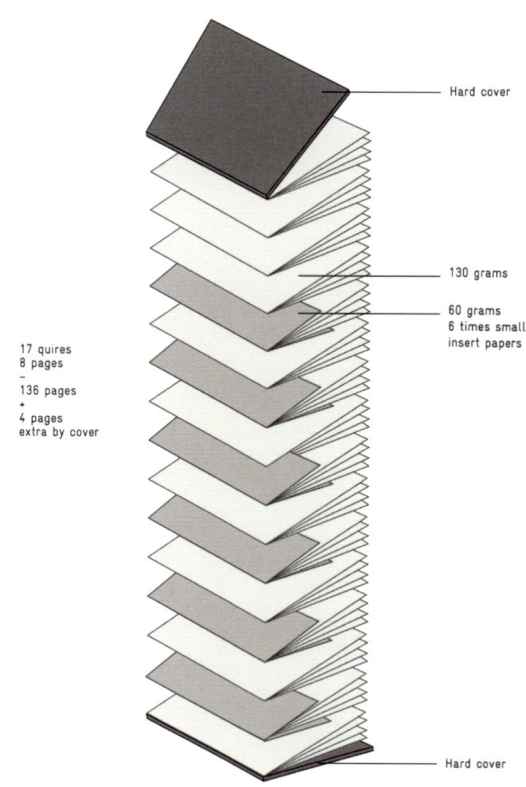

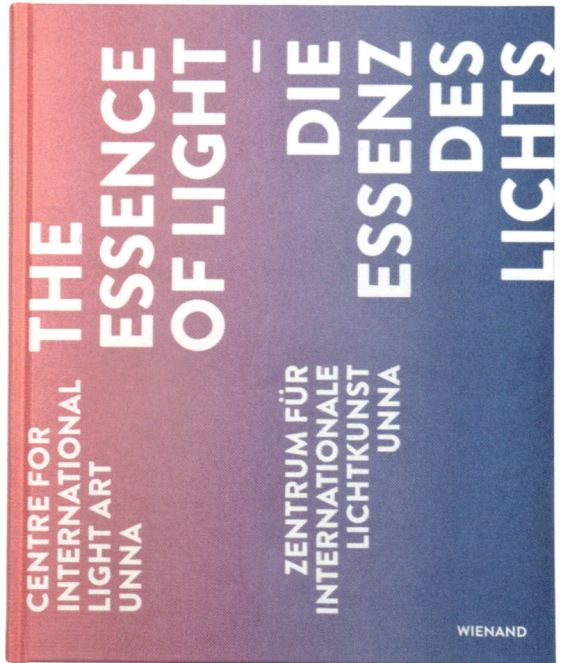

Technique

This book *The Essence of Light* for the Centre for International Light Art Unna, Germany, features a collection of the museum's installations. Starting with the floor plan, the book takes the reader through the space, and features multiple types of paper.

For the *The Essence of Light*, photos were printed on 150 gram glossy coated paper while the introductory texts are printed on 60 gsm uncoated paper that partly covers the photographs.

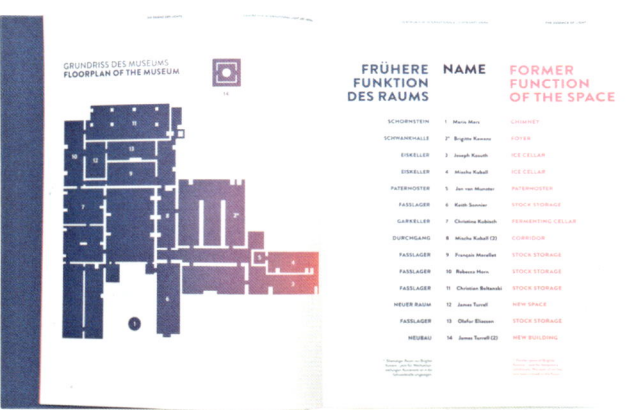

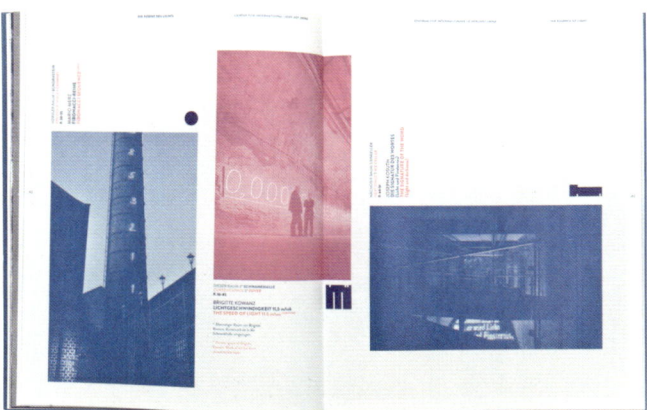

TEXTIELLAB YEARBOOK 2012

Open spine
Double covers
Special sewing

Paper Material: Paper Cyclus, paper Ivolin
Size: 210mm x 270mm

Raw Color [The Netherlands]

Yearbook TextielLab 2012 – expanded view

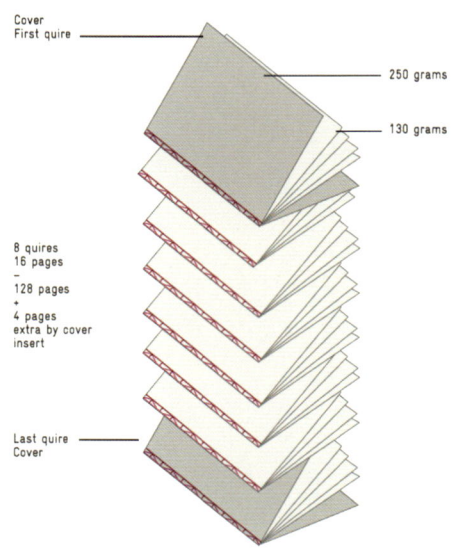

Cover
First quire
— 250 grams
— 130 grams

8 quires
16 pages
–
128 pages
+
4 pages
extra by cover
insert

Last quire
Cover

○ Technique

●

The 2012 yearbook continues the identity of the TextielLab (of TextielMuseum) series. TextielLab a knowledge centre that specializes in providing workshops for producing experimental knits and woven fabrics. The year book features the most interesting projects developed during the year.

The book was created with an open spine, to which a distinguishing pattern of the initials of "TextielLab" and "TextielMuseum" was added. There is a double cover application, incorporating the first with last sections of the book. Due to this the cover returns on the inside page displaying the clients of TextielLab. The mix of different types of papers and thickness adds a tactile dimension to the publication. An elastic cord was specially developed in TextielLab to keep the smaller inserted booklet in its place in the center of the book.

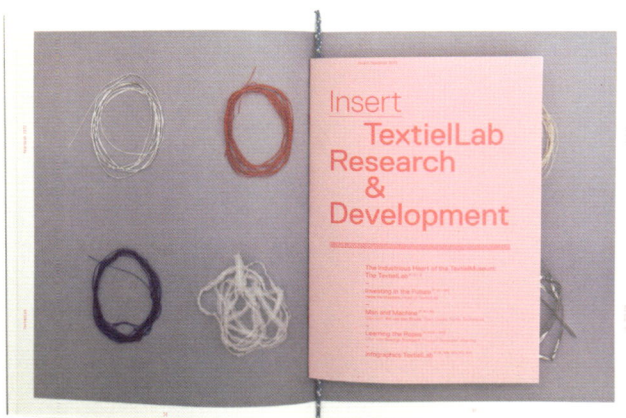
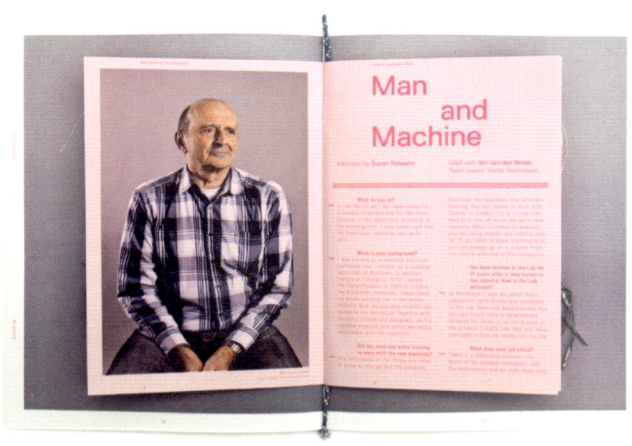

CONTEMPORARY GLASS ARCHITECTURE BOOK

Secret Belgain Binding
Laser-cut cover

Paper Material: Perspex(cover), Mold-made creme paper
Size: 200mm x 260mm

Coraline Chane, CMC-Concept [UK]

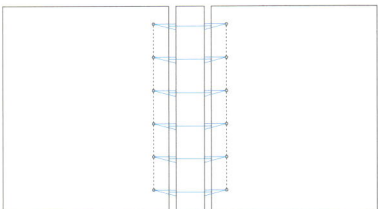

Binding /
Secret Belgian Binding > Outside view cover

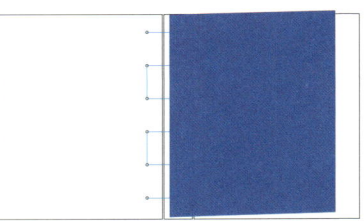

Binding /
Secret Belgian Binding > Inside view cover

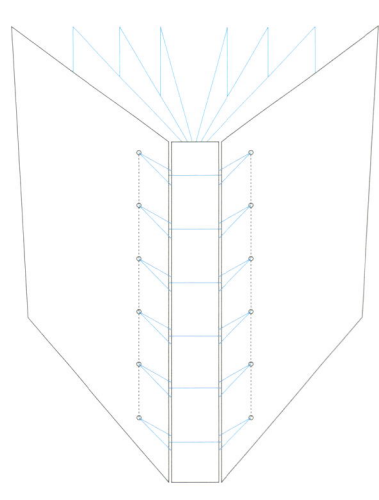

Binding / Secret Belgian Binding
Cover / Lasercut perspex

○ *Technique*

●

The *Contemporary Glass Architecture Book* presents some recent architectural projects that feature transparent materials. The layout and the binding of the book reflect this idea of reflection and transparency.

The book features Secret Belgian Binding and the design was inspired by the characteristics of glass, which is reflected in the symmetry of the drawings on the laser-cut cover, the use of a grid system based on mirrors and the use of transparent materials.

ОДИН (THE ONE)

Sewing
Screen printing
Vinyl sticker
Unique package design

Paper Material: Cyclus Offset, CP Fuchsia Pink, 100% ECF Virgin Fibre, FSC Accredited
Size: 297mm x 420mm

Nina Gudz [UK]

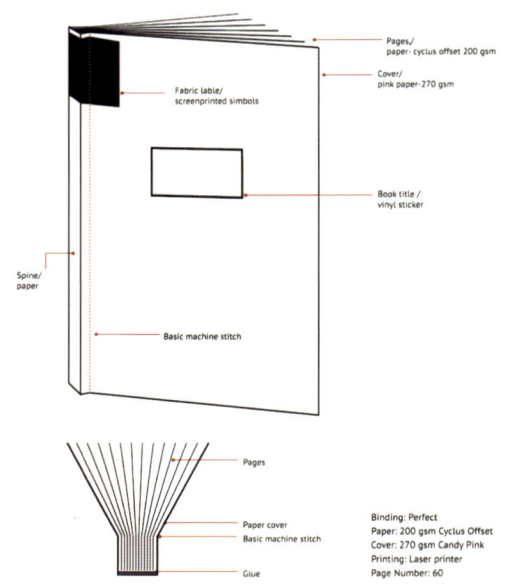

This book is a non-commercial, visual research project for Southampton Solent. It sets out to explore the relationship between fashion and human identity. The designer used the sewing machine stitching as a part of the visual languages as a reference to mass production in the fashion industry as well as to plastic surgery and artificial beauty. The stitches create a sense of distortion when they run across the works of art in the book.

Basic machine stitches on the cover connect it with the interior which is attached with fabric labels. The paper was chosen to make the book look like a fashion magazine. For this book, perfect binding was used with a thermally activated adhesive. The binding was then secured with a sewing machine stitch 7mm from the spine, using 3-ply, corespun thread made from polyester fibres. The fabric label was glued to the spine of the book, and then stitched over. The stitch plays an important role not only in securing the perfect binding, but also in communicating the central idea of the book.

○ *Technique*

CFDA BRAND BOOK

Jewelry decorated spine
Special binding
Embossing

Paper Material: Mohawk; black leather
Size: 229mm x 279mm

Lucie Kim for MyORB [USA]

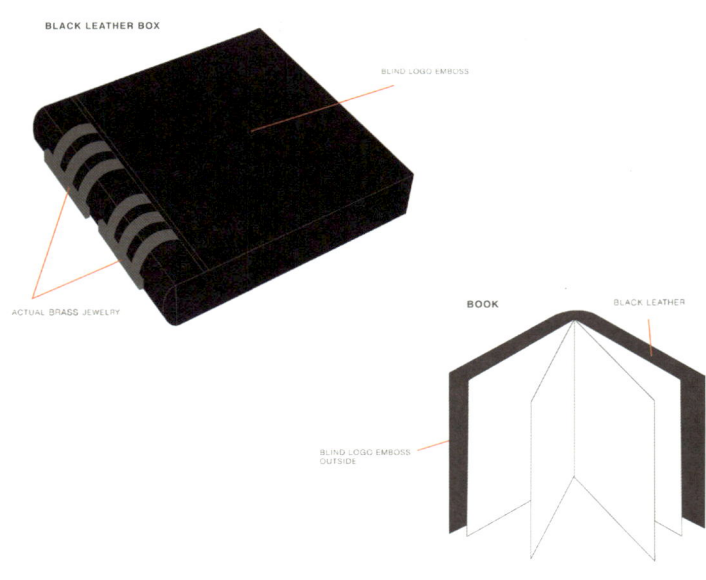

BLACK LEATHER BOX

BOOK

212

◉ Technique

● In a collaborative effort to woo the judges, who included Anna Wintour and Diane von Furstenberg, the authors worked together to create this 1.5" thick leather box and book for the CFDA Vogue Fashion Fund. The work paid off as one of the authors became a finalist and since then has collaborated on many new projects with the CFDA and Vogue.

⁖ One of the most outstanding design details of the book is its binding with real brass jewelry. Blind embossing and inkjet printing were used.

THE MORE I REALIZE

Coptic binding
Bow stitching
Cut-out photo frame

Paper Material: Cartridge paper, embossed paper
Size: 260mm x 160mm

Bethany Johnson   [UK]

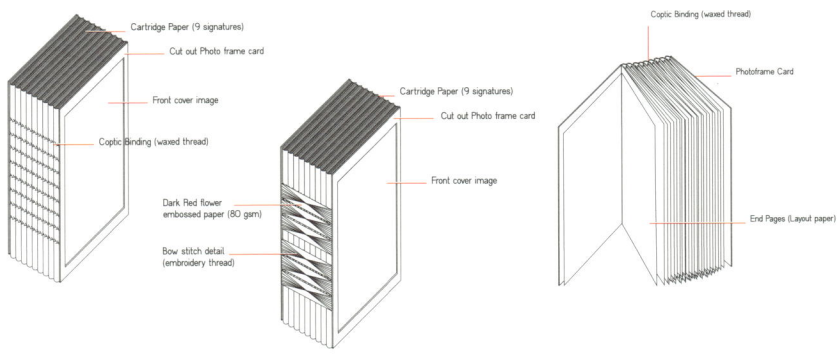

Technique

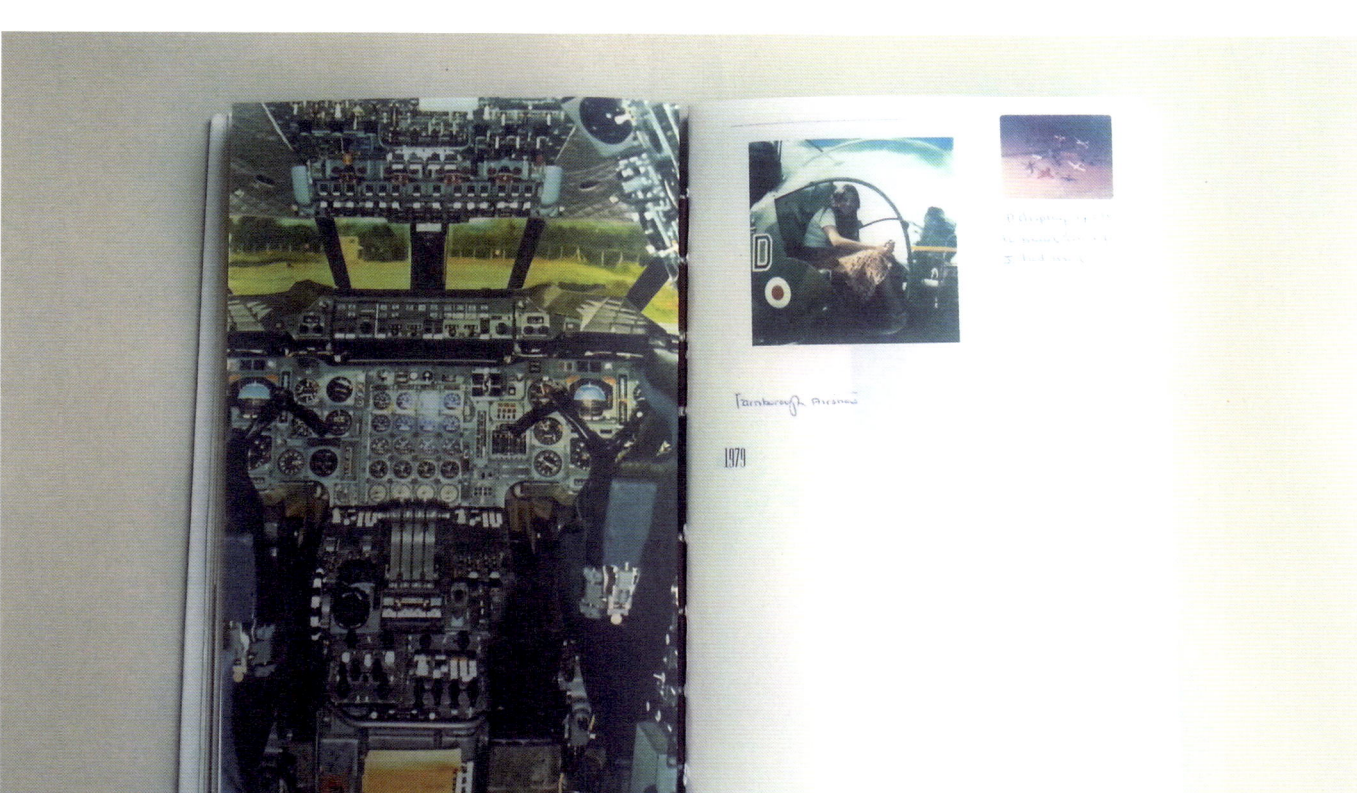

- This work originated from the intention to create a publication with powerful content that experimented with layout, paper stock and production techniques as well as ways of communicating. Its content is based on photographs collect by the designer's mother. When put in sequence, the photographs create a timeline of the designer's mother's life.

- *The More I Realize* unites handwriting and computer type. The handwriting allows the reader to connect with the designer's mother while the type signifies the voice of the artist. The deep red on the spine represents the color of the uniform her mother had throughout her career as a flight attendant and exudes warmth and love. A lot of attention was paid to the spine sewing process, which gives it even more meaning. Some space on the spine is exposed to show the beautiful colors left by signature creases and to create a sense of openness.

215

Foiling
Inserts
Cutting

Paper Material: Light-weight paper, kraft paper
Size: 140mm × 203mm

Hangqingtang Design [China]

SOUL OF A PAINTER

Technique

Soul of a Painter is a story about famous Chinese female painter, Pan Liang-yu.

"Frame" was the governing concept for the design of this book. It helped determine several parts of the design, including color choices. The use of kraft paper and the foiled frame on the cover are intended to remind the viewer of oil painting, as are the canvas-like inserts and typographic styles.

"30" - MONOGRAPH

Half-open spine

Paper Material: Glossy paper, uncoated paper, hardboard
Size: 170mm x 217mm

250 Gramm [The Netherlands]

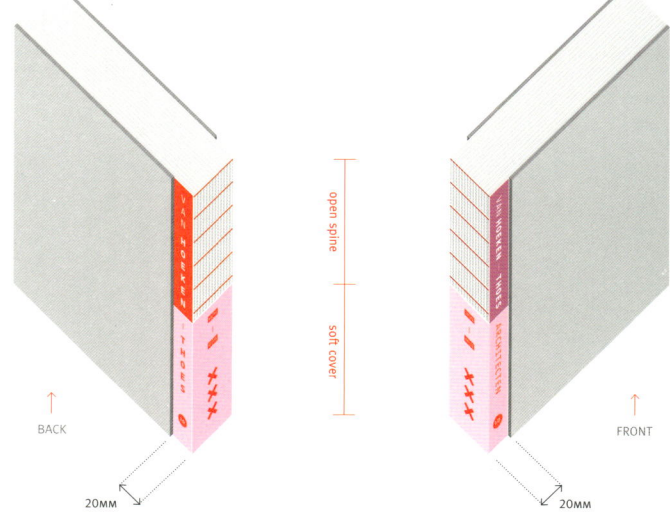

◉ *Technique*

● The book title, "30," refers to 30th anniversary of the client. This number has been translated into the book's structure by dividing the content into 30 sections. The main section is organized chronologically, proividing an accurate timeline of the company's creative voyage.

The archive section is designed in an organic manner, creating a reading experience much like browsing through a file-cabinet, due to the half-open spine design. A secret of the book will only be revealed when you read it in the dark. The striking fluorescent colors on the open spine will be fully revealed.

NAKAJIMA MONOGRAPH

Thread binding
French fold

Paper Material: Hardboard, transparent rice paper
Size: 200mm x 265mm

250 Gramm [The Netherlands]

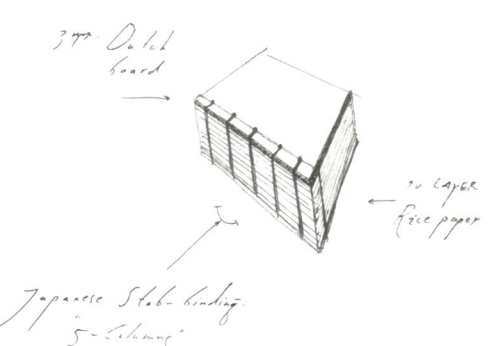
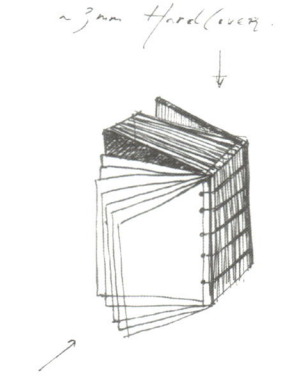

Technique

● The book is a monograph on renowned Japanese graphic designer Hideki Nakajima. This bilingual book contains an overview of his oeuvre and is divided into ten categories.

 The book can be read from back to front and vice versa, thus having no distinction between cover and back. A dynamic grid provides freedom in composition and was inspired by the artist's unfinished project, a poster series created by sampling his previous versions, constructing an interconnected, on-going process of layering.

DREBBEL

Sewn binding

Monochromatic printing

Paper Material: Wood-free book paper, recycled paper, sewing
Size: 216mm × 171mm

250 Gramm [The Netherlands]

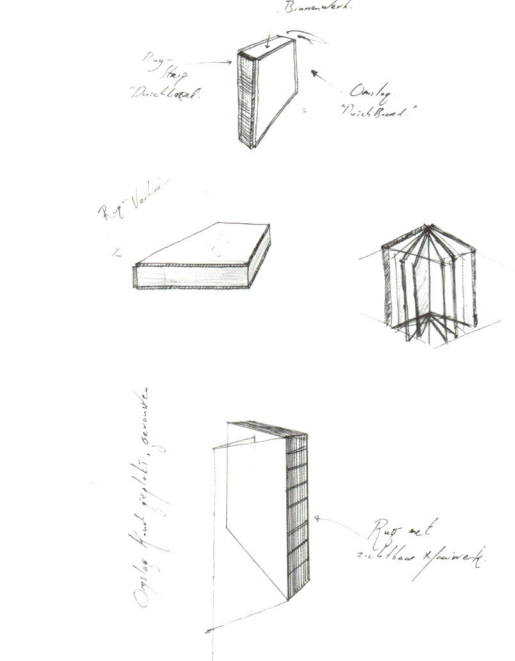

Technique

● This publication for an opera contains the libretto, interviews with cast and crew, as well as historical essays. The main section features the opera's libretto and original texts and poetry, highlighting the narrative. Production related information and cast and crew content are placed at the end of the book as an appendix.

⋮ Custom made stamps in red ink were applied manually on the cover and inside pages. The spine of the book stands out because it is open and features red thread. This binding choice served to lower costs but increase distinctiveness. The color is also frequently echoed on the interior page. A flexible grid system has been created specifically to enable multiple typographic styles, formats and sizes to accommodate the heavy libretto.

DAS GROSSE VIEL UND DAS KLEINE DICKE WENIG

Open spine
Special thread stitching
Illustrations

Paper Material: Cream-colored paper, greyboard
Size: 180mm x 250mm

Lara Bispinck [Germany]

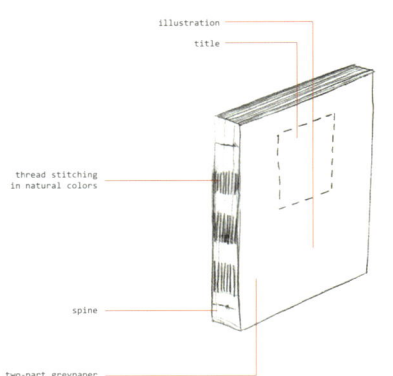
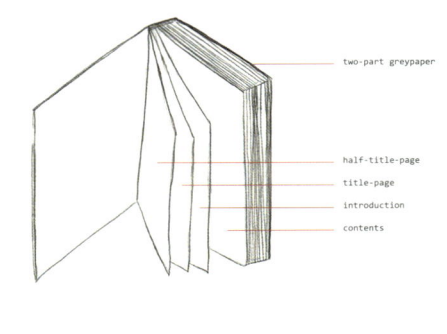

Technique

This children's book, "The Big Plenty and the Wee Tubby Sparsely," is a bachelor's thesis about child poverty in Germany. Despite the fact that Germany is a developed country, many children live in poverty and don't have access to healthy food or education. There are two monsters in the story: the Big Plenty has many toys and can go to school, whereas the Wee Tubby only has its cuddly monster toy and envies the Big Plenty. But their good friendship shows that material status is not always the most important thing in life.

The 200-page children's book is printed on cream-colored 300g paper. There are two versions of the spine: thread stitching in different colors and greyboard/thread stitching for the white hardcover. The illustrations in the book are in natural pastel colors throughout in order to maintain a unified look. The handmade character of the binding technology was very important to the designer. The book's size was determined such that it would be easy for children to hold.

TYPE FAST / TALK FADES

Format

Sewing

French fold

Paper Material: Recycled paper; Newspaper
Size: 260mm x 215mm

Sibyl Cherry Lai [Hong Kong, China]

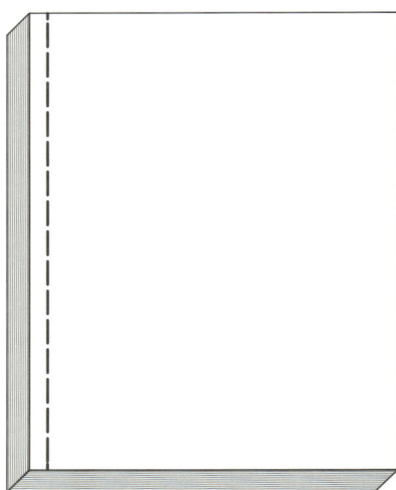

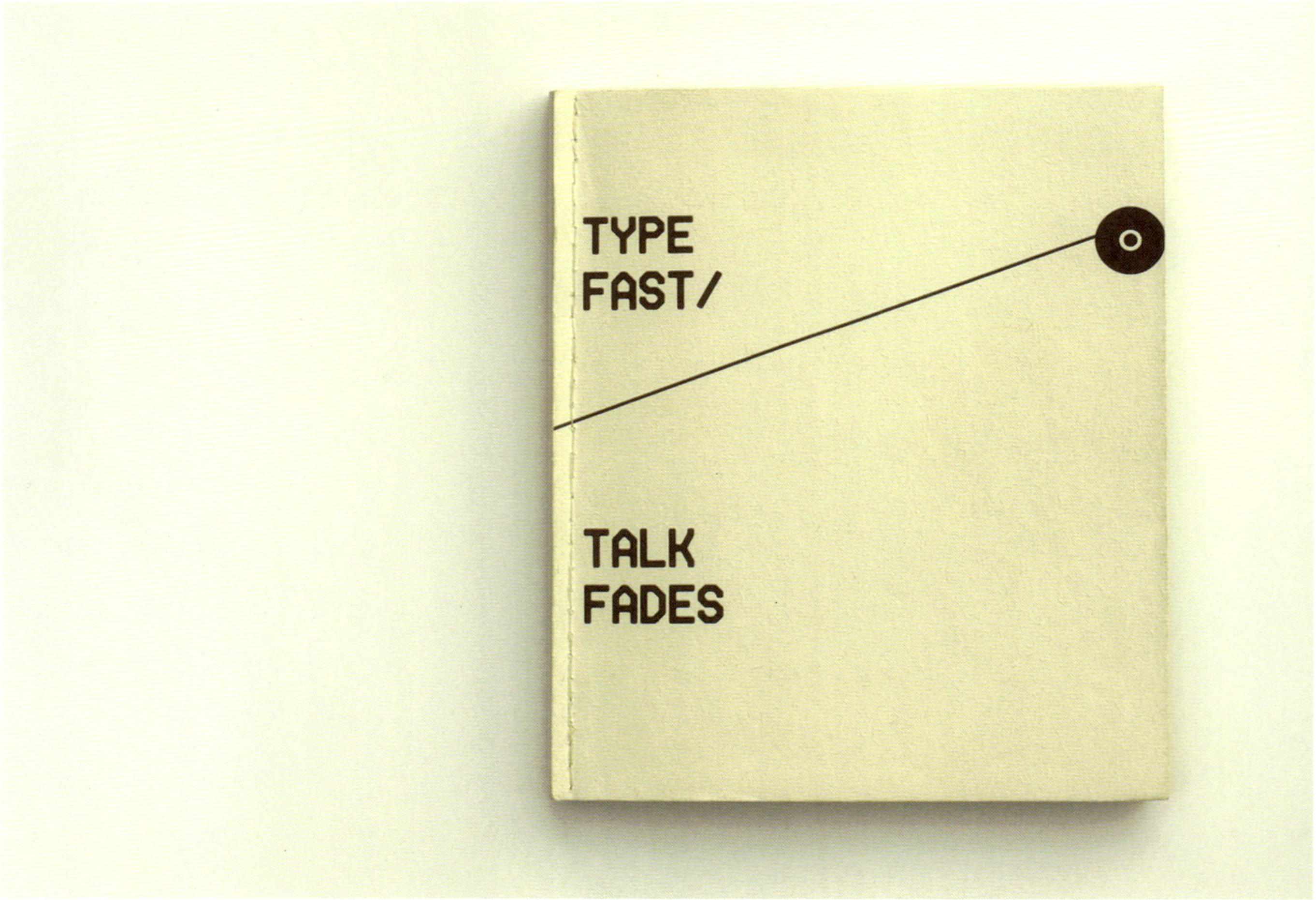

Technique

This book is a reflection on the social network, Facebook, which is thought of as a medium that facilitates communication. The ideology and practical functions of the network are presented via editorial and typographic media, showing the contents of the site from the perspectives the designer gained through her observation of its communities.

The book is divided into 12 sections. Each section demonstrates one feature of Facebook. The intention was that the readers could form their own opinions about whether Facebook promotes or hinders communication. The book is a printed representation of the site. Most of the paper used inside is similar to newsprint as an expression of the contrast between the virtual and the actual.

CONSTRUCTIVE

Special binding
Hand-sewn binding

Paper Material: Biotop pure white
Size: 177mm x 230mm

Luc van Kan [The Netherlands]

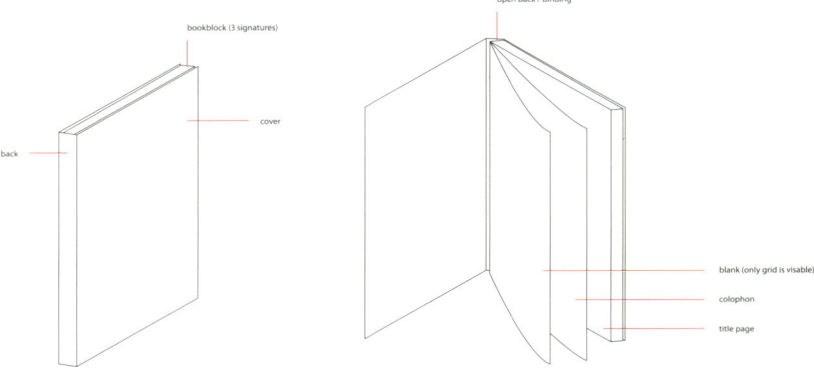

For this project the designer conducted research on the word "constructive" and has published the results in this book. The book features constructive colors, constructive pictures, constructive grids, constructive typography, and constructive binding.

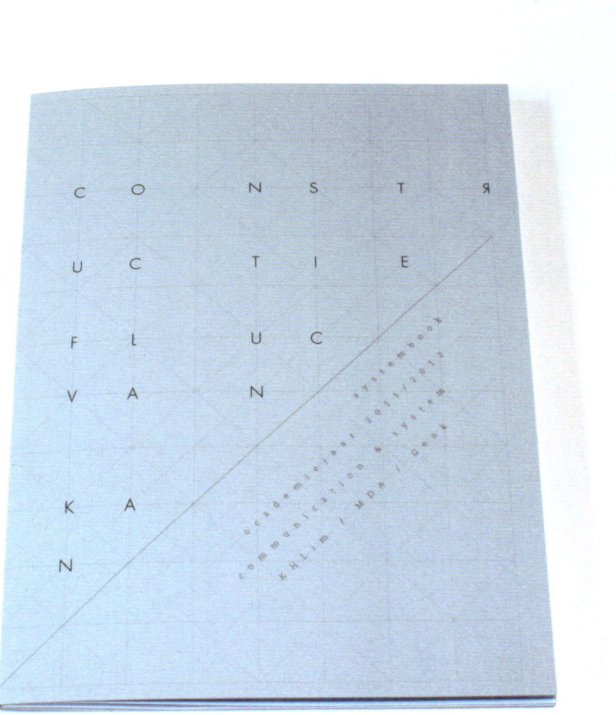

Technique

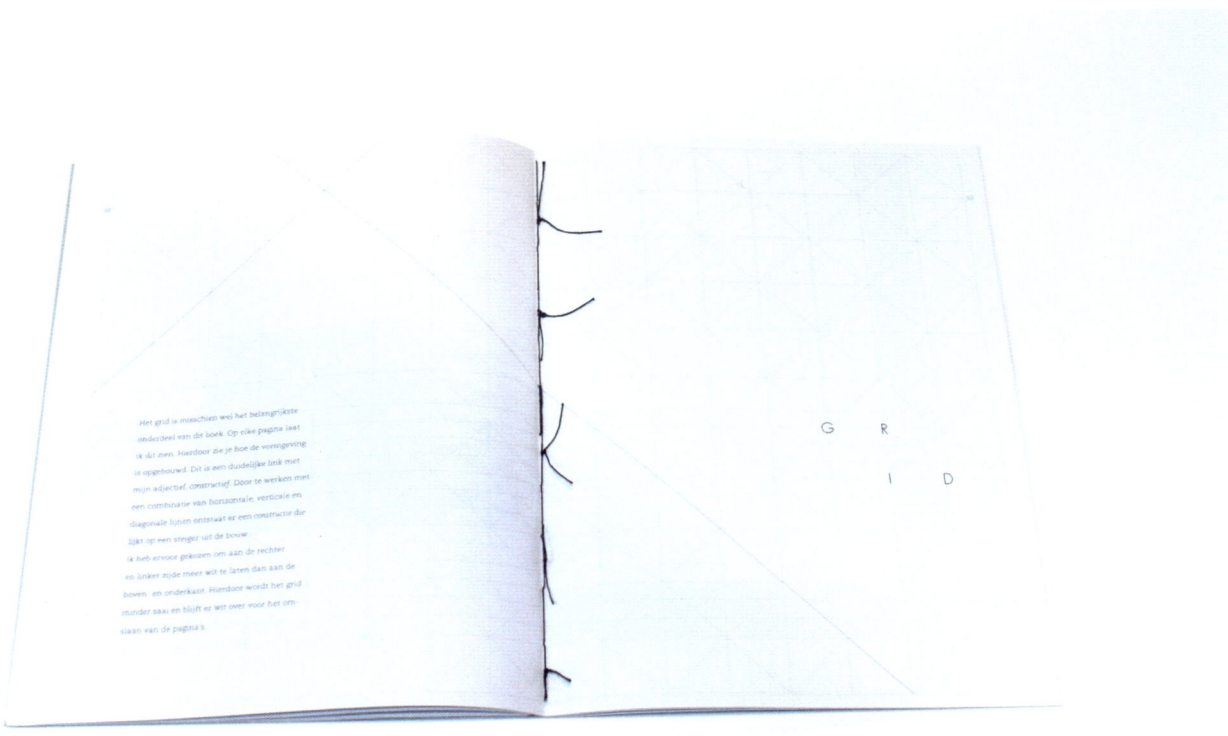

Constructive is laser printed. The hand-made binding the designer chose is consistent with the constructive theme. He has also made a special packaging for a designer's edition, in the same constructive style.

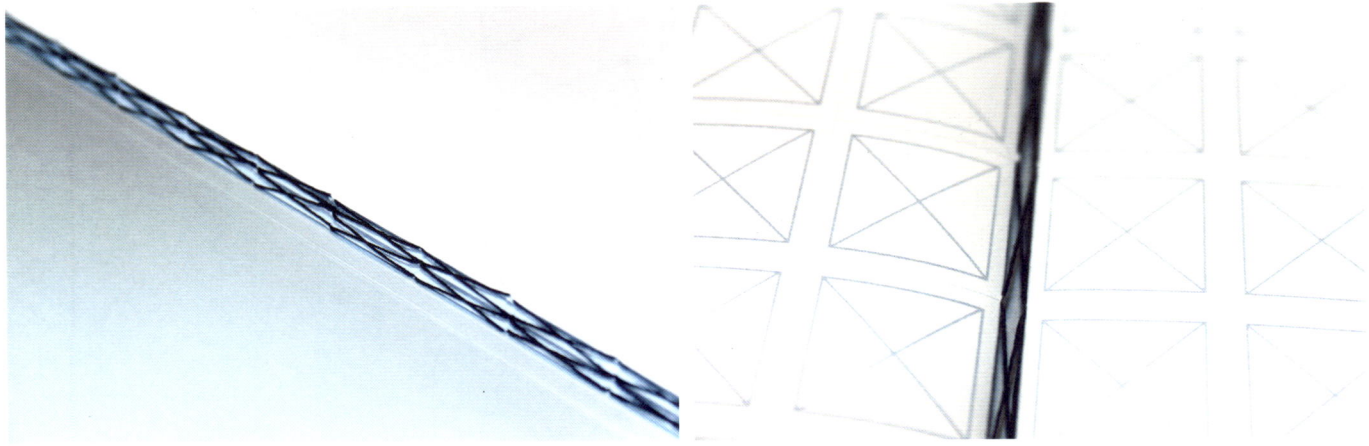

SALON DES
MÉTIERS D'ART DU QUÉBEC

Unique layout design

Monochromatic printing

Hand bound

Paper Material: Recycled paper stock
Size: 184mm x 184mm

Fanny Roy   [Canada]

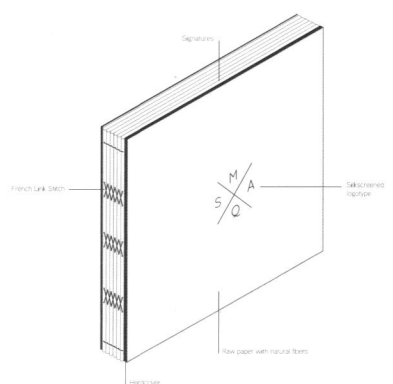
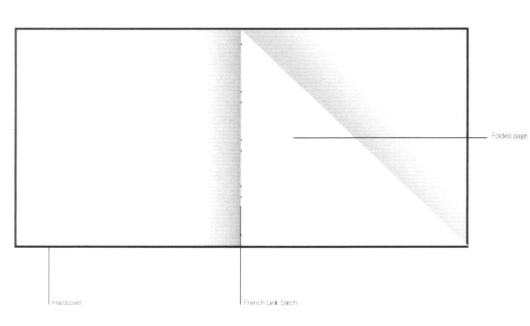
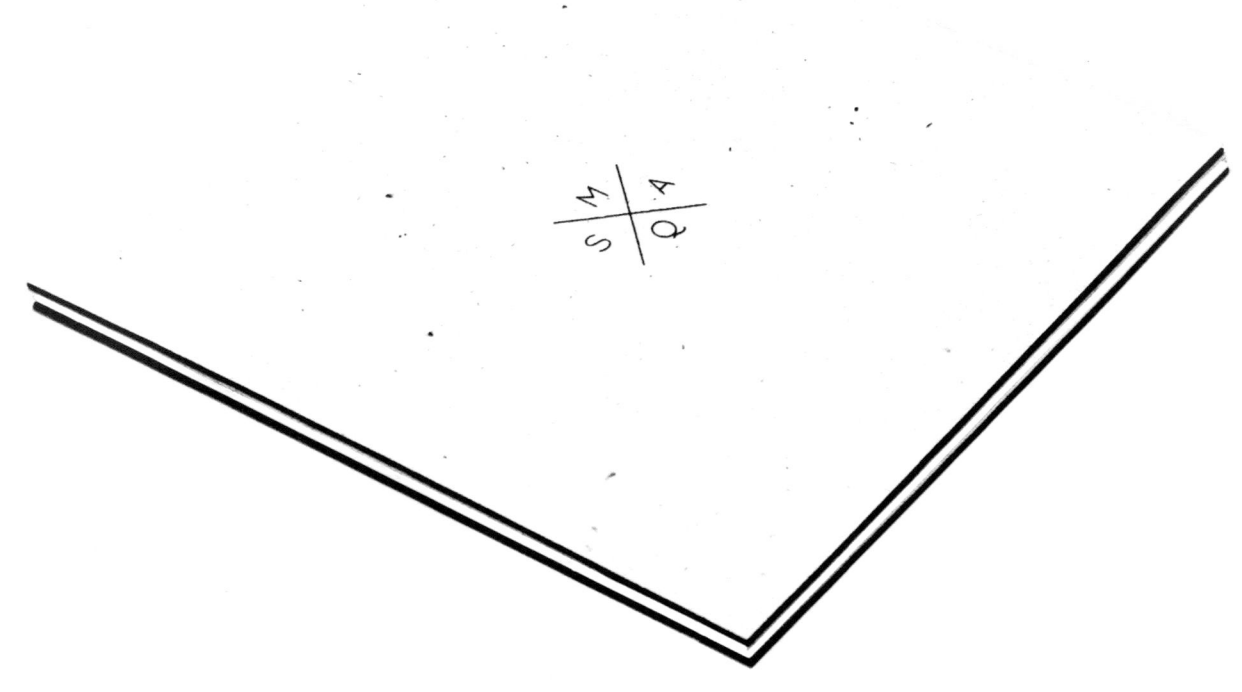

○ Technique

●

This design is part of a new visual identity for Salon des Métiers d'Art du Québec. It is a student work that puts raw materials and craftsmanship center stage.

⋮⋮⋮

The book was assembled using two separate hardcovers, leaving the book spine visible. The covers are made from recycled paper that was mounted on thick, black, natural fiber cardboard, emphasizing the natural character of the print and at the same time adding rigidity to the book. The content is laid out in 6 parts, which are bound together with a strong yet delicate French Link. On the spine, the X-patterned sewing mimics the company's new black logotype, which is silkscreened on the front cover. The inside pages feature composite images created with the use of diagonally folded pages and juxtapositions of raw material.

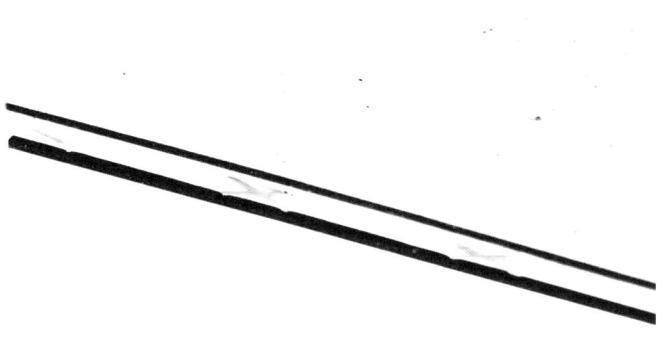

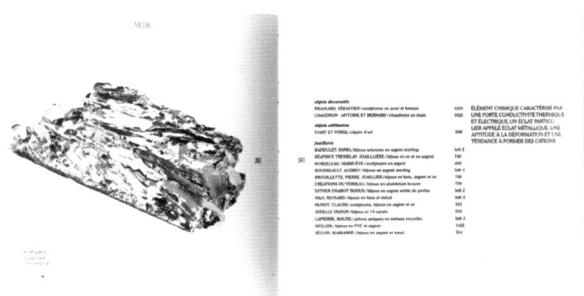

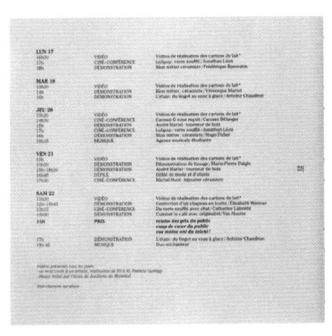

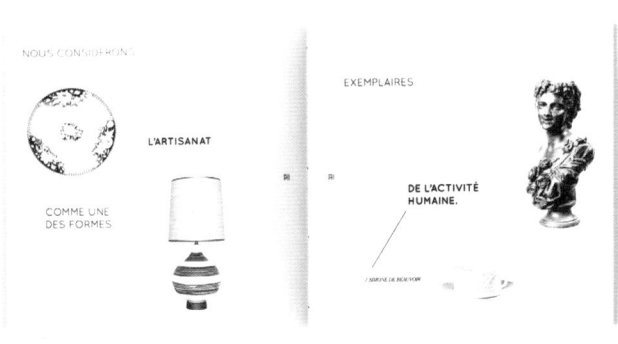

AUSTRIAN DESIGN DETAILS

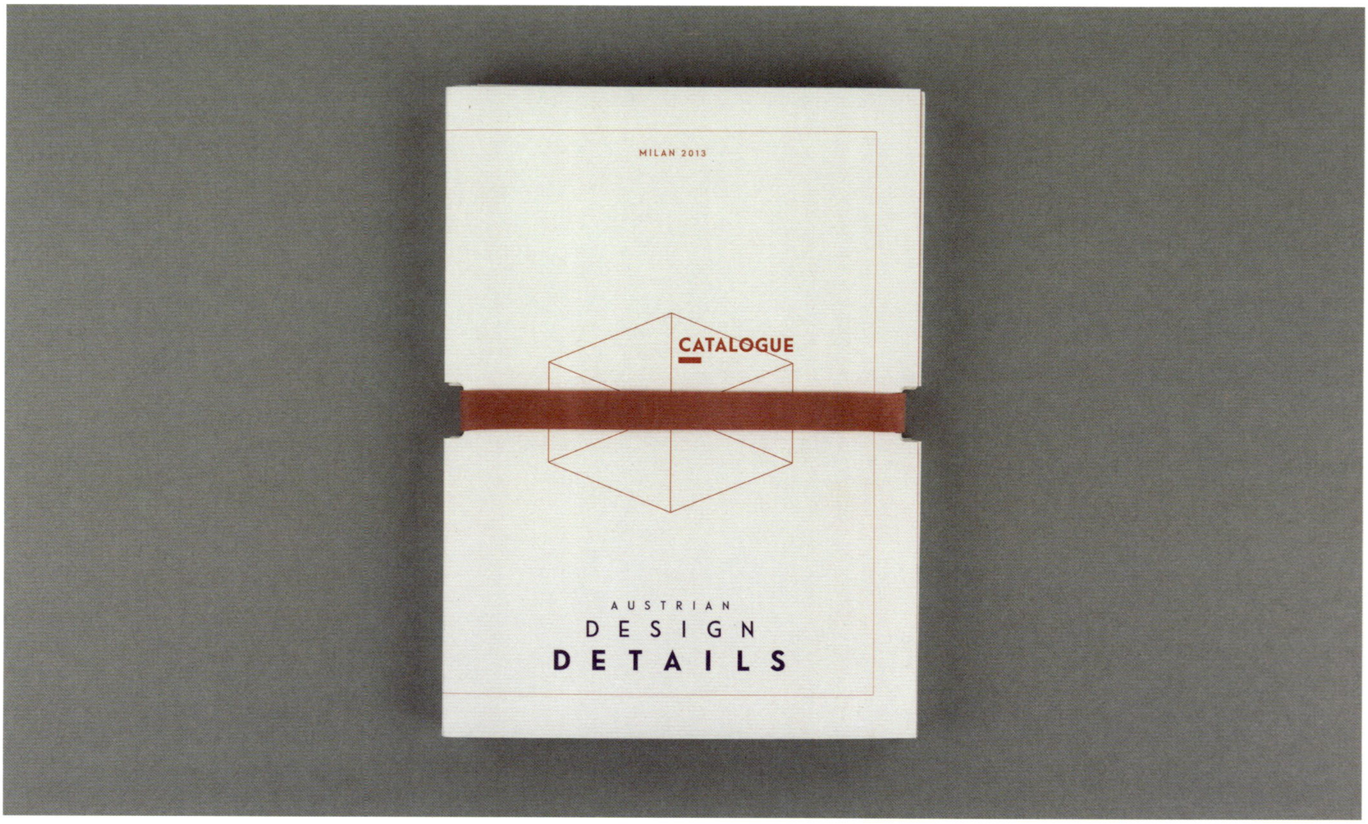

Special binding

Paper Material: Algrodesign duo white
Size: 473mm x 210mm

MOOI [Austria]

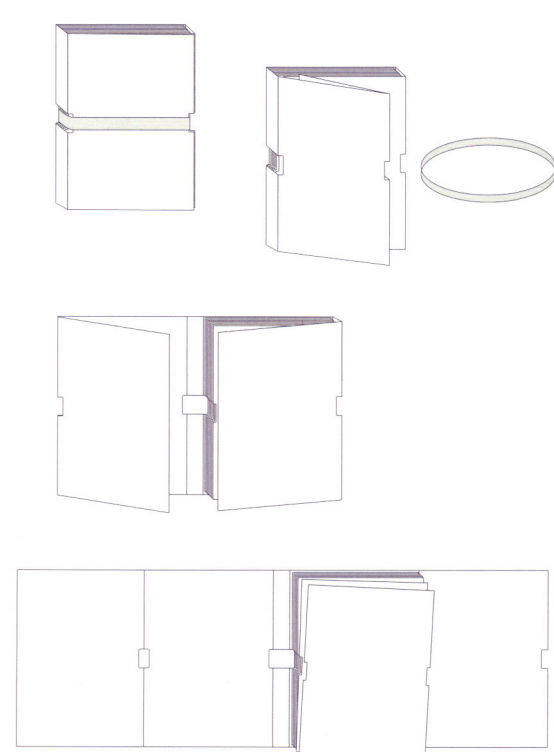

Technique

• Salone Internazionale del Mobile is the most important furniture fair in the world. In this context, ADVANTAGE AUSTRIA is organizing a large-scale group show for interior designers, producers and craftsman to present their work to an international audience. The concept of the exhibition catalog was to magnify an interesting detail of the products, as if they were being looked at through a microscope. Each visitor of the exhibition was able to customize his catalog by varying the product focus. By collecting only his or her favorite pieces, each visitor's catalog became a unique object. A special display wall at the entrance offered 57 cards to choose from.

 To enable the cards to come together to form the book and to integrate the cover, an unconventional binding method was developed. A rubber band was made of caoutchouc and matching die cuts. In this way the exhibition catalog was transformed into a multifunctional "book"—the cards could be used as business cards, product folios or even memory cards. The logo on the cover is a Necker cube, which represents the concept of the exhibition: the sum is greater than its parts.

AMBIDEX COMPANY BOOK

Offset printing

Rubber binding

Paper Material: Woodfree paper
Size: 320mm × 190mm

Kamimura Typografie Gestalten
[Japan]

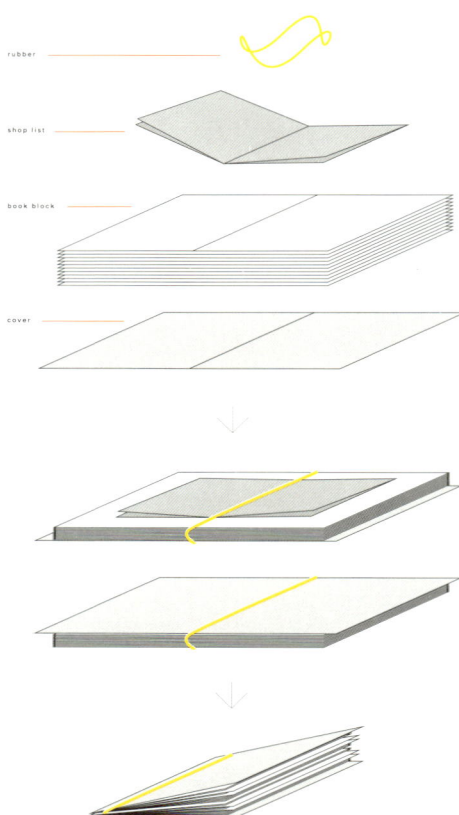

● This publication is a company brochure for AMBIDEX Co., Ltd, a multiple-brand entity.

⋮ The brochure contains descriptions of its various brands, which are bound together with a rubber band.

○ Technique

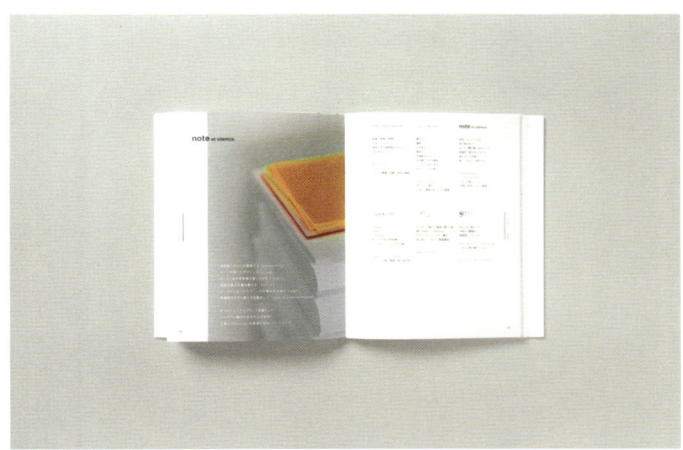
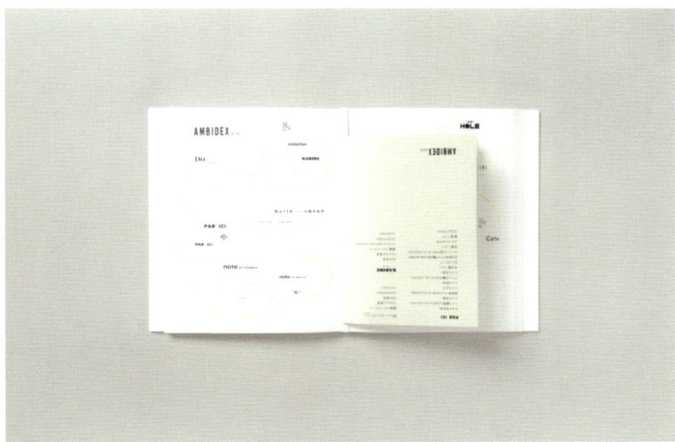

235

ISTD BRIEF: BOOKS STILL?

Minimalist typography
Screw and post binding
Raster images

Paper Material: Munken Lynx Rough, GF Smith Mandarin
Size: 286mm x 256 mm

Mykolas Puodžiūnas [Lithuania]

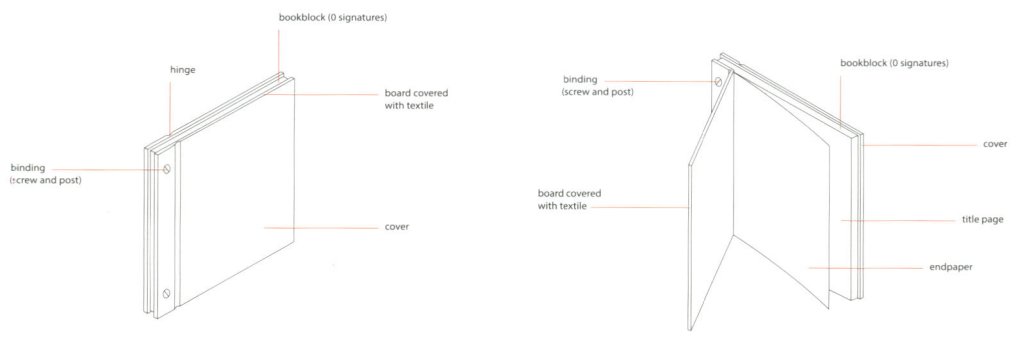

This project is a modern graphical interpretation of Bertrand Russell's "War Crimes in Vietnam." It is a response to the 2013 International Society of Typographic Designer's topic, "Books Still?".

○ *Technique*

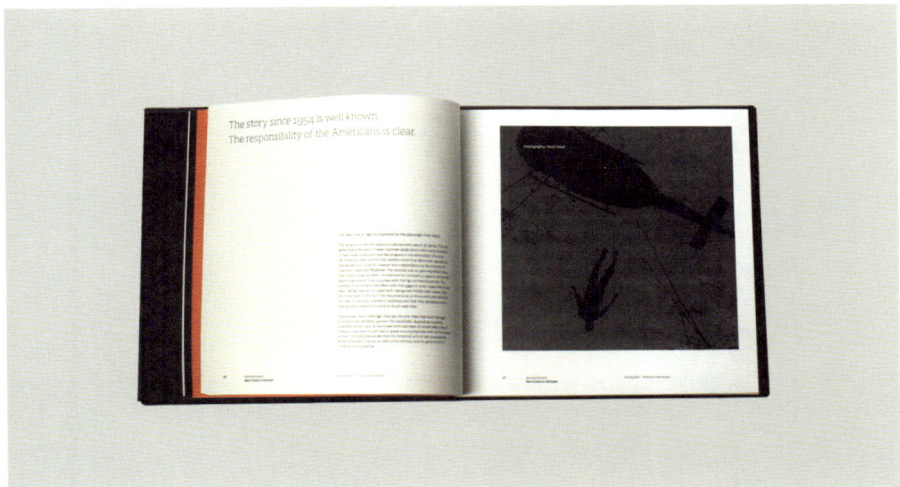

One of the main objectives of this book design was to escape from regular pages filled with continuous text from top to bottom. Clear typography, generous amounts of white space and panoramic raster images allow the reader to browse through the book without being challenged with information overload. The content of the book is complemented by an unusual book cover that is covered with a rough black textile. Slightly off-white book block paper is paired with eye-catching orange-colored paper which is used as an inbuilt bookmark to separate chapters.

CASA DA MÚSICA ANNUAL PROGRAMME BOOK, 2013

Offset printing
Open spine
UV ink silk screening
UV varnish
Printed open spine
Sewing

Paper Material: Munken Lynx, Coral Book White
Size: 156mm x 213mm

Sara Westermann [Portugal]

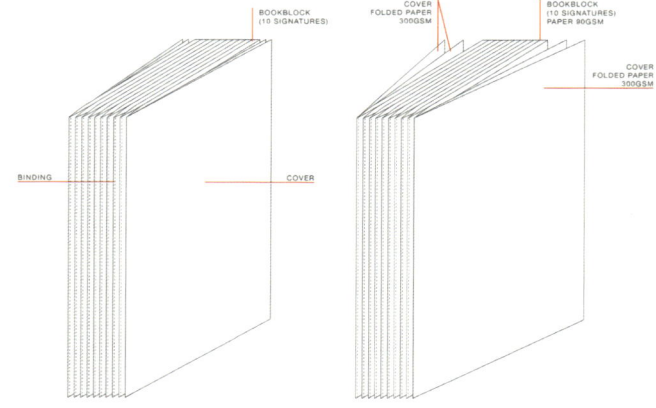

○ Technique

●

Casa da Música showcases a vibrant music program. This publication groups Casa da Música's 2013 programs and presents them through a course of 12 narratives, each photographed as a staged display.

Simple, Casa da Música's institutional font (designed by Norm), is used in the publication. Colors used on the cover are also present inside to separate the programming blocks. The spine enables a better handling of the book as well as a clear view of entire spreads. In general, this approach aims to facilitate readability while retaining the complexity and density of the contents.

239

CONTEMPORARY APPROPRIATIONS OF THE PAST

Thread binding
Fold-out page
Screen printing

Size: 230mm x 275mm

Wang Zhi-hong [China]

Technique

• The book is a compilation of the work of 23 Taiwanese contemporary artists who have springboarded their creative explorations from local historical and cultural contexts, as well as individual life experiences, since the 1990s. Based on the subject matter of the appropriated works, the exhibition is divided into seven categories, harkening back to the classification system of dynastic China. The seven categories are landscapes, Taoism and Buddhism, human figures, tales of the mysterious, calligraphy, flowers, birds and beasts, and photographic images.

JOAN BROSSA, CARRER DE JOAN PONÇ

> Cutting
> Stamping
> Inserted pages
> Folded page

Paper Material: Recicled Keaycolour tiza, Embossing Geltex K 111 snow white, Munken Pure, Courius Touch arches, Creator Gala
Size: 194mm x 239mm

SETANTA [Spain]

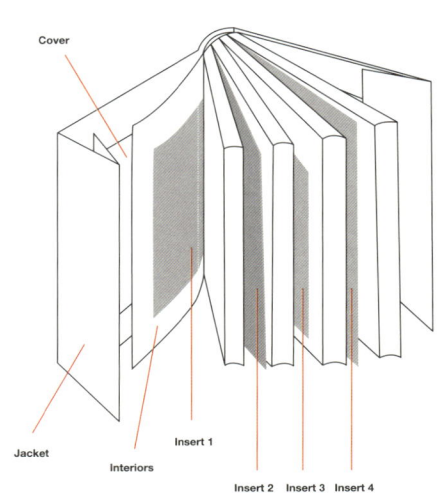

• This book focuses on the relationship between two important Catalan artists of the 20th century, Joan Brossa and Joan Ponç. Brossa is a notorious artist and poet and Ponç a great painter. During their friendship, they produced a lot of pieces dedicated to each other as a kind of correspondence between them, creating an artistic dialogue that lasted for forty years.

Technique

The book shows the extraordinary conversations between the two artists through their poems, plays, paintings, illustrations and correspondence. The book, a hardcover with 3mm cardboard with a vaulted spine and black sewing, features a stamped laminated jacket. The exterior is selectively varnished, as are the four inserts.

UNTOPIA

Embossing
Stamping
Black edging

Paper Material: Heavy weight paper
Size: 200mm x 150mm

JvV by Joost van Vredendaal
[The Netherlands]

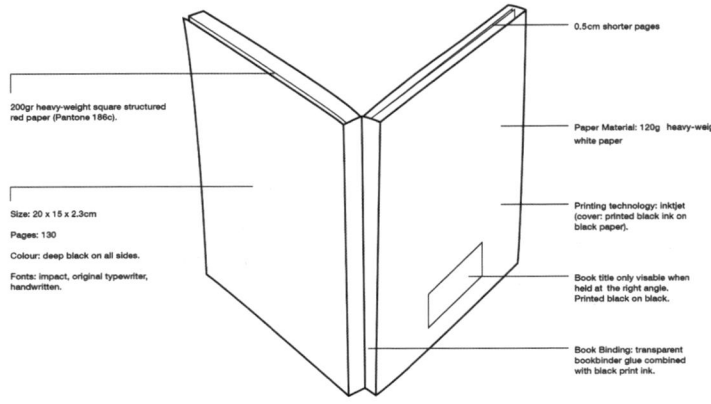

200gr heavy-weight square structured red paper (Pantone 186c).

Size: 20 x 15 x 2.3cm
Pages: 130
Colour: deep black on all sides.
Fonts: impact, original typewriter, handwritten.

0.5cm shorter pages

Paper Material: 120g heavy-weight white paper

Printing technology: inktjet (cover: printed black ink on black paper).

Book title only visable when held at the right angle. Printed black on black.

Book Binding: transparent bookbinder glue combined with black print ink.

Technique

● This photo book for photographer Alex Brandon contains pictures of his lifestyle and the environments that inspire him. The storyline in this book is depicted through the letters between the designer and Brandon.

 This publication is printed in black with red accents on heavy-weight paper. You can actually scratch the ink off. Because of this, it has a very raw feeling. Its temporary presence fits the ever changing mood of the book's content. The main title can only be seen when you hold the book at the right angle. Some pages are hidden when you look quickly through the book, since these pages are a bit smaller than the rest of the pages.

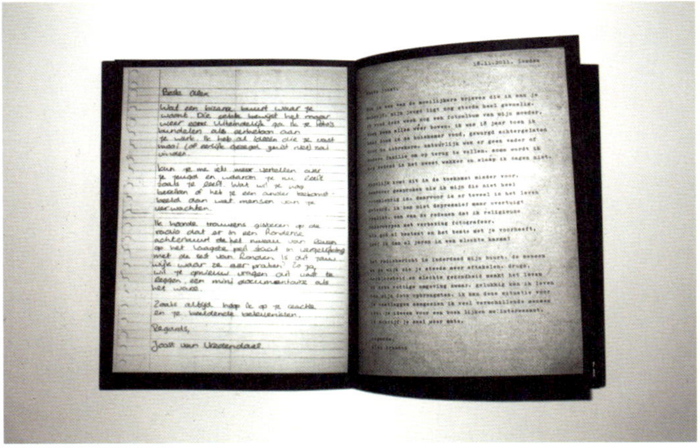

CHIBOUGAMAU

Screen printing
Hand-sewing
Headband

Paper Material: Post-consumer fiber matt paper
Size: 286mm x 203mm

Justin Lortie [Canada]

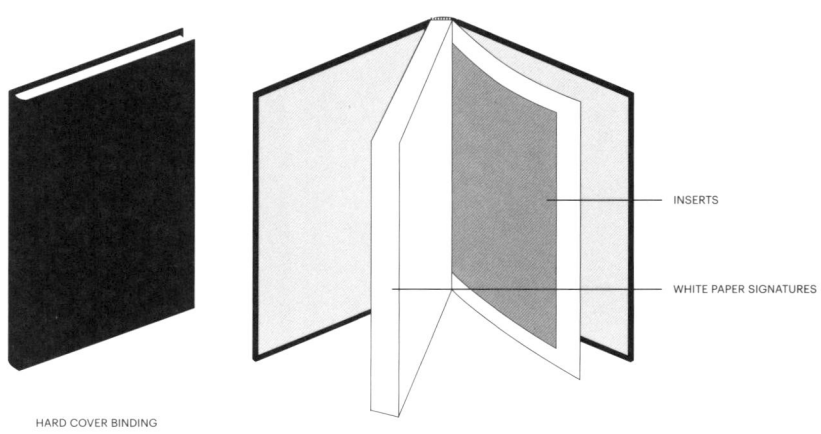

JUSTIN LORTIE - CHIBOUGAMAU

INSERTS
WHITE PAPER SIGNATURES
HARD COVER BINDING

Technique

The book was inspired by the Chibougamau region in northern Canada. It presents a Canadian restaurant with a contemporary menu featuring local products. In addition to food photography, scenery is shown to exhibit the natural context that inspired the cuisine.

The binding of the book was made using a traditional hardcover. The booklets were sewn by hand with black thread and a two-color headband was added to the finishing. The cover is made of black canvas and was screenprinted with black and white inks. The interior was printed on matte paper (Enviro 100 by Cascade) using a color laser printer. The inserts were printed on a light gray paper using a black and white laser printer.

CLOSED CITIES

Wrapped open spine
Unique layout
Flap design

Paper Material: Arctic + plastic coating, Cyclus Offset
Size: 240mm x 300mm

Manuel Radde [Austria]

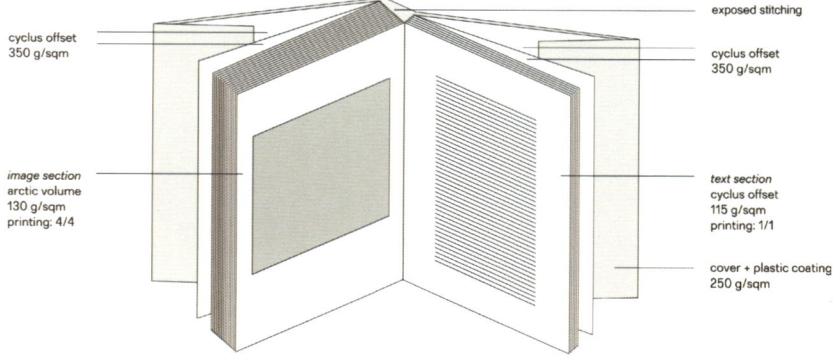

Technique

•

In his impressive photo series, Gregor Sailer examines the forms taken by so called "closed cities" in Siberia, Azerbaijan, Qatar, Chile, Algeria/Western Sahara and Argentina. The term "closed city" was originally coined for the Soviet Union, where, for various reasons, the existence of numerous towns was long kept secret. Even today, there are still places that are being discovered including military sites, refugee camps and even gated communities for the affluent, hidden away from the mainstream. Forms of urban settlement highlight questions connected to dwindling resources, climate change, political conflicts and a demand for security.

The book is divided into an image section, which consists of 6 series of images, and a text section containing 3 essays and the appendix. The image and text sections are printed on different paper so that the separation of the textual content is also discernible through the material used. At several points in the book the layout refers to the geographical location of the cities. Since many closed cities have long been kept secret and not marked on maps, the cartographic representation itself remains invisible and the cities are located solely through the use of a geographical coordinate system. The cover of the book has an unusual, synthetic feel which emphasizes the character of the artificially created urban zones.

INNER EXFOLIATION

Special layout

Varied paper size

Paper Material: Vellum; white paper
Size: 200mm x 200mm

Mina Zarfsaz [USA]

●

Inner Exfoliation is a two-part project. The first part is the process of looking at the idea of "self" in retrospect, deconstructing a 3 x 3 matrix of three agents - family, society and regime, in relation to three voices, in three time periods. The second is a video installation that visualizes the concepts of distress, suppression, and isolation, which are drawn from the above-mentioned matrix. This video is an attempt to visualize the concepts that shape this narrative.

∴

The process of creating this visual narrative required reconstructing layers of thoughts and emotions that relate to each targeted agent. This pattern is woven into the design of the book itself, from the paper to the layout, creating a presentation unique to the thought process.

Hand-sewing

Varied paper size

Special layout

Paper Material: Brown Kraft paper, white paper
Size: 190mm x 240mm

Mina Zarfsaz [USA]

RE { }

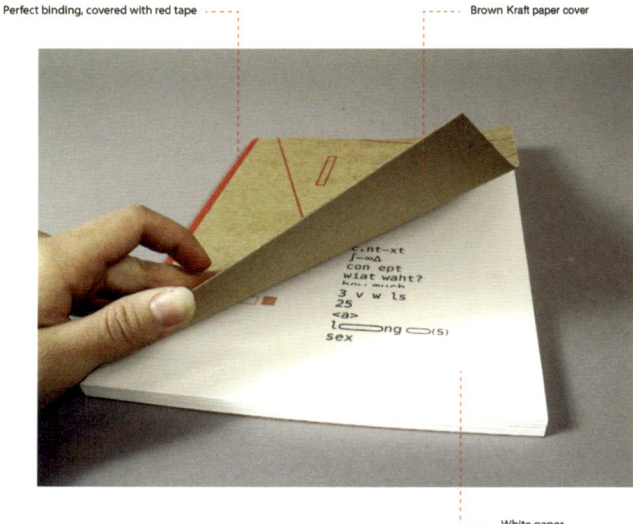

Perfect binding, covered with red tape · · · · · Brown Kraft paper cover

White paper

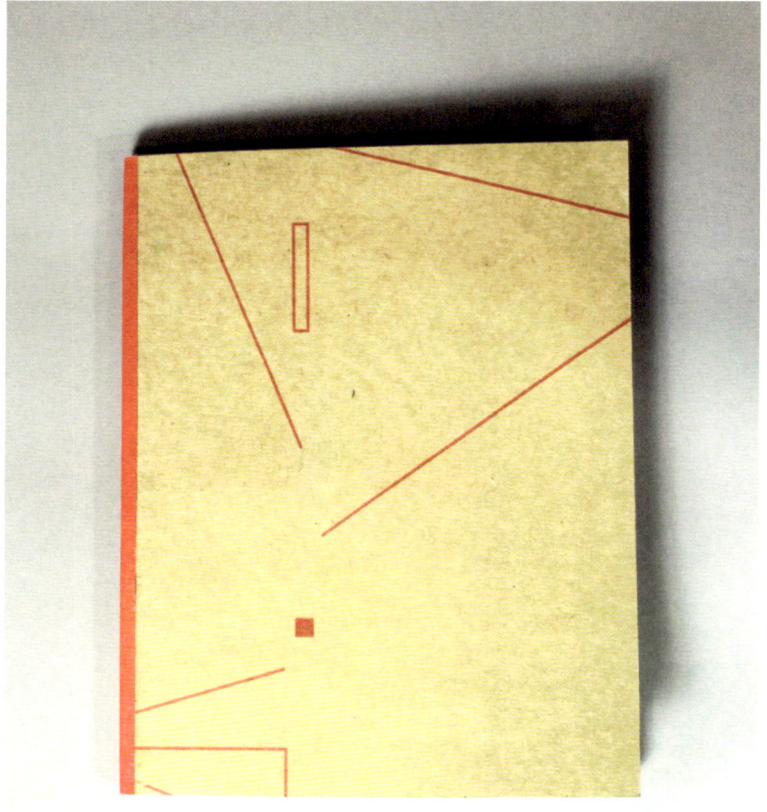

●

This book sets out to introduce new written forms and structures based on a minimalist linguistic concept. Using different approaches, the designer focuses on something lost (old structures of written language), and gives prominence to something new (new language structures). She presents the lost as mundane, uniform, repetitive, ordinary, or understood, and the found as the opposite to create a guidebook that reconsiders the ordinary.

⁘

The layout of the pages of this book also suggests new forms in support of the concept of restructuring. Each page is trimmed in a specific way, and the heavy-weight paper used in this book brings a steady foundation to the physical structure.

Technique

253

INDEX

250 Gramm
www.250g.nl
P218, P220, P222

A

A beautiful design
www.abeautifuldesign.com.sg
P138

ACST Design
acstdesign.asia
P172, P176

Akos Polgardi
www.akospolgardi.com
P78

Alba Miralles Blanch
P90

Alberto Hernández
www.hereigo.co.uk
P10, P110

Aris Zenone Studio
www.ariszenone.ch
P168

Autobahn
www.autobahn.nl
P140, P142

B

Beste Bibi
P64

Bethany Johnson
www.behance.net/BethJohnson
P214

Buenos días
www.buenosdias.info
P144

C

Carmentrino & Zafir Pri/Emir hakim Design
www.carmentrino.com
www.emirhakim.com
P178

Carolina Vargas
www.carolina-vargas.com
P128

Caroline Andersson
www.behance.net/carolinegasten
P24

Chong Yee Cher Cheryl
www.behance.net/hellobighair
P106

Christer Dahlslett
www.behance.net/dahlslett
P122

Coraline Chane CMC Concept
P208

D

Dan Lawrence
www.dan-lawrence.com
P112

Danielle Muntyan
www.behance.net/daniellemuntyan
P126

David Newman
P148

Derrick Li Hua
www.behance.net/derricklihua
P108
P194
 -Design Office, Art Center College of Design Creative Directors:
 Winnie Li and Simon Johnston
 -Designers:
 Eliana Dominguez and Andrea Carrillo

E

Esen Karol Tasarım Ltd
esenkarol.com
P76

F

Fanny Roy
www.behance.net/fannyroy7
P230

Festina Lente Libros
P22

G

Gabrielle Guy
www.gabrielleguy.com
P92

Guangzhou Zhengdian Advertisement
www.gzdad.com
P74

H

Halbye Kaag JWT
www.halbyekaagjwt.dk
P20

Haller Brun
www.hallerbrun.eu
P94

Hanqingtang Design
www.hanqingtang.com
P96, P198, P200, P216

Happycentro
www.happycentro.it
P8, P50, P192

I

Isabel Seiffert
P158

Ivo Ferreira, Bruno Viegas
www.behance.net/iferreira
www.brunoviegas.com
P52

J

Jasper Jongeling
www.jasperjongeling.nl
P46

Jess García
www.behance.net/jessgarciastuff
P88

Jiani Lu
www.lujiani.com
P32, P56, P174

Joél Valdez
www.joel-valdez.com
P82

Jooey Lek
www.behance.net/jooeylek
P132

Jorge Fernández Puebla
www.jpuebla.com
P12

José Luís Sousa Dias
www.behance.net/zeluisousadias
P188

Justin Lortie
www.jlortie.com
P246

JvV by Joost van Vredendaal
www.joostvanvredendaal.com
P28, P34, P244

K

Kamimura Typografie Gestalten Makoto
www.typgestalt.com
P234

KAN & LAU DESIGN
www.kanandlau.com
P26

Karolien Pauly
www.karolienpauly.be
P58, P120

Katharina Schiessler
www.ka-tinka.de
P184

Klára Balázs
www.behance.net/search?search=kittyom
P98

K.S.U
Dept. of Visual Communication Design/Mixed Media Studio
P146
 -Art Director: Cheng Chung-yi
 -Designers:
 Wu Mu-chang, Dai Yi-jing,
 Yang Shi-ching, Liu Zhi-yu
 -Copy Writer: Zue Bo-Yen

L

Lara Bispinck
www.behance.net/LaraBispinck
P224

Luc van Kan
www.lucvankan.nl
P30, P228

Lucie Kim
www.myorangebox.com
P212

M

Mak Yu Jing
www.makyujing.com
P164

Manuel Radde
www.manuelradde.com
P248

Marcin Hernas/tessera – graphic design
www.tessera.org.pl
P66, P68

Marton Borzak
www.martonborzak.com
P150

Metaklinika
www.metaklinika.com
P202

Milan Janic
www.milanjanic.net
P196

Mina Zarfsaz
www.behance.net/minazarfsaz
P130, P250, P252

Mircea W. Gutu
www.mwgutu.de
P42

MOOI
www.mooi-design.com
P232

Morphoria design collective
www.morphoria.com
P60

Mykolas Puodžiūnas
www.vagabond.lt
P236

N

Nina Gudz
www.ninagudz.co.uk
P210

O

Oliver Ward
www.oliverward.co.nz
P124

R

Raw Color
www.rawcolor.nl
P204, P206

Riccardo Zecchini & Giorgio Fanecco
www.riccardozecchini.com
P62

RM&CO
www.rossimazzei.com
P190

Robert Urban
www.roberturban.sk/
P180

Roman Dzyvulskyi
Bird of Happiness
P182

S

Sagmeister & Walsh
www.hubertfischer.com
P104
 -Art Direction:
 Stefan Sagmeister
 -Book Design:
 Philipp Hubert (Hubert & Fischer)

Sandra Weber Grafikdesign
www.sandraw.de
P86

Sara Westermann
www.sarawestermann.com
P238

Say What Studio
www.saywhat-studio.com
P14

SendPoints Publishing
www.sendpoints.cn/
P156, P160, P162

SETANTA
www.setanta.es
P142

Shenzhen Huathink Design Company
www.huathink.net
www.liuyongqing.com
P48, P114, P170

Sibyl Cherry Lai
www.cargocollective.com/sibylcherry
P118, P226

Somewhere Else
www.somewhere-else.info
P152, P154

Stan Van Steendam
www.stanvansteendam.be
P80

Stefen Clark
www.behance.net/stefenclark1
P16

Studio Sarah Schwarz
www.sarahschwarz.de
P84

U

Umut Altıntaş
www.behance.net/umutaltintas
P70

United Design Lab
www.u-d-l.com
P116

Urban Tribe
www.urbantribe.cn
P54

V

Viktorija Leleive
www.behance.net/ViktorijaLeleive
P44

W

Work in Progress
www.workinprogress.no
P166

Wang Zhi-hong
www.wangzhihong.com/
P36, P38, P40, P240

Y

Ye Sheng-hao
shenbinima.zcool.com.cn/
P72

Yolaine Codjovi
www.behance.net/yolainecodjovi
P186

ACKNOWLEDGEMENTS

We would like to thank all the designers and contributers who have been involved in the production of this book. Their significant contribution is indispensable in the compilation of this book. We would also like to express our gratitude to all the producers for their invaluable opinions and assistance throughout this project. And to the many others whose names are not credited but have aided in the production of this book, we thank you for your continuous support.